KAREN BROWN'S

French

Country Bed & Breakfasts

KAREN BROWN TITLES

California Country Inns & Itineraries

English Country Bed & Breakfasts

English, Welsh & Scottish Country Hotels & Itineraries

French Country Bed & Breakfasts

French Country Inns & Itineraries

German Country Inns & Itineraries

Irish Country Inns & Itineraries

Italian Country Bed & Breakfasts

Italian Country Inns & Itineraries

Portuguese Country Inns & Pousadas

Spanish Country Inns & Paradors

Swiss Country Inns & Chalets

KAREN BROWN'S

French
Country Bed & Breakfasts

Written by

CLARE BROWN and KIRSTEN PRICE

Sketches by Barbara Tapp
Cover Painting by Jann Pollard

Travel Press

Karen Brown's Country Inn Series

Travel Press editors: Karen Brown, June Brown, Clare Brown, Kirsten Price, Susanne Lau Alloway
Iris Sandilands; Technical support: William H. Brown III; Aide-de-camp: William H. Brown
Illustrations: Barbara Tapp; Cover painting: Jann Pollard
Maps: Brenden Kootsey of Cassell Design

This books is written in cooperation with Town & Country-Hillsdale Travel, San Mateo, CA 94401

Distributed USA & Canada: The Globe Pequot Press
P.O. Box 833, Old Saybrook, CT 06475-0833, USA; tel: 203-395-0440

Distributed Europe: Springfield Books Ltd.
Norman Road., Denby Dale, Huddersfield HD8 8TH, Yorkshire, England; tel: (0484) 864 955

A catalog record for this book is available from the British Library

Library of Congress Cataloging-in-Publication Data

Brown, Clare.
     Karen Brown's French country bed & breakfasts / written by Clare
    Brown; sketches by Barbara Tapp; cover art by Jann Pollard..
    Updated and rev. 3rd ed.
        p. cm. -- (Karen Brown's country inn series)
     Rev. ed. of : Karen Brown's French country bed & breakfasts /
    Kirsten Price and Clare Brown.
     Includes index.
     ISBN 0-930328-47-7 : $13.95
     1. Bed and breakfast accommodations--France--Guide-books.
    2. France--Guide-books. I. Brown,Karen. II. Price, Kirsten, 1956-
    Karen Brown's French country bed & breakfasts. III. Title.
    IV. Title: French country bed & breakfasts. V. title: French
    country bed and breakfasts. VI. Series.
    TX907.5.F7B75 1993
    647.944403--dc20

                          92-39208
                             CIP

Dedicated to
My Best Friend, Bill,
and to Fritz.

Contents

Introduction

Travellers with a sense of adventure can truly experience France, and get to know the French people by journeying beyond Paris and exploring the countryside. The way of life outside Paris (in "the provinces," as the French say), is a fascinating reflection of French history and culture: the impact of modern civilization is felt, but a pronounced respect for traditions and quality of life remain. Beyond Paris, the land is like a treasure chest: royal forests still harboring stags and wild boars, graceful castles casting their images into serene lakes; picturesque stone and half-timbered villages; vineyards outlined with rose bushes; meadows of fragrant lavender, fields of vibrant yellow sunflowers, medieval walled cities perched upon mountain tops; and wild, salty coastlines—all waiting to be discovered.

The Bed and Breakfast formula is for any traveller who wants to experience the "real" France, its people and culture. There is a social flavor to Bed and Breakfast travel that is not found in the normal tourist experience; you have ample opportunities to meet and exchange ideas with other travellers (usually Europeans) as well getting to know the hosts and their families, many times making lasting friendships. Single travellers will love the social aspect of Bed and Breakfast stays because they will not feel "alone." Bed and Breakfast travel is also tailor-made for families with children—the informality, convenience and reasonable rates make travel a pleasure. (Note: Many places also offer special family accommodations with several bedrooms and small kitchens.)

Bed and Breakfasts are called "Chambres d'Hôtes" (literally "guest bedrooms") in French, and are usually found in rural settings. This guide offers lodging selections in or near major tourist sites, as well as in unspoilt, less-visited regions. Most hosts prefer that their Bed and Breakfast guests take the time to unwind by staying at least two nights. (Americans have a reputation for always being in a *HURRY*.) Frequently stays of a week or longer are discounted, but the advantages of longer stays in one place are far greater than just financial; it is great fun to become friends with the owners and other guests, to just "settle in"—no packing and unpacking every night. We strongly feel you should choose one place to stay and make it your hub, going off in a different direction each day to explore the countryside.

European hotels, in a price range comparable to most Bed and Breakfasts, tend to all be cut from the same cloth: sterile—sometimes even dingy and depressing. For the same price or less, a Bed and Breakfast accommodation is personal, usually superior in cleanliness and comfort, and as varied as the landscape. Perhaps spend a few nights in a chateau dating from the Middle Ages whose stone walls evoke dreams of knights and their ladies. Then move on to experience the sights and sounds of a simple farm surrounded by bucolic pasture lands. Careful reading of the descriptions in this guide will ensure that the homes you select are in line with the type of welcome and accommodation you prefer. Each home is, of course, unique, offering its own special charm, yet all share one wonderful common denominator: the welcoming feeling of being treated as a cherished guest in a friend's home.

Over 3,800 Bed and Breakfasts in France belong to a national organization named GÎTES DE FRANCE. Members of this organization usually display the green and yellow Gîtes de France logo (shown below).

Bed and Breakfasts that are members of Gîtes de France have passed an inspection by the organization and conform to set standards of welcome and comfort. We have worked very closely with this organization that has given us tremendous cooperation in helping us select the finest places to stay from an overwhelming list of possibilities. The majority of Bed and Breakfasts featured in this guide are part of this association. However, we also visited and have included many excellent places to stay that have chosen not to belong to the Gîtes de France. In the hotel description section of this guide, we have indicated by each Bed and Breakfast if it is a member of the Gîte organization. If it is a member, we have put (GÎTE DE FRANCE) by its name. Gîtes de France has a head office in Paris that offers information and a complimentary reservation service. An English speaking staff is usually available to answer questions. In addition to the head office in Paris, there are also regional Gîtes de France branches located throughout France. Following are a few offices in key tourist locations:

PARIS, Head office

Gîtes de France, National Office
35 rue Godot de Mauroy
75009 Paris, France
tel: 1 47.42.20.92, fax: 1-47.42.73.11

LOIRE VALLEY, Regional office

Gîtes de France
38, rue Augustin Fresnel
37171 Chambray les Tours, France
tel: 47.48.37.46, fax: 47.48.13.39

DORDOGNE-PÉRIOGORD, Regional Office

Gîtes de France
16, rue Wilson
24009 Périgueux, France
tel: 53.53.44.35, fax: 53.09.51.41

We personally visited over 500 Bed and Breakfasts throughout France, inspecting not only those that are members of Gîtes de France, but also independent Bed and Breakfasts that do not belong to this affiliation. We made our personal selection based on their individual charm, old-world ambiance and warmth of welcome, choosing each place to stay on its merit alone—no one paid to be included in this guide. We selected in each region the most outstanding accommodations in various price ranges. Our choices are very subjective: we have "hand-picked" for you those places that we liked the most and thought you would also enjoy.

ACCOMMODATION

Bed and Breakfast accommodation, in most cases, means a bedroom rented in the home of a French family. Throughout this guide, the French term "chez" used before a family name translates as "at the home of" and is an accurate phrase when describing the type of accommodation and ambiance that one can expect. Do no feel that to travel the "Bed and Breakfast" route means you will be roughing it. Although some of the least expensive choices in our guide offer simple rooms without a private bathroom, it is possible to choose places to stay that offer sumptuous accommodations—as beautiful as you will find in the most luxurious hotels in France, at a fraction of the cost. So, this guide is not just for the budget conscious traveller, but for anyone who wants to meet the French people and experience their exceptional hospitality.

Levels of comfort and luxury are as individual and varied as the people and homes you will be visiting, so look at the rates and read the descriptions carefully in order to ensure finding the desired type of accommodation. All of the Bed and Breakfasts listed in this guide are clean and tidy and, unless otherwise specified, have at least a basin area in the bedroom if there is no private bath. Sometimes in the least expensive Bed and Breakfasts, toiletries are not provided, not even soap; so bring your own. (On the other hand, some of the more elaborate Bed and Breakfasts offer every nicety including shampoo and hair dryer.) Besides soap, two other items that are a good idea to pack are a wash cloth and a flashlight. The former is almost unheard of in France, and the latter can be helpful for a middle-of-the-night trip to the hallway WC.

Hosts cover the entire spectrum of French society, from titled counts and countesses to country farmers. All who are listed in this guide are hospitable and have a true desire to meet and interact with their guests. It takes a special kind of person to open his home to strangers, and the French who do so are usually genuinely warm and friendly. Bed and Breakfast accommodation is actually a relatively new trend in France, only gaining popularity in the last five to ten years. Although by nature, the French are reserved and private, they exude an outstanding hospitality to guests in their home.

CREDIT CARDS

Most Bed and Breakfasts do not accept credit cards. If they will accept credit cards, we have indicated this in the description of the Bed and Breakfast using the following codes: AX (American Express), EC (Eurocard), MC (MasterCard), VS (Visa).

DRIVING AND DIRECTIONS

It is important to understand some basic directions in French when locating Bed and Breakfasts. Signs directing to Chambres d'Hôtes are often accompanied by either "1ère à droite" (first road on the right) or "1ère à gauche" (first road on the left). Chambres d'Hôtes signs can vary from region to region, but most have adopted the national green and yellow sign of the Gîtes de France as previously shown on page 3.

Maps will label the roads with their proper numbers, but you will find when driving that signs usually indicate a direction instead of a road number. For example, instead of finding a sign for N909 north, you will see a sign pointing in the direction of Lyon, so you must figure out by referring to your map whether Lyon is north of where you want to go and if N909 leads there. The city that is signposted is often a major city quite a distance away. This may seem awkward at first, but is actually an easy system once you get your bearings.

Most Bed and Breakfast homes and farmhouses are located outside whatever town or village under which they are listed. To make finding your destination easier, specific driving instructions are given in each hotel description. However, if you become lost while looking for a Bed and Breakfast, you can always find the nearest post office or public phone box (usually in the central town square or in front of the post office) and call your hosts for directions—is a good idea to keep a few francs handy for phone calls. In a pinch, bars and petrol stations will usually allow you to use their phones (they will charge you after the call). An added suggestion: Always plan to arrive at your destination before nightfall—road signs are very difficult to see after dark.

LANGUAGE

Language is only sometimes a barrier, but a good idea is to take a traveller's French course before departure. Possessing even the most rudimentary knowledge and exposure to French will make your trip a thousand times more rewarding and enjoyable. One can always "get by": usually there is someone around who speaks at least a little English, and the French are accustomed to dealing with non-French-speaking travellers. It is helpful to carry paper and pencil to write down numbers for ease of comprehension, as well as a French phrase book and/or dictionary. If pronunciation seems to be a problem, you can then indicate the word or phrase in writing. If you are having difficulty, above all keep your sense of humor; becoming frustrated or angry only makes matters worse.

The level of English spoken in the Bed and Breakfasts in this guide, runs the gamut from excellent to none at all. Because some of you would have fun practicing your high school French while others would feel more comfortable freely communicating, we have indicated under each Bed and Breakfast description what you can expect. Levels of the host's English are indicated according to the following guidelines:

NO ENGLISH SPOKEN—a few words at best.

VERY LITTLE ENGLISH SPOKEN—a little more than the most rudimentary, or perhaps their children speak schoolroom English. More is understood than spoken.

SOME or GOOD ENGLISH SPOKEN—basic communication is possible, but longer, involved conversations are not. Speak slowly and clearly. Remember, they may understand more than they can articulate.

VERY GOOD ENGLISH SPOKEN—easy conversational English. More understood than able to express verbally.

FLUENT ENGLISH SPOKEN—can understand and communicate with ease, frequently the person has lived in Britain or the United States.

MAPS

In the back of this guide (on pages 219–230) there are eleven maps pin-pointing the location of each Bed and Breakfast. However, these are not detailed enough to be sufficient on the road. Because places in the countryside are so very difficult to find, it is vital that you supplement our maps with more detailed ones. The finest are made by Michelin who publishes two sets of regional maps—we recommend and cross-reference the series numbered from 230 to 245. So that you will know what to purchase, we have put the corresponding Michelin map number at the bottom of each hotel description. Every place to stay featured in this guide can be found on these maps. (Another bonus with the Michelin maps is that historical monuments are indicated and scenic routes are highlighted in green.) Nothing can surpass the accuracy and detail of the Michelin maps, but sadly, they lack an index; so it is helpful to supplement the Michelin maps with a Hallwag map (distributed by Rand McNally) that covers an amazing number of small towns and also has an index that is very useful. Michelin and Hallwag maps can be purchased or special-ordered from travel oriented book stores.

MEALS

BED AND BREAKFASTS usually provide a Continental-type breakfast, including a choice of coffee (black or with hot milk), tea or hot chocolate, bread (sometimes a croissant or wheat bread for variety), butter and jam. The evening before, hosts will customarily ask when you want breakfast, and what beverage you prefer. Sometimes they will offer a choice of location such as outside in the garden, or indoors in the dining area or kitchen. (Breakfast is rarely served in the bedroom.)

"TABLE D'HÔTE" means that the host serves an evening meal, usually joining you for dinner, though certainly not always. Of all the special features of a Bed and Breakfast experience, this is one of the most outstanding attributes. If you see "Table d'Hôte" offered under the Bed and Breakfast description in the back of this guide, be sure to take it! You will not have a choice of menu, but you will have a delicious, home-cooked dinner (usually the ingredients are fresh from the garden) and be able to meet fellow guests. Prices quoted are always per person and sometimes include a table wine. The price depends upon how elaborate the meal is, the sophistication of the service, the number of courses, if wines are included, etc. But, whether the meal is simple or gourmet, whenever you take advantage of the "Table d'Hôte" option, you will discover a real bargain and have a truly memorable experience.

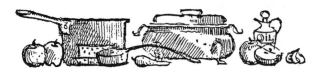

Most frequently meals are served at one large table with the hosts joining you and the other guests for dinner. Sometimes though, meals are served at individual or shared tables. Expect at least three courses (an appetizer, a main course and dessert), often four or five courses (with salad and cheese being served between the entree and dessert). Contrary to popular belief, salad is not always served after the main course and thus may appear before or accompanying the main meal. Even when it is indicated in the Bed and Breakfast description that Table d'Hôte is available, it is *ALWAYS* only by prior arrangement. So, if you want to dine, make a dinner reservation when you book your room and check to see what time the meal will be served (be sure to call your host from along the way if you are running late). The French do not have large freezers stocked with frozen supplies nor microwaves to defrost a quick meal—food is usually selected and purchased with care the day it is prepared, so, it is difficult to produce an impromptu meal. If you are a late arrival and have not eaten, sometimes your host will offer a plate of cold cuts, salad and bread, but do not expect this as it is not standard procedure. A few other French terms to describe food services are listed below:

"DEMI-PENSION" includes breakfast and dinner with prices quoted per person. This usually saves you money. Be sure to eat dinner, as hosts plan on it.

"PENSION COMPLET" includes breakfast, lunch and dinner with prices quoted per person. This formula is rarely an option since most travellers prefer to be on their own for lunches.

"FERME AUBERGE" is a family-style restaurant, open to the public, on a working farm. These inns are actually controlled by the French government insofar as the products served must come mainly from the farm itself. The fare is usually simple and hearty, utilizing fresh meats and vegetables. The hosts do not usually sit down and share meals with their guests because sometimes they are too busy serving.

RATES

In each hotel listing, rates are given for two persons in a double room, including tax, service and continental breakfast. Often rooms can accommodate up to four to six persons at additional charge. Cribs and extra beds are usually available for children. Prices frequently go down if a stay is longer than three to five nights. Many places to stay also offer small apartments or separate houses with cooking facilities that are ideal for families. Apartment rates do not include breakfast and are based on a week's stay (reservations are rarely accepted for time periods less than a week). When budgeting, a rule of thumb to remember is that usually the farther out in the country and away from large towns or tourist regions, the more inexpensive the accommodation will be. Beautifully furnished country homes and castles can be real bargains; although they will cost more if located in one of the prime tourist centers. Rates quoted were given to us at the time of publication and are subject to change. Be sure to verify the current price when making a reservation.

RESERVATIONS—GENERAL INFORMATION

Reservations are vital, especially during the busy summer months—particularly for Bed and Breakfasts in the most popular tourist regions. Even if you do not make a reservation before leaving home, it is important that you do call in advance. Bed and Breakfasts are not hotels, they are private homes, so as a rule, it is not appropriate to just knock on the door and expect accommodation. Therefore, if you want to be "footloose" and not confined to a rigid schedule, phone from along the way to see if space is available.

RESERVATIONS—DEPOSITS: Deposits are preferred if you are reserving several months ahead of your arrival date and should be paid in French francs. This is for your own protection against fluctuating exchange rates. Money orders in French francs can be purchased at the main branch of many large banks. Credit cards are rarely accepted at Bed and Breakfast homes. Payment should always be in French francs, not traveller's cheques.

RESERVATIONS BY FAX: A few of the more sophisticated Bed and Breakfasts have installed fax machines. If so, this is a very efficient way to request a reservation. (You can use the reservation letter in French found on page 14.) Sending a fax is like telephoning: use the international code (011 from the United States), then the country code for France (33) followed by the fax number. (Remember to give your fax number for their response.)

RESERVATIONS BY MAIL: Writing a letter is the most popular method for booking accommodations, but allow plenty of time. It is advisable to write two months in advance so that you will have time to write to your second choice if your first choice is unavailable. Allow at least a week each way for air mail to and from France. If you do not speak French, you can make a photo copy and use the reservation letter supplied on page 14 (at the end of this introduction section).

RESERVATIONS BY TELEPHONE: If you speak French (or if we have indicated under the Bed and Breakfast description that fluent English is spoken by the owner), we recommend you call for a reservation. With a telephone call you can discuss what is available and most suited to your needs. It is best to always follow up with a letter and a deposit in French francs if requested. Telephone reservations are accepted by most Bed and Breakfast homes, but if there is a language barrier, it will be frustrating and difficult to communicate your wants. (Remember the time difference when calling.)

RESERVATIONS THROUGH THE GÎTES DE FRANCE OFFICES: Many of the Gîtes de France offices will make reservations for you (see page 4 for a few local Gîte contacts).

The Gîtes de France office in the Loire Valley has indicated to us that they will make reservations any where in France for *ANY* Chambre d'Hôte (Bed and Breakfast) in our guide that belongs the Gîtes de France affiliation. To take advantage of this service, when making your reservation you must prepay with your credit card (accepted for payment are Visa, MasterCard or EuroCard). The booking fee will range from 50F to 100F (please contact the Loire office directly for futher details). If you do not speak French (or even if you do), this one telephone call to make reservations throughout France seems to be a very handy arrangement (we would appreciate your feedback on how well this system works). To use this service, contact Philippe Bordet (fluent English) at GÎTES DE FRANCE, 38, rue Augustin Fresnel, 37171 Chambray les Tours, France; telephone 47.48.37.46, fax 47.48.13.39. Remember, to call or fax to France, first dial the international code (011) and then the country (33) and then the telephone or fax number. (Please note: we are in no way affiliated with any of the Gîtes de France offices and cannot be responsible for any bookings made through them.)

RESERVATIONS AND CHECK IN: The Bed and Breakfasts are not hotels, they are private homes, and there is not always someone "at the front desk" to check you in. Therefore, it is a great courtesy to call the day you are expected to reconfirm your reservation and to advise approximately what time you expect to arrive. You can call from along the way from a public telephone (they are easy to use in France) or else call from where you stay the previous night.

RESERVATIONS AND CANCELLATIONS: If it is necessary for you to cancel your reservation for any reason, *PLEASE PHONE* (or write far in advance) to alert the proprietor. Bed and Breakfasts often only have one or two rooms to rent, and are thus severely impacted financially if they hold a room for a "no-show". It is embarrassing to hear stories from gracious innkeepers who have stayed up until late at night, waiting to welcome the guest who never came.

TOURIST INFORMATION

"Syndicat d'Initiative" is the name for the tourist offices found in all towns and resorts in France. When you are on the road, it is very helpful to pop into one of these tourist offices that are sign-posted with a large "I" (which stands for "information"). The agents gladly give advice on local events, timetables for local trains, buses and boats, and often have maps and brochures on the region's points of interest. They can also help with locating Bed and Breakfast accommodation. Before you depart for France, additional information can be obtained by writing to one of the tourist offices listed below:

French Government Tourist Office, 610 Fifth Avenue, Suite 222, New York, NY 10020, U.S.A.

French Government Tourist Office, 9454 Wilshire Blvd., Beverly Hills, CA 90212, U.S.A.

French Government Tourist Office, 2305 Cedar Springs Road, Suite 205, Dallas, TX 75201, U.S.A.

French Government Tourist Office, 645 N. Michigan Avenue, Chicago, IL 60611, U.S.A.

French Government Tourist Office, 178 Piccadilly, London W1V OAL, England

French Government Tourist Office, 1981 Avenue McGill College, Suite. 490, Montreal, Quebec, H3A 2W9, Canada

The above tourist offices can only be contacted by mail. If you want to call for specific information, in the United States you can telephone 1-900-990-0040. Calls to this number will be charged to your phone bill at the rate of $.50 (fifty cents) per minute. When you are in France, the French government in conjunction with American Express has an outstanding service available from May through October. From anywhere in France dial 05-201-202 (a toll-free "Hotline") to speak to an English-speaking travel adviser.

SAMPLE RESERVATION LETTER

To: Bed and Breakfast name and address

Monsieur/Madame:

Nous serons _____ personnes.   Nous voudrions réserver pour _____ nuit(s)
We have (number) of persons in our party. We would like to reserve for (number of nights)

du _____   au _____
from (date of arrival)   *to   (date of departure),*

une chambre à deux lits _____,   une chambre au grand lit _____
a room(s) with twin beds   *a room(s) with double bed(s)*

une chambre avec un lit supplémentaire _____
room(s) with an extra bed

avec toilette et baignoire ou douche privée _____
with private toilet & bathtub or shower

Veuilliez confirmer la réservation en nous communicant le prix de la chambre et la somme d'arrhes que vous souhaitez. Dans l'attente de votre réponse, nous vous prions d'agréer, Messieurs, Mesdames, l'expression de nos sentiments distingués.

Please advise availability, rate of room & deposit needed. We will be waiting for your confirmation & send our kindest regards.

Your Name and Address

14

Descriptions of Places to Stay

Madame Guervilly's ivy-covered manor house, dating from the 1700's, is filled with a collection of wonderful country antiques. She is an antique dealer and, fortunately for her guests, displays some splendid pieces in her historical home. The breakfast room is particularly lovely, with old tile floors, high beamed ceiling and a massive stone fireplace, all complemented by period furniture. Madame enjoys entertaining friends and serving intimate Table d'Hôte dinners in this lovely room. On warm mornings, guests are treated to breakfast on the garden terrace; a peaceful setting interrupted only by an occasional bird song. The charming guest rooms are found in a separate wing of the house where a restful night's slumber is assured after you are lulled to sleep by the rustling sound of the wind in the poplar trees. Picturesque surroundings, a gracious hostess and reasonable rates all combine to make Le Grand Talon a truly marvelous find. *Directions:* Andard is located 10 km east of Angers. From Angers, take N147 in the direction of Saumur. After about 10 km, you will see a green and yellow Chambres d'Hôtes sign. After 10 km, you see a large sign pointing to Sarrigne. Turn as if you were indeed going to Sarrigne, go through the stop sign and the driveway will be 20 meters later.

LE GRAND TALON (Gîte de France)
Hostess: Madame Annie Guervilly
Route National 147
49800 Trelaze, Andard, France
tel: 41.80.42.85
2 rooms, both with private bath/share WC
Single: 180F, Double: 230F, Triple: 280F
Table d'Hôte: 100-120F per person
Open all year
Very little English spoken
Region: Loire Valley, Michelin Map 232

Although close to Avignon, one almost seems in another world approaching through the barren, rock studded landscape to Le Rocher Pointu, a lovely old stone farmhouse softened by dark brown shutters and huge terra cotta pots brimming with flowers. It must have seemed an overwhelming task to make the house livable when Annie and Andre Malek bought it a few years ago, there was not even running water. Now, not only is there running water, there is a beautiful swimming pool (if you are somewhat prudish, be forewarned that you might find most of the guests swimming au natural). The interior has been renovated maintaining the natural appeal of the original old farmhouse: white walls, massive beamed ceilings, and country antiques add to the appealing ambiance. Upstairs are four bedrooms—my favorite is the Clair de Lune room with a handsome wood French Provençal headboard and a pretty view from the casement windows. There are a kitchen and barbecue area for guests use. *Directions:* Aramon is located about 10 km southwest of Avignon. From Avignon, follow the D2 south along the west bank of the Rhône. Turn right, in the direction of Saze, when you come to D126. After 2.3 km you will come to the sign for Le Rocher Pointu. Turn left at the sign and follow the road to the Rocher Pointu.

LE ROCHER POINT (Gîte de France)
Hosts: Annie & Andre Malek
Plan de Deve
30390 Aramon, France
tel: 66.57.41.87 fax: 66.57.01.77
4 rooms, with private bathrooms
Double: 310-350F, Triple: 410-500F
No Table d'Hôte
Open all year
Good English spoken
Region: Provence
Michelin Maps 240,245,246

In a region where pretty Romanesque churches and medieval villages dot the rolling hills, very near the lovely and historic Fontenay Abbey, the Clergets offer modest and home-like accommodations in their pretty stone house. A charming front garden leads into Madame Clerget's friendly kitchen where her grandchildren often visit for a taste of her famous rhubarb pie. Guest bedrooms are located upstairs and are all unique, filled with an eclectic collection of knickknacks and antiques, old family photos, pictures and paintings. The house dates from 1807 and the rooms all have their own individual character, most with exposed beams and rafters. Monsieur and Madame Clerget are a retired couple who extend a warm welcome to guests and are happy to aid in planning sightseeing excursions or even wild mushroom-hunting forays in the nearby forest. *Directions:* Arrans is located approximately 80 kilometers northwest of Dijon. Take auto route A38 in the direction of Paris, exiting at Sombernon and continuing on D905 towards Vitteaux and Montbard. At the town of Montbard, turn right onto D5 towards Arrans. About 9 kilometers later, just before entering the village of Arrans, look for the Clerget's ivy-covered house on the left and marked with a Chambres d'Hôtes sign.

L'ENCLOS (Gîte de France)
Hostess: Mireille Clerget
Arrans, 21500 Montbard, France
tel: 80.92.16.12
4 rooms, 3 with private bathrooms
Double: 200-250F, Triple: 300-350F
Table d'Hôte: 75-95F per person
Open March 1 through November 30
No English spoken
Region: Burgundy, Michelin Map 243

Christiane and Serge Maurel's Ferme Auberge is built in a style typical of the more southern regions of France, with light stone walls and a warm tile roof. Accommodation consists of a suite in the main house and five rooms in a pavilion-style annex, each with French doors opening out to the swimming pool and lawn area. Rooms are clean and functional with cool tile floors and private bathrooms. The Maurels have created an idyllic setting, building their pool on a terrace overlooking a spectacular vista of faraway gorse- and oakcovered hills. Le Mas de Clamouze is well-known for its delicious meals served in generous portions. Days begin with a breakfast buffet of ham, yogurt, regional cheeses, fresh fruit, croissants, two kinds of bread, juice and a choice of coffee, tea or hot chocolate. In the evenings, Christiane's hearty, five-course meals featuring fresh farm produce are served in the spacious country dining room. *Directions:* Asprières is located approximately 16 kilometers southeast of Figeac. Take N140 towards Rodez as far as Bouillac, turning right onto D40 towards Villeneuve and Asprières. Go through the village of Asprières and follow Chambres d'Hôtes signs to the Maurel's farmhouse. The driveway is on the left-hand side of the road.

LE MAS DE CLAMOUZE (Gîte de France)
Hosts: Christiane & Serge Maurel
12700 Asprières, France
tel: 65.63.89.89
6 rooms, with private bathrooms
Single: 206F, Double: 306F, Triple: 434F
Table d'Hôte: 80F per person
Open May to September 30
Very little English spoken
Some Italian & German spoken
Region: Lot, Michelin Map 235

The small country village of Availles Limouzine is the peaceful setting for the 200-year-old home of Marie-Reine and Andre May. A shady front yard and sunny front terrace lead to the entrance of this quiet home where a warm welcome and comfortable quarters await. The Mays are still in the process of renovating some parts of their interesting house, but most of the public areas are freshly painted and home-like. Bedrooms are simply furnished and very clean, with artful touches adding life and charm. The entire family seems to have an artistic streak, and artwork by Madame's uncle, son and daughter is displayed throughout the house. The living room and dining room adjoin and are furnished in a pleasing mixture of country antiques and comfy seating accented by family photos. An adjoining terrace provides a pleasant spot for breakfast on sunny mornings. The modest Logis de la Mothe is recommended for travellers who are seeking quiet, comfortable accommodation in a village environment. *Directions:* Availles Limouzine is located approximately 56 kilometers southeast of Poitiers. Take D741 through Gençay, continuing to Pressac where you will turn left onto D34 to Availles Limouzine. Once in the village, go to the church at the top of the hill where the road splits: take the left fork. Look for the May's house on the right. A few hundred feet later—the gatepost is marked with a Chambres d'Hôtes sign.

LOGIS DE LA MOTHE (*Gîte de France*)
Hosts: Marie-Reine & Andre May
86460 Availles - Limouzine, France
tel: 49.48.51.70
4 rooms, 2 with private bath/WC
Single: 125F, Double: 190, Triple: 250F
No Table d'Hôte
Open all year
No English spoken
Region: Limousin, Michelin Map 233

If you choose to make Les Ecureuils your "home" while exploring the Loire Valley, you will be warmly welcomed as friends by Françoise and Lionel Menoret, who take great pleasure in making each guest feel special. Their small, symmetrical, two-storey home with a steeply pitched roof and twin chimneys, is located in the pretty little village of Cheille (well known for its very old church that miraculously has a tree growing within the wall). As you enter the front hallway, on the right is an intimate parlor that guests are welcome to use. To the left is the dining room where Françoise serves delicious meals that are lovingly prepared and artfully presented. A doorway off the hall leads to the one bedroom, with the shower and wash basin in a curtained off area and a private WC. located in a separate room. The bedroom is small, but impeccably clean and very sweet in tones of soft green and rose with "Laura-Ashley-like" wall paper and pretty coordinating fabric used for the headboard and drapes. Lionel, whose business is tourism, is a wealth of information on what to see and do in the area, and will happily help you plan each day's adventure. His lovely young wife, Françoise, keeps busy managing the B&B, caring for their little girls, Pauline and Gaille (who will win your heart), and tending the garden where she grows fresh vegetables for the table. *Directions:* From Azay le Rideau take D18 northwest towards the Chateau d'Ussé. After about 5 km, turn left at Cheille. Go past the church. Continue 150 meters. You will see Les Ecureuil's sign on your left.

LES ECUREUILS (*Gîte de France*)
Hosts: Françoise & Lionel Menoret
Cheille, 37190 Azay le Rideau, France
tel: 47.45.39.74 fax: 47.48.13 39
1 room with private bathroom
Double 240F
Table d Hôte 90 F per person, includes wine
Open all year, 2 night minimum
Fluent English by Lionel, Françoise learning
Region: Loire Valley, Michelin Map 232

La Bihourderie, a characterful long, low home, with a heavily-tiled roof, has a storybook charm. With ivy covering almost the entire farm house, La Bihourderie is extremely appealing, and also well located for visiting the fabulous chateaux of the Loire Valley. It has white shuttered windows peeking out from a lace of greenery and gabled windows prettily accentuating its steep roof. The front courtyard abounds with beautifully tended flower gardens. Everything is meticulously kept: neat and tidy. A separate door leads into the guest quarters where there is a parlor and four bedrooms, each named for a Van Gough painting. My favorite room is "Les Iris," attractively decorated with fabrics blending with the framed copy of Van Gough's painting. Although the farm house is very old, the decor is a bit bland and not antique in feeling, but everything is exceptionally well-kept and immaculately clean—Mignès Epaud is a wonderful housekeeper. All the food is fresh from the family's farm. When the days are warm, both breakfast and dinner are served at tables set outside on the lawn behind the house, so wonderfully close to the fields, that wheat almost tickles your nose. *Directions:* Take N143 north in the direction of Tours. In about 10 km, turn right at the Chambres d'Hôtes sign toward Azay-sur-Indre. La Bihourderie will be signposted on the left side of the road.

LA BIHOURDERIE (Gîte de France)
Hosts: Mignès & Philippe Epaud
37310 Azay-sur-Indre, France
tel: 47.92.58.58
4 rooms, with private bathrooms
Double: 220-240F
Table d'Hôte: 85F per person, includes wine
Open all year
Good English spoken
Region: Loire Valley, Michelin Map 238

Nestled in the rolling hills and farmlands of the Lot region, the Chambert's 150-year-old farmhouse has a regional red tile roof made remarkable by its twin pigeon towers at either end. Guests have complete independence and privacy as the Chamberts live next door in a more recently constructed home. Monsieur tends to his primary occupation of farming, while Madame capably handles all guest needs. A home-like, comfortable ambiance reigns, especially in the evenings when Madame serves her family-style Table d'Hôte dinners in front of the large open-hearthed fireplace. Beamed ceilings, hanging copper pots and rustic family antiques add warmth and charm to the homespun decor. Bedrooms are equally charming, furnished in a mix of antiques and more contemporary pieces. One particularly quaint room has a brass bed, exposed support beams and a pretty, round antique table adorned with an earthenware pot of dried flowers. Located near the spectacular hillside village of Rocamadour, Domaine de Bel Air offers a quiet retreat into French farm life. *Directions:* Le Bastit is located approximately 18 kilometers south of Rocamadour. Take N140 towards Gramat and Cahors: at Gramat follow directions for Cahors and Le Bastit on D677. At Le Bastit, look for a series of small, hand-made arrows directing you through the village and down a country lane to Domaine de Bel Air.

DOMAINE DE BEL AIR (Gîte de France)
Hostess: Francine Chambert
Le Bastit, 46500 Gramat, France
tel: 65.38.77.54
6 rooms, 2 with private bathrooms
Double: 200F, Triple: 260F
Table d'Hôte: 65F per person
Open all year
Very little English spoken
Region: Lot, Michelin Map 235

Arlette Vachet's English-style country cottage is at the top of our list for romantic and atmospheric Bed and Breakfast accommodation. Arlette is a painter and former antique dealer who has filled her cozy, ivy-covered house with a potpourri of country antiques and used her artistic talents to decorate the interior to charming perfection. Her salon is a virtual treasure trove of paintings, old furniture and objets d'art, set off by low, beamed ceilings and an old stone hearth. A comfortable couch and a crackling fire are the perfect accompaniments to an evening's aperitif before sampling one of the region's many restaurants, renowned for their fine wines and gourmet cuisine. French doors open from the garden to the ground floor bedroom (that has an adjoining rose-tiled bathroom) is prettily decorated in tones of forest green and pink. The upstairs bedroom is small and intimate, its walls and low, sloping ceiling covered by beautiful flowered wallpaper. *Directions:* Baudrières is located approximately 20 kilometers northeast of Tournus. Leave Tournus on N6 towards Sennecey le Grand and Chalon sur Saône. Just after passing through the town of Sennecey le Grand, turn right onto D18 in the direction of Gigny. Cross the river Saône and follow signs to the small village of Baudrières: Arlette Vachet's picturesque cottage is on the corner.

CHEZ VACHET (Gîte de France)
Hostess: Madame Arlette Vachet
Baudrières,
71370 St-Germain du Plain, France
tel: 85.47.32.18
2 rooms, with private bathrooms
Double: 300F
No Table d'Hôte
Open all year
Good English spoken
Region: Burgundy, Michelin Map 243

Ludovic and Eliane Cornillon have struck the perfect balance between rustic ambiance and luxurious comfort in their charming farmhouse found in the countryside of northern Provence. The entire farm complex dates from 1769 and is rectangular in shape, forming a tranquil central garden sheltered by weathered stone walls. A low doorway leads into the historic entry salon that has a large old hearth decorated with dried flower bouquets and interesting antique furniture including a petain, a piece somewhat like a large chest used for both storing flour and kneading bread dough. The adjoining dining room, formerly the stables, still displays a stone feeding trough and little stairway to the attic where the hay was stored. Eliane's fresh style of cuisine features regional herbs and is complemented well by Domaine de St-Luc wines, as Ludovic is a talented wine maker. After dinner, a good night's rest is assured in charming bedrooms, all with spotless private baths. *Directions:* La Baume de Transit is located about 24 kilometers north of Orange. Take auto route A7 and exit at Bollene, following directions for Suze la Rousse on D94. Leave Suze la Rousse on D59 towards St-Paul Trois Chateaux, but turn off almost immediately onto the small country road CD117 towards La Baume de Transit. Look for signs for Domaine de St-Luc.

DOMAINE DE ST-LUC **(***Gîte de France***)**
Hosts: Eliane Ludovic & Cornillon
Le Gas du Rossignol, La Baume de Transit
26130 St-Paul-Trois Chateaux, France
tel: 75.98.11.51 fax: 75.98.19.22
5 rooms, with private bathrooms
Single: 200F, Double: 260F, Triple: 300F
Table d'Hôte: 125-130F per person
Open all year
Good English spoken by Eliane
Region: Provence, Michelin Maps 245, 246

As the road winds down the rocky barren incline from Les Baux, an oasis suddenly opens up where luxury hotels and handsome homes peek out from the shrubbery of verdant gardens. Here you will find La Burlande, the home of Jenny Fajardo de Livry: lawyer, mother, and talented hôtelier. At the moment she no longer practices law—her four children, along with the day to day operation of La Burlande as a Bed and Breakfast keep her more than occupied. The house is newly built and does not attempt to closely emulate the typical provençal antique style. Instead, the ambiance is of a modern home with large picture windows and spacious, bright airy rooms. The furnishings, that are accented by oriental carpets on cool tiled floors, are sophisticated rather than country-cute. There are only three guest rooms plus a suite comprised of two guest rooms sharing a bathroom. This suite is an ideal set up for a family because it also has its own little terrace that opens out to a beautiful swimming pool and the impeccably tended, prize winning gardens. *Directions:* As you leave Les Baux on the D78F you will see La Burlande sign-posted on the left-hand side of the road.

LA BURLANDE (Gîte de France)J
Hostess: Jenny Fajardo de Livry
Le Paradou
13520 Les Baux, France
tel: 90.54.32.32
3 rooms, with private bathrooms
1-2 bedroom suite sharing a bath
Double 350-630F, Suite 630-720F
Table d'Hôte: 135F per person, without wine.
Open all year
Good English spoken
Region: Provence, Michelin Maps 245, 246

The Chateau d'Arbieu is filled with family antiques, paintings, and objets d'art, yet also manages to convey a comfortable, lived-in feeling. Titled hosts Count and Countess de Chenerilles are a young, friendly and unpretentious couple who happily welcome guests to their historic family home. Delicious and carefully prepared Table d'Hôte dinners are enjoyed with the de Chenerilles in their pleasant dining room. Furnishings are a mix of contemporary and antique pieces accented by home-like touches such as large color photos of their five children above the mantelpiece. The guest bedrooms that are found upstairs, affording lovely views of the countryside, contain beautiful antique furnishings and are decorated with tasteful, period-style wallpapers, fabrics and artwork. Fresh flower arrangements and in-room phones add thoughtful touches of luxury. Extensive grounds include a refreshing swimming pool and convenient pool-house kitchenette for guest's use. *Directions:* Bazas is located 48 kilometers southeast of Bordeaux. Take auto route A62 in the direction of Agen and Toulouse. Exit at Langon and follow signs to Bazas via D932. From Bazas, take D655 towards Casteljoux and less than 1 kilometer outside town look for a Chambres d'Hôtes sign that marks the long driveway to the Chateau d'Arbieu.

CHATEAU D'ARBIEU (Gîte de France)
Hosts: Count & Countess de Chenerilles
Arbieu 33430 Bazas, France
tel: 56.25.11.18 fax: 56.25.90.52
3 rooms, 1 suite, all with private bathroom
Single: 365-420F, Double: 395-450F
Table d'Hôte: 150F per person
Open all year (reservations required in winter)
Some English spoken
Region: Lot & Garonne, Michelin Map 234

The picturesque Alsatian town of Beblenheim is the quaint setting for Stefan Klein's half-timbered antique shop, winebar, and Bed and Breakfast. Guests enter a flower-filled courtyard and then go down worn stone steps leading through an old archway to the atmospheric cellar bar where many convivial evenings are spent listening to music and sampling regional wines and beers. A light menu offers tasty gourmet fare such as quiche, salads and selections of regional cheese and sausage. Inviting guest rooms are located upstairs and are charmingly furnished with polished pine furniture, antique paintings, dried flower arrangements and cheerful, dainty, flowered bedspreads and pillowcases. Beamed ceilings and windows opening out onto flower-filled window boxes complete the German country feeling. *Directions:* Beblenheim is located about 15 kilometers north of Colmar. Take N83 through the village of Ingersheim where you will turn right onto D10 and follow La Route des Vins (wine route) towards the town of Riquewihr. Turn off into the village of Beblenheim and follow the main street past a little fountain and the post office (PTT). Take the next right on to rue Jean Mace, followed by an immediate right onto rue des Raisins. The narrow street dead-ends, and Chez Klein is found at the end on the left.

CHEZ KLEIN (Gîte de France)
Host: Monsieur Stephan Klein
4, rue des Raisins
68980 Beblenheim, France
tel: 89.49.02.82
5 rooms, with private bathrooms
Double: 245-270, Triple: 375F
Convivial, casual restaurant
Open all year
Good English spoken, also fluent German
Region: Alsace, Michelin Map 242

High in the French Alps, life in the small, remote villages remains very much unchanged from generation to generation. A stay with the Pasquier family offers a chance to experience a real slice of mountain farm-life: no frills, but plenty of old-fashioned hospitality and simple comforts. Their traditional farmhouse is found nestled in a narrow valley flanked by green meadows and jagged peaks. The region is a paradise for hikers and skiers, all of whom the Pasquiers enjoy welcoming to their home and table. Madame's Table d'Hôte dinners feature substantial home-cooked fare typically including soup, a main course of meat and potatoes, a selection of cheeses, green salad and fresh fruit for dessert. Bedrooms are small but adequate with basic, yet pleasant decor; each with the convenience of its own tiny bathroom and WC. *Directions:* Bellevaux is located approximately 50 kilometers northeast of Geneva. Take D907 from Geneva for about 35 kilometers to the town of St-Jeoire. Exit the national route and go into town, looking for a turnoff about halfway through town for Megevette. Continue through Megevette and look for a turnoff to the right just before the town of Bellevaux marked Chevrerie and Lac de Vallon. Pass the several chalets that make up the hamlet of Clusaz and look for a Chambres d'Hôtes sign marking a driveway on the right to the Pasquier's farm.

CHEZ PASQUIER (Gîte de France)
Hosts: François & Geneviève Pasquier La Clusaz
74470 Bellevaux, France
tel: 50.73.71.92
5 rooms, with private bathrooms
Single: 90F, Double: 166F, Triple: 240F
Table d'Hôte: 65F per person
Open all year
No English spoken
Region: French Alps, Michelin Maps 243, 244

This old stone farmhouse once belonged to the nearby chateau and is now an ideal stop for travellers seeking a familial, countryside Bed and Breakfast at a delightfully inexpensive price. Andre and Arlette Vermes and their three children welcome guests into their farmhouse with enthusiasm, always happy to assist guests by helping with sightseeing plans, loaning bicycles or even offering their playroom to children. The former stables comprise a separate wing for Bed and Breakfast guests that includes a large dining room/salon and three guest bedrooms. Downstairs, a rustic flavor still remains with a collection of old farm implements displayed on the natural stone walls. Breakfasts and Table d'Hôte dinners are served here at a long pine table. The family-style meals feature regional dishes such as chicken in cream sauce and delicious apple tarts. Four bedrooms are found upstairs and one on the ground floor. Each is charmingly individualized with pretty details such as brass beds, pine armoires, pretty print wallpapers and matching bedspreads. Bathroom facilities are modern, well equipped and very clean. *Directions:* Bernières d'Ailly is located approximately 30 kilometers southeast of Caen, 10 kilometers northeast of Falaise on D511. In Bernières d'Ailly, follow the Chambres d'Hôtes signs that will direct you to the Verme's farm.

FERME D'AILLY (Gîte de France)
Hosts: Arlette & Andre Vermes
14170 Bernières d'Ailly, France
tel: 31.90.73.58
5 rooms, with private bathrooms
Double: 165F, Triple: 210F
Table d'Hôte: 60F per person
Open all year
Good English spoken
Region: Normandy, Michelin Map 231

Jean Masdoumier is a sculptor and former theater artist who has a great love for his native Limousin countryside. He has converted an old farm complex dating from 1550 into a Bed and Breakfast that functions also as a small conference center and a retreat for stress reduction. Monsieur Masdoumier's Bed and Breakfast enterprise is complemented by his wife Anna's homeopathic medicine practice in an adjoining part of their charming old house. Monsieur Masdoumier has taken great care and pride in renovating the historic building, displaying its lovely stone floors, massive fireplaces and an ancient tower stairway original to the complex. Bedrooms are small and functional, and guests are encouraged to spend time in the public areas. A comfortable, attractively decorated study upstairs leads to the bedrooms and is a cozy room for a relaxing read or chat. Downstairs guests may choose to spend time in the peasant salon or the convivial dining room. There is also a wonderful gymnasium in an adjoining converted barn for guest's use and ponies are available for treks in the enchanting countryside. *Directions:* Travel northeast of Limoges approximately 35 kilometers on N20. Turn onto D28 at Bessines. Follow directions for Bersac sur Rivalier and Laurière. Turn left after the railroad bridge, then follow arrows to Domaine du Noyer.

DOMAINE DU NOYER (Gîte de France)
Hosts: Anne & Jean Masdoumier
Bersac sur Rivalier
87370 St-Sulpice Lauvière, France
tel: 55.71.59.54
4 rooms, with private bathrooms
Double 250F
Table d'Hôte: 85F per person, includes wine
Open all year
Very good English spoken
Region: Limousin, Michelin Map 239

Betschdorf is a picturesque, half-timbered town that has always been known for its distinctive blue-toned stoneware. Traditional pottery methods are handed down from generation to generation, and host Christian Krumeich represents the ninth generation of potters in his family. He and his artistic wife Joelle have installed charming guest quarters above their large pottery workshop, offering independent, stylish accommodation to travellers. Rooms are small yet very attractive, furnished in highly tasteful combinations of contemporary and antique furniture. Artful decor includes pastel upholstery, Monet prints, dried flower arrangements and colorful durrie rugs. The guest salon, decorated with Oriental rugs, antique furniture, well-chosen objets d'art and bookshelves stocked with interesting reading, offers a refined, comfortable ambiance for relaxation and meals. *Directions:* Betschdorf is located approximately 44 kilometers northeast of Strasbourg. Take N63 past Hagenau, continuing on D263 towards Hunspach and Wissembourg. After about 10 kilometers, turn right onto D243 to Betschdorf. Soon after entering town, on the main street, look for the Krumeich's driveway on the right, marked by a sign for Poterie and Chambres d'Hôtes.

CHEZ KRUMEICH (Gîte de France)
Hosts: Joelle & Christian Krumeich
23, rue des Potiers
67660 Betschdorf, France
tel: 88.54.40.56
3 rooms ,with private bathrooms
Double: 200-240F
No Table d'Hôte
Open all year
Some English spoken by Joelle
Region: Alsace, Michelin Map 242

La Grande Métairie, a characterful 16th-century stone farmhouse, belonged to Christine Moy's grandfather. Happily, very little has been changed except for the necessary modernization of plumbing and electricity. The beamed-ceilinged dining room is a gem: an enormous fireplace, copper pots, fresh flowers, antique fruitwood side-board and stone floors gleaming with the patina of age and walls three feet thick. Here Christine sets the table with a checkered table cloth and serves on Limoges china simple, yet superb meals from food almost totally grown on their organic farm—even the butter, meat, cheeses and vegetables come from their property. There are two tastefully decorated bedrooms plus a 2-bedroom apartment. La Grand Métairie is a simple working farm, yet the accommodations, ambiance, and genuine warmth of welcome far outshine the modest price (there is even a swimming pool on a back terrace). *Directions:* Ruffec is located 147 km NE of Bordeaux via the N10. Go to Ruffec and take D740 east toward Confolens. After the road crosses the river, take D 197 toward Bioussac. In 1.3 km turn left toward Oyer. Soon you will see La Grande Métairie on your left.

LA GRANDE MÉTAIRIEGîte de France)
Hosts: Christine & Jean Louis Moy
Oyer, 16700 Bioussac, France
tel: 45.31.15.67
2 rooms, with private bathrooms
Double: 200F
Also, 2-bedroom apt 1,800F/week
Table d'Hôte 65F per person, includes wine
Credit cards: None
Open April 7 through October 31
Swimming pool, bicycles
Fluent English spoken
Region: Limousin, Michelin Map 233

The Chateau de Cheman is a wonderfully enchanting castle dating from the 14th Century where Madame Antoine has made her home since 1941. She takes great pride in her historic home and the rosé and red wines produced here. The ancient, arched stone entry leads up to circular slate steps, worn by generations of use. Old wooden doors set in the tower stairwell lead into the Antoine's two guest apartments. The first is very spacious, with a sitting room and fully equipped kitchen area: walls and floors are stone, warmed by soft Oriental carpets, tapestries and wallpaper. The bedroom is furnished with elegant antiques and old prints, gilt light fixtures and gold trimmed furniture. A stone archway leads to the bathroom that is thoughtfully stocked with fresh towels, soap, and cottonwool. The second apartment is smaller, but also contains lovely furnishings and has a private terrace. Guests may choose to stay at the Chateau de Cheman either on a Bed and Breakfast basis, or for longer stays, at a weekly rate. *Directions:* Blaison is located 19 kilometers east of Angers on the south bank of the Loire. Take D751 to St-Jean des Mauvrets, then take D132 through St-Sulpice. Look for a hard-to-see sign indicating Chambres d'Hôtes that marks the chateau's long driveway.

CHATEAU DE CHEMAN (*Gîte de France*)
Hostess: Madame Alvina Antoine
Blaison Gohier
49320 Brissac Quince, France
tel: 41.57.17.60
2 apartments, with private bathrooms
Double: 550F
No Table d'Hôte
Open all year
No English spoken
Region: Loire Valley, Michelin Map 232

The Le Quéré family lives in a lovely old manor house dating from the 1700's that is also a working farm. The large, ivy-covered home is set back behind a tranquil green lawn and approached by way of a long, shady drive. The sunny dining room is furnished with tapestry chairs, a long wooden table and a Parisian marble fireplace and is a pleasant place to linger over breakfast. The guest bedrooms all have lovely hardwood floors and harmonious wallpapers, bedspreads and curtains. Most are simply furnished with family antiques and comfortable, contemporary chairs and tables. The three first-floor bedrooms share a common bath and WC, while the two third-floor bedrooms share a communal shower room and WC. The Le Quéré's farm Bed and Breakfast is not located near any well-known tourist areas, but offers instead tranquil, countryside surroundings providing many opportunities for scenic drives, walks or cycling tours. Guests can experience a true slice of French country life enhanced by a warm welcome and reasonable prices. *Directions:* The Le Quéré's farm is located approximately 40 km north of Limoges. Take N147 to Bellac and then follow N145 in the direction of La Souterraine. After about 1 km, turn left onto a small road across from a John Deere farm machinery dealership. Signs point the way to the Le Quéré's farm.

CHEZ LE QUÉRÉ (Gîte de France)
Hosts: Monsieur & Madame Le Quéré
Commune de Blanzac; RN 145 Rouffignac
87300 Blanzac, France
tel: 55.68.03.38
5 rooms, all share 2 bathrooms
Double: 180F
Table d'Hôte: 75F per person, without wine
Open all year
Good English spoken
Region: Limousin, Michelin Map 233

A mountain road winds through rustic Alpine hamlets and grassy fields of wildflowers to reach the Bertrand's contemporary home. Circular in shape, the house was designed by Monsieur, an architect by trade, and built on a ridge overlooking mountain ranges on either side. Inside, all bedrooms are built around a central living area that has picture windows showing off the lovely view. Floral-print drapes bring a breath of spring into the attractive living area that contains inviting couches and a cozy fireplace. Guest bedrooms are small but comfortable and are accessible either through the Bertrand's living area or via French doors leading out to a garden and tree-covered hillside. Monsieur and Madame Bertrand and their teenage children are friendly and solicitous hosts who also enjoy sharing home-cooked family meals with their guests. *Directions:* Bois Barbu is located about 30 kilometers southwest of Grenoble. From Grenoble, go through Sassenage, then take D531 to Villard de Lans. Just before the village of Villard de Lans, turn right towards Cote 2000 and Corrençon. After 1 kilometer, turn right following signs for Bois Barbu and Val Chevrière. At Bois Barbu take the left-hand fork of the road that will climb up slightly. Turn left again just before L'Auberge des Montards, then follow the winding road up to Col du Liorin and look for the Bertrand's low white house on the left.

CHEZ BERTRAND (*Gîte de France*)
Hosts: Monsieur & Madame Bertrand
Bois Barbu, 38250 Villard de Lans, France
tel: 76.95.82.67
2 rooms, both with private sink/WC/share shower
Double: 200F
Demi-pension: 180F per person
Open all year
No English spoken
Region: French Alps, Michelin Map 244

The Bon's romantic Alpine cottage is found high in a meadow filled with wildflowers and bordered by dark pine trees. Dominique and Agnes are a young, attractive couple who have lovingly restored and decorated their 250-year-old farmhouse, adding modern comfort while accenting its rustic country charm. Agnes is a wonderfully creative cook and enjoys preparing healthy, gourmet meals for guests. We enjoyed a friendly meal with the Bons and their three children that featured a crisp green salad, a delicate pork dish made with plenty of fresh eggplant and garden tomatoes, a selection of regional cheeses and homemade custard topped with ripe strawberries. Upstairs bedrooms are all freshly renovated with dainty flowered wallpapers and matching coverlets, complemented by country antiques and bouquets of field flowers. Rooms are small, but guests are invited to make themselves at home in the pretty downstairs sitting room with a cozy wood stove and well-stocked bookshelves. *Directions:* Bois Barbu is located about 30 kilometers southwest of Grenoble. From Grenoble, go through Sassenage, then take D531 to Villard de Lans. Just before the village of Villard de Lans, turn right towards Cote 2000 and Correncon. 1 kilometer later turn right following signs for Bois Barbu and Val Chevrière. Continue 3 kilometers and turn left opposite the cross-country ski center onto the Bon's gravel driveway.

CHEZ BON (Gîte de France)
Hosts: Dominique & Agnes Bon
Bois Barbu, 38250 Villard de Lans, France
tel: 76.95.92.80 fax: 76.95.56.79
3 rooms, with private bathrooms
Double: 230F, Triple: 340F
Table d'Hôte: 80F per person
Open all year
Some English spoken
Region: French Alps, Michelin Map 244

Built by monks in the late 1400's to early 1500's, this half-timbered manor house is filled with historic ambiance. Madame Delort has lived here for 45 years and has been hosting travellers since 1978. She obviously loves having personal contact with her guests, but unfortunately speaks no English. We arrived on a damp day in early spring, and were immediately ushered into the dining room to warm our feet beside the large open stone hearth. Breakfast is served at one long table in this atmospheric room framed by half-timbered walls and a beamed ceiling. The country antique furnishings are dominated by a huge chest filled with a colorful collection of old plates. A winding wooden staircase leads to the first floor where Madame Delort's guest rooms can sleep up to five and six people respectively. Bedrooms are not elegant, but they impart an authentic sense of the past, with beautiful original tile floors and antique armoires. Madame Delort's Bed and Breakfast is a reasonably priced, picturesque base from which to explore the Normandy area. *Directions:* La Boissière is located 8 kilometers west of Lisieux. Take N13 towards Caen, and you will see a Chambres d'Hôtes sign before reaching the town of Boissière that directs you to turn to the left. About 1 kilometer later another sign will indicate a long driveway to the right and you will see this typical Norman manor house set behind a pretty front garden.

CHEZ DELORT (*Gîte de France*)
Hostess: Madame Delort
La Boissière 14340 Cambremer, France
tel: 31.32.20.81
2 rooms, with private bathrooms
Double: 210F
No Table d'Hôte
Open April 1 to November 1
No English spoken
Region: Normandy, Michelin Map 231

Monsieur and Madame Letrésor, the attractive couple who own the Manoir du Champ Versant, thoroughly enjoy welcoming travellers into their 450-year-old, half-timbered manor house. It is not surprising that over the years they have built up a very faithful, repeat clientele. One of their returning guests is a New York artist who visits once a year and stays for a month at a time in order to paint the surrounding countryside: his pretty watercolors are found adorning the walls of the Letrésor's home. This home is full of character inside and out. The well-kept grounds consist of wide grassy areas, a pond, miscellaneous buildings, horses and chickens. Inside there are huge, open-hearthed stone fireplaces in both the salon and breakfast room, complemented by country antique furniture. Upstairs, the bedrooms are also very inviting with stone fireplaces, antique beds and armoires. Our room was the smaller of the two, cozy and intimate with an ancient cupboard, convenient writing table, and window with pretty view of the garden. We highly recommend the Letrésor's picturesque home, particularly to those travellers who value authentic charm and a warm welcome over luxurious comfort. *Directions:* Bonnebosq is located about 32 kilometers east of Caen. Three kilometers north of Bonnebosq on **D16** look for a "Manoir du Champ Versant" directing you to turn right onto a country road. Another sign marks the Letrésor's driveway to the left.

MANOIR DU CHAMP VERSANT (Gîte de France)
Hosts: Monsieur & Madame Letrésor
Manoir du Champ Versant
14340 Bonnebosq, France
tel: 31.65.11.07
2 rooms, with private bathrooms
Double: 210F, Triple: 280F
No Table d'Hôte
Open April 1 to November 1
Very little English spoken
Region: Normandy, Michelin Map 231

Chateau de Bouesse is a stunning turreted 13th-century castle, just brimming with romance. Not only is the castle fabulous, but its magical return to splendor is a story in itself. Jacqueline and Harry Courtot-Atterton (who are Canadians) loved to holiday in France. Seeing so many once-splendid castles falling into ruins, they decided to purchase one and restore it for future generations to enjoy. Two years of searching and 30 castles later, they found their dream. The lovely, but dilapidated, Chateau de Bouesse. With unbelievable love and tireless labor, they have transformed the castle to its original glory, and now share their home with a few lucky guests. When one enters the reception hall, to the right is a comfortable lounge where guests linger before dinner in front of the massive carved fireplace. Beyond the lounge is the bright and cheerful dining room, a real beauty with paneled walls painted a soft gray blue with white trim. The chef and meals are outstanding (using produce from the chateau's own garden). The bedrooms are all dramatic, particularly the large rooms in the tower reached by the circular stone staircase. As special as this castle is, the outstanding hospitality of the Courtot-Attertons is what will make your visit most memorable. Special note: Harry is a born story teller and a wealth of information on the castle and history of the area. His tales of the castle truly make history "come alive". *Directions:* Take N20 south from Chateauroux to Argenton. Then take D 927 east for about 13 km to Bouesse. The chateau is in the village.

CHATEAU DE BOUESSE
Hosts: Jacqueline & Harry Courtot-Atterton
36200 Bouesse, France
tel: 54.25.12.20 fax: 54.25.12.30
5 rooms, 3 suites, with private bathrooms
Doubles 430-530F, suites 730F
Restaurant: from 125F per person, without wine
Open all year except January
Fluent English spoken
Region: Berry, Michelin Map 238

An old stone house dating from 1700 is the site of the Trickett's intensive language school, translating service and Bed and Breakfast. They have renovated the entire house; preserving the old stone walls, large walk-in fireplaces and beamed ceilings. Bedrooms are functional with sparse, yet tasteful furnishings and each has its own very clean shower and sink area. Dried flower arrangements, dainty Laura Ashley print wallpapers and crocheted lace curtains add charm and warmth to the cool stone architecture. The Tricketts offer Bed and Breakfast on a nightly basis or week-long stays combining language programs with leisure time. These enjoyable and effective courses are offered at every level and are limited to six persons per class. Ian and Christiane are from England and France respectively and form an energetic and talented teaching and translating team. *Directions:* Bourdeilles and the small hamlet of La Rigeardie are located about 24 kilometers northwest of Périgueux . From Périgueux take D939 towards Brantôme and Angoulême turning left onto D106 following signs for the Chateau de Bourdeilles. Continue rough the village of Bourdeilles without crossing the bridge over the river, then turn left onto D78 towards Lisle and Riberac. After passing the sign for the hamlet of La Rigeardie, the Trickett's is the first house on the left.

LA MÉTAIRIE (Gîte de France)
Hosts: Christiane & Ian Trickett
La Rigeardie
24310 Bourdeilles, France
tel: 53.03.78.90 fax: 53.04.56.95
6 rooms, all w/private shower/sink, share 2 WC
Double: 220-240F
No Table d'Hôte
Open all year
Fluent English spoken
Region: Périgord, Michelin Map 233

This storybook château is actually located in the small town of Port Boulet on the road between Chinon and Bourgueil. Built by the same family who went on to build the well known châteaux Azay-le-Rideaux and Chenonceaux, the Château des Réaux could be out of a fairytale with its twin, red-checked towers and pretty setting. Inside, Madame Goupil de Bouillé establishes a friendly atmosphere and is present to genuinely welcome all her guests. Climb the well-worn turret stairs to the salon where aperitifs are served round a table amidst elegance and comfort. Madame's feminine touch is evident throughout and she has managed to make every room an inviting haven of antiques, paintings, polished silver and authentic memorabilia. Many friendships are made and congenial hours spent in the comfy salons and at the large oval dining table where all the guests may share a meal. The twelve bedrooms in the château and five in a neighboring annex all have private baths and are charmingly decorated with antiques set off by delicate floral print bedspreads, curtains and wallpapers. We look forward to returning to the Château des Réaux, a historical monument that radiates warmth, hospitality and beauty. *Directions:* Travelling south from Bourgueil on D749, turn right immediately after the bridge over the railroad tracks where a sign is posted for the chateau.

CHÂTEAU DES RÉAUX
Hosts: Florence & Jean-Luc Goupil de Bouillé
Le Port Boulet, 37140 Bourgueil, France
tel: 47.95.14.40 fax: 47.95.18.34
17 rooms, with private bathrooms
Double: 550-1050F
Table d'Hôte: 250F per person
Open all year
Good English spoken
Region: Loire Valley, Michelin Map 232

The Moulin Bleu is perched on a scenic vantage point above the Loire Valley, looking out over vineyards and farmlands below. Round tables with bright blue umbrellas, blue and white checked placemats and napkins dot the flagstone terrace where guests may enjoy breakfast and light snacks throughout the day. Madame Breton is an energetic and lively hostess who welcomes guests as if they were visiting friends. The Moulin Bleu (Blue Windmill) actually used to be two old mills side by side, one of which has been converted into Madame's cozy cottage. The two guest bedrooms are furnished with a mix of family antiques and more contemporary furniture, creating a home-like, familial feeling throughout. The windmill next door is still in its original state, and it is here in an wonderful old room with vaulted, stone ceilings that Madame offers wine tastings, samplings of patés and cheeses and savory Table d'Hôte dinners to tour groups and her Bed and Breakfast guests. *Directions:* Bourgueil is located 21 kilometers east of Saumur on the north bank of the Loire. From Saumur, take N147 north in the direction of Longue, then at the roundabout turn right onto D10 (that changes to D35) towards Bourgueil. Look for signs pointing the way to Le Moulin Bleu to the left—the blue windmill on the hill is visible from afar.

LE MOULIN BLEU (Gîte de France)
Hostess: Françoise Breton
37140 Bourgueil, France
tel: 47.97.71.41
3 rooms, with private bathrooms
Double: 210F
Table d'Hôte: 65F per person
Open all year
Very little English spoken
Region: Loire Valley, Michelin Map 232

The 200-year-old Domaine de Monciaux, set in well manicured gardens, is positively beguiling—not at all foreboding as some castles tend to be. The facade is of a creamy tan stone, laced with ivy and accented by white shuttered windows. Two turrets with peaked slate gray roofs frame the building and add a jaunty, proper French appeal. The castle has new owners, Helga and Klaus Schröder who are from Germany (where they were in the antique business). They loved France, particularly the Périgord, so when the Domaine de Monciaux came on the market, they bought it and moved there with their four young children. It was not their intention to open a Bed and Breakfast, but previous guests kept knocking on the door, so they decided they might as well "try it" and found they enjoyed meeting people from around the world. I have not had the opportunity to meet the new owners, but they sound very nice, and I am delighted that they have decided to keep the fairy-tale-like Domaine de Monciaux open as a Bed and Breakfast. In the gardens are a pretty swimming pool and tennis court. *Directions:* Bourrou is located 27 km southwest of Périgueux. Take N21 south from Périgueux for about 23 km. Turn west on D24 toward Villamblard. Go 3 km and turn right. Go through the tiny village of Bourrou, following signs to Domaine de Monciaux.

DOMAINE DE MONCIAUX
Hosts: Helga & Klaus Schröder
Bourrou, 24110 St. Astier, France
tel: 53 82 94 12 fax: 53 82 94 13
7 rooms, all with private bath/WC
Single 400F, Double: 500-550F
No Table d'Hôte
Credit cards: none accepted
Closed in winter (except by special request)
Very good English spoken
Pool, tennis
Region: Dordogne, Michelin Map 233

Monsieur and Madame Pochat are charming and cultivated hosts who welcome guests with enthusiasm and warmth into their lovely, historic home. It was purchased in a state of uninhabited disrepair, but the Pochats have carefully restored the main house, its authentic pigeon tower and nearby outbuildings to form a harmonious ensemble of exposed stone walls and warm tile roofs that look much as they must have when originally built in the mid 1600's. Bedrooms are beautifully furnished in highly polished antiques and decorated with soft-hued fabric wall coverings, old paintings and objets d'art. Details such as fresh fruit and flower bouquets upon guest's arrival are typical of the Pochat's thoughtful and personalized welcome. They are happy to pamper guests by serving breakfast in the rooms and invite all who visit Les Vignes to be seduced by the bird songs, wildflowers and serenity of the countryside. *Directions:* Brassac is located about 38 kilometers east of Agen. Take N113 in the direction of Moissac, turning left onto D953 at Valence. Continue to the hamlet of Fourquet, turning left onto D7 to Brassac. Go through Brassac, staying on D7 towards Bourg de Visa, and after 3 kilometers turn left onto CV3 towards Le Bugat. Travel 1 kilometer then turn right onto CV10—the driveway to Les Vignes is about 500 meters farther on the right.

LES VIGNES (Gîte de France)
Hosts: Monsieur & Madame Pochat
Brassac, 82190 Bourg de Visa, France
tel: 63.94.24.30
2 rooms & 1-2 bedroom. suite, all w/pvt baths
Double: 300F (after 1 night, rate 250F)
Suite: 600F (after 1 night, rate 500F)
No Table d'Hôte (guest kitchen available)
Open May 1 to October 1
Good English spoken, also German
Region: Tarn & Garonne, Michelin Map 235

The Chateau de Brélidy is located in central Brittany, in an area surrounded by quiet woods and fishing streams. Monsieur and Madame Yoncourt are the gracious hosts who solicitously attend to their guest's every need. Brélidy is a chateau hôtel offering luxurious hôtel-type accommodation, and, fortunately for travellers with smaller pocketbooks, the Yoncourts offer more modest Bed and Breakfast accommodation as well. These guest bedrooms are located up the grand stone staircase on the third floor and were formerly attic rooms. Newly renovated and redecorated, the rooms are not particularly large but are very home-like, comfortable and spotlessly clean. Guests are invited to relax in the castle's salon where tapestry chairs, a huge open fireplace, vases of fresh flowers and objets d'art create a refined setting. A stay here is as comfortable as it is atmospheric, for, although the castle dates from the 16th Century, the Yoncourt family has worked hard to restore it to its current polished state of perfection. *Directions:* Brélidy is located approximately 40 kilometers northwest of St-Brieuc. From Guingamp, take D8 towards La Roche Derrien, turning left after 11 kilometers onto D15 to Brélidy. Directions to the chateau are well marked once you arrive in the village; thus you need only follow signs for the Chateau de Brélidy.

CHATEAU DE BRÉLIDY (Gîte de France)
Hosts: Yoncourt Family
Brélidy,0 Begard, France
tel: 96.95.69.38 fax: 96.95.18.03
4 rooms, with private bathrooms
Double: 470F
Table d'Hôte: 170F per person, without wine
Open all year
Very good English spoken
Region: Brittany, Michelin Map 230

Le Chateau, although not old, is built in the traditional Norman style architecture and is built on the site of a fortified small castle. In fact, the original tower gates are still standing and remnants of the encircling wall can still be seen. Best of all, the entrance is over a small bridge, because the original moat still wraps completely around the castle. Inside, many materials used in construction were old, such as ceiling beams and floor tile giving an old world ambiance. There is even a tower, although it looks quite new with modern stone work. Your gracious hostess, Maryvonne Legras, who lives here with her three small poodles and several cats, has created a very homey atmosphere with plump sofas, comfortable chairs, Oriental carpets, country antique furniture, oil paintings, personal knick knacks on the tables, and abundant arrangements of colorful flowers. Stairs wind up the tower leading to three small bedrooms, each decorated with different wallpapers and color coordinated fabrics. Sloping roof line and casement windows create a cozy ambiance. Each of the rooms has a private shower and washbasin, but all share one toilet that is down the hallway. The price seems a little high for rooms without any private bathrooms, but plans were underway for one to be installed in one of the bedrooms. *Directions:* From Breteuil, take road D141 west. After the road leaves the forest, just before entering the village of Bémécourt, you will see a Chambres d'Hôtes sign on the right side of the road. After the sign, turn left at the first lane that leads to the chateau.

LE VIEUX CHATEAU (*Gîte de France*)
Hostess: Maryvonne Legras
27160 Bémécourt, Breteuil, France
tel: 32.29.90.47
3 rooms, with shower & wash basin
Double 350F
Table d'Hôte - sometimes on special request
Open all year
Very good English spoken
Region: Normandy, Michelin Map 231

Lacy wisteria vines cover the facade of the Coulon's old mill that dates from 1729. The setting is extremely peaceful, next to a cool stream, in the middle of wooded countryside. A stay at the Coulon's could be likened to a visit to one's grandparent's home in the country, and is recommended for those travellers seeking simple accommodation in a quiet, dignified house. Rooms are furnished and decorated in an old-fashioned style and are comfortable and homelike rather than luxurious: most bathrooms are shared. A small upstairs sitting area furnished in family antiques offers guests a cozy spot in which to relax. Breakfast is enjoyed in the downstairs dining room at an intimate round table adorned with a large bouquet of garden flowers. A former bread oven and stone fireplace reflect the history of the room. Located about a two hour's drive from Paris, Chez Coulon is a good choice for a stopover heading south or west. *Directions:* Briarres sur Essonne is located approximately 35 kilometers southwest of Fontainebleau. Take N152 towards Orleans and just before Malesherbes, follow the road to Puiseaux. At the first round-about, take D25 to Briarres sur Essonne. Chez Coulon is between Briarres sur Essonne and Villereau. Turn off at the small sign for Francorville, then travel past an old farm to the river where you will see the Coulon's home.

CHEZ COULON (Gîte de France)
Hosts: Monsieur & Madame Bernard Coulon
Francorville
45390 Briarres sur Essonne, France
tel: 38.39.13.59
2 rooms, share 1 large bath, separate WC
Double: 270F, Triple: 260F
No Table d'Hôte
Open April 1 to November 1
No English spoken
Region: Loire Valley, Michelin Map 237

If you want to experience genuine French hospitality in a storybook chateau, the Chateau de Brie is perfection. Do not be intimated by the titles of the owners: Comte and Comtesse du Manoir de Juaye's welcome is so warm, so genuine, that you will feel right at home. The castle was used for many years only for holidays, but now it is the family's permanent home. And, although the four daughters live away, they too love the chateau and come home as often as possible. The rooms of the castle are elegant yet comfortable. The furnishings are gorgeous—all family antiques that have been in the castle forever. One of the most endearing qualities of this castle, is, that although the walls are 2 meters thick, light streams through the many windows giving the rooms a light and airy ambiance. The Chateau de Brie is surrounded by pretty gardens and grassy lawns that stretch out behind the castle to tranquil views of trees and farmland. Beyond the manicured park dominated by the picture-perfect castle, the family owns 1000 acres of forest—a haven for walking. *Directions:* Brie is located 45 km southwest of Limoges. From Limoges go southwest on N21 for 35 km. Exit at Chalus and follow the D 42 west toward Cussac. In about 8 km you will see the Chateau de Brie well signposted on the right side of the road.

CHATEAU DE BRIE (Gîte de France)
Count & Countess Pierre du Manoir de Juaye
Brie
87150 Champagnac la Riviere, France
tel: 55.78.17.52 fax: 55.78.14.02
4 rooms, with private bathrooms
Double: 550-650F
Table d'Hôte: 250F per person, with wine
Open May to November
Fluent English spoken
Region: Limousin, Michelin Map 233

The Chateau de la Bourgonie is absolute perfection combining all the ingredients to make a stay in France unforgettable: fabulous old stone chateau dating back to the 14th-Century, breathtaking antiques, stunning decor and a marvelously interesting history. As if this weren't enough, the owners, Christine and Hubert de Commarque, open their hearts as well as their home to their guests. The chateau is a quadrangle, built around a large central courtyard. One wing can either be used as a complete home with kitchen, dining room, living room and four bedrooms (perfect for stays of a week or more) or, the four bedrooms are also available on a Bed and Breakfast basis. When I asked the charming Christine how long the chateau had been in her family, the answer was very simple, "forever". Just a short drive away, perched on a hillside above the Dordogne River, the de Commarque family owns the Chateau de la Poujade, an equally gorgeous home available to rent by the week. Either of the chateaux you choose offers peace and utter tranquilty near the prehistoric caves of Lascaux and the medieval town of Sarlat. *Directions:* Le Buisson is located 128 km east of Bordeaux. From Le Buisson take D25 toward Siagrac. As you leave Le Buisson, take the first road to the right that goes over the railroad tracks and up the hill. When the road splits, go left. The road dead ends at Chateau de la Bourgonie.

CHATEAU DE LA BOURGONIE
Hosts: Christine & Hubert de Commarque Paleyrac
24480 Le Buisson, France
tel: 53.22.01.78
4 rooms, with private bathrooms
Double: 750F; 4 bedroom apt 8,000F week
No Table d'Hôte
Open May to mid-November
Fluent English spoken
Region: Dordogne, Michelin Map 235

Madame Boyer de Latour lives in her ivy-covered family home that dates from the 1700's. The house has some lovely antique furniture, interesting artifacts and objets d'art from her 20 years of living in North Africa and the Far East while her husband was in the diplomatic service. Old paintings and prints decorate the walls and Oriental rugs cover the handsome wood and tile floors. The house is not luxurious: in fact, if one looks closely it is rather frayed at the edges, yet the elegant furnishings speak of better days gone by. The two guest bedrooms in the main house display some beautiful antique pieces and have private baths. The other two rooms are in an adjoining building and are less appealing. Madame Boyer de Latour appreciates advance reservations for Bed and Breakfast guests. *Directions:* The Bus St-Rémy listing of this Bed and Breakfast is misleading, since it is actually found closer to the village of Bray et Lu. Travel 56 kilometers northwest of Paris via A15, changing to N14 to Mangy en Vexin, then taking D86 to Bray et Lu. In Bray et Lu look for a Chambres d'Hôtes sign directing you to leave the village on D146 towards St-Rémy. At the edge of town look for a large gate with a Chambres d'Hôtes sign on it. Be careful not to drive right by, as there is no driveway; the gate is flush with the road.

LA JONQUIÈRE: (Gîte de France)
Hostess: Madame Boyer de LaTour
Le Petit Beaudemont, 34 route de la Vallee
Bus St-Rémy 27630 Ecos, France
tel: 34.67.72.40
4 rooms, 2 with private shower or bath/WC
Double: 250F
No Table d'Hôte
Open all year
Very little English spoken
Region: Ile de France, Michelin Map 237

Located in the open countryside south of the Loire Valley, the imposing Chateau du Boisrenault sits in a grove of lush, green trees. Hostess Sylvie du Manoir is a charismatic hostess who is also a picture framer. She has decorated her guest bedrooms with plenty of artistic flair and sometimes a touch of whimsy, assigning each its own distinctive theme. The informal Tahitian room has painted murals of tropical scenes, blue sky and clouds, while the highly traditional English country room is an understated blend of lovely antique furniture, rugs and framed prints. All the bedrooms are very tasteful with a strong emphasis on guest comfort. Downstairs public areas are spacious and have lofty high ceilings, yet the du Manoirs have fortunately managed to maintain a warm, comfortable feeling so that one is not overwhelmed by the sheer size of the rooms. A wood-paneled library offers ping-pong, television and a selection of English books. *Directions:* Buzançais is located approximately 25 kilometers northwest of Chateauroux. Take N143 in the direction of Tours until reaching Buzançais. Once in the village, turn right towards Vierzon on D926 and continue for about 3 kilometers. You will find the alley leading to the chateau on your right with a Chambres d'Hôtes sign.

CHATEAU DU BOISRENAULT (*Gîte de France*)
Hosts: Sylvie & Yves du Manoir
36500 Buzançais, France
tel: 54.84.03.01 fax: 54.84.10.57
6 rooms, all w/private shower or bath, 3 share WC
Single: 300-350F, Double: 350-450F
Suite for 4 persons 750F
Table d'Hôte 130F* per person
*only on request, minimum 4 persons
Open all year except January
Swimming pool
Good English spoken
Region: Loire Valley, Michelin Map 238

Located in a beautiful area of wooded hills about an hour's drive southwest of Carcassonne is the fabulous 16th-century Chateau de Camon where Dominique du Pont welcomes guests into his home. The picture-perfect chateau (really more like a castle) encloses one side of Camon, a jewel of a walled medieval village that has been designated as one of France's prettiest towns. From the moment you walk into the impeccably groomed inner courtyard, a garden brimming with flowers, you are immersed in the romance of days gone by. This is definitely not the place to take your exuberant youngsters, but rather the kind of elegant retreat to pamper yourself for a few days. Every detail of the castle has been beautifully restored with an eye for perfection. The decor is also delightful with authentic antiques enhancing the fairytale mood of the castle. An added bonus is the beautiful swimming pool—luring guests to linger on a summer day, but if you want more strenuous activities, there is hiking, fishing, or prehistoric caves to explore. *Directions:* Mirepoix is located 47 km southwest of Carcassonne. From Mirepoix go south on D625 for 4 km. Turn east toward Chalabre on D7. In about 10 km you will come to Camon. he chateau dominates the small town—you cannot miss it.

CHATEAU DE CAMON
Hostess: Dominique du Pont
Camon, 09500 Mirepoix, France
tel: 61.68.14.05 fax: 61.68.81.56
7 rooms, with private bathrooms
Double: from 800F
Table d'Hôte: 300F per person, includes wine
Credit cards: all major accepted
Open March to November
Fluent English spoken
Region: Midi Pyrénées, Michelin Map 235

A friendly ambiance pervades the Bohic's turn-of-the-century manor house near the port town of Carantec. Perhaps because they share their visitor's love of travel, Monsieur and Madame take great pleasure in welcoming travellers into their home. We were fascinated to hear of their own far-flung adventures in exotic locales such as Brazil, Argentina, Ireland, Israel and the United States. Spend a lazy afternoon exchanging stories on the Bohic's flagstone terrace that looks out over the surrounding artichoke fields to the distant sea. Equally inviting for a chat or a cup of tea is the cozy, antique-filled sitting room where Madame also serves breakfast. Guests are treated to more than just a typical breakfast, as Madame Bohic also offers warm crêpes, fresh croissants and three kinds of homemade preserves. Guest bedrooms all provide a high level of comfort, with fluffy towels, soft sheets and warm blankets. Kervezec is truly a Bed and Breakfast where guests are made to feel at home. *Directions:* Carantec is located on the coast approximately 55 kilometers northeast of Brest, 15 kilometers north of Morlaix via D58 in the direction of St-Pol de Leon. Turn right onto D173 towards Carantec, and just before entering village look for a Chambres d'Hôtes sign directing you to turn at the first left. Continue to the Bohic's large, gray stone manor house that will be on the right.

KERVEZEC (Gîte de France)
Hosts: Monsieur & Madame Bohic
29660 Carantec, France
tel: 98.67.00.26
6 rooms, with private bathrooms
Double: 260-320F
No Table d'Hôte
Open all year
Very little English spoken
Region: Brittany, Michelin Map 230

Deep in the enchanted hill country of the Dordogne is an inviting and affordable Bed and Breakfast. Centuries ago a fortified castle stood on the site where young Patrick Guittard and his parents now raise livestock and produce a local red wine. The old stone farmhouse has been in the Guittard family for three generations: in fact Patrick's grandmother and father were both born in the house. Guest quarters are completely independent and are entered through an oak door off a small flagstone terrace. Guests enjoy breakfast in a modest room whose focal points are a massive, open-hearth fireplace and a lovely view out over the countryside. Patrick has equipped this room with a discreet corner kitchenette plus basic dishes and cooking utensils so that guests may cook their own evening meals if desired. Bedrooms are clean and basic in their furnishings. This is a special place where the simplicity of the accommodation and the fairy-tale quality of the surrounding landscape cast a magic spell from the past. *Directions:* From Sarlat, take D704 towards Cahors. About 2 km outside of town, turn left on the D704a towards Souillac. Stay on this road for 20 km. The route number changes to 703 along the way. A little over 3 km after Roussillac, turn left on a tiny road (D61a) signposted "Orliaguet, 3,5". Go about a half kilometer and turn right. There is a "Chambres d'Hôtes" sign, but the tiny sign for Castang can't be seen from this direction. Keep winding up this tiny road for 4 kilometers. At the hilltop where the road deadends, go left. Guittard's is the first farm on the left.

CHEZ GUITTARD (Gîte de France)
Host: Patrick Guittard
Castang, near Orliaguet, 24370 Carlux, France
tel: 53.28.84.0 3
3 rooms, none with private bathroom
Double: 140F
No Table d'Hôte
Open April to November 30
Very little English spoken
Region: Dordogne, Michelin Map 235

The Chateau du Foulon is an absolute dream: a beautiful small chateau surrounded by a one hundred acre park complete with 25 handsome peacocks and one naughty swan. Inside, the rooms without exception are furnished with exquisite antiques, many dating back to the 17th Century. The essence is of a fine home, elegant, yet very comfortable, with a "lived-in" ambiance—photographs of beautiful children and grandchildren prove this is indeed a family dwelling. The five guest rooms, each beautifully decorated with pretty wallpapers and attractive fabrics, look out over the gardens from large casement windows. In addition to the five bedrooms, there are also two charming apartments, each with its own little kitchen, bedroom and living room. The Chateau du Foulon, built in 1840, is the home of Vicomte and Vicomtesse de Baritault du Carpia, who although they do not speak much English, exude a great warmth of welcome. If you want to explore the Médoc wine region, or just enjoy an interlude in the French countryside, I can think of no lovelier base: this is a place you must plan to stay for a while. And, one of the happiest surprises is the price that is one of the best values we saw in France. *Directions:* Take D1 north from Bordeaux for about 28 km. When you reach Castelnau de Médoc, at the first traffic lights turn left and almost immediately you will see the sign for Chateau du Foulon on your left.

CHATEAU DU FOULON
Hosts: Vicomte & Vicomtesse de Baritault du Carpia
33480 Castelnau de Médoc, France
tel: 56.58.20.18 fax: 56.58.23.43
5 rooms, with private bathrooms
Double: 350-400F
2 one bedroom apts, 500-600F per night
No Table d'Hôte
Open all year
Very little English spoken
Region: Médoc, Michelin Map 233

A scenic drive through green vineyards and hillsides covered with flaming gorse bushes leads to the village of Le Caylar. The Clarissac's gray, two-storey house is found just at the edge of the village, making for quiet, tranquil accommodation. Guest rooms are separate from the main house in an adjoining wing that fronts a shaded garden. French doors lead from an arched gallery into the peaceful rooms, that the Clarissacs have been offering to travellers for the last 15 years. The decor is a bit dated, but still attractive, with matching bedspreads and curtains complemented by antiques or reproduction furniture. On the ground floor of the main house is a handsome dining room and a lounge filled with the flavor of days gone by. Vaulted ceilings and walls are of exposed regional stone, as is the large open-hearthed fireplace. Country antique furniture, hanging copper pots and dried flower bouquets add warmth and charm, creating a cozy ambiance. A Table d'Hôte dinner enjoyed here with the Clarissac family is a treat to be long remembered. *Directions:* Le Caylar is located approximately 60 kilometers northwest of Montpellier. Take 9 through Lodève and continue 18 kilometers towards Millau to Le Caylar. In the village, turn left just before the restaurant L'Hostellerie du Roc Castel and there will be a sign for Chambres d'Hôtes on the right.

LE BARRY DU GRAND CHEMIN (Gîte de France)
Hosts: Maryvonne & Bernard Clarissac
34520 Le Caylar, France
tel: 67.44.50.19
5 rooms, with private bathrooms
Single: 205F, Double: 275
Table d'Hôte: 85F per person
Open all year
No English spoken
Region: Provence, Michelin Map 240

Vanessa and John McKeand, a delightful, handsome young couple from England, decided to take a break from their hectic careers as professional musicians and move to the quiet of the French countryside. They bought an old stone farmhouse set in a lovely meadow with a sweeping view over a patchwork of fields fringed by trees and have transformed it into a little jewel. The interior is refreshingly light and airy, reflecting the ambiance of an English cottage. Each room is different, but each is absolutely charming and decorated with antique country furniture and pretty fabrics that Vanessa has sewn into color coordinated drapes and bed covers. Vanessa and John also operate a small restaurant, very attractively decorated—refreshingly bright and cheerful. In one corner of the dining room is a beautiful harp, a reminder of the days when Vanessa was on the circuit as a professional musician. Now she is the chef, combining the best of English and French cuisine. Soon to be completed is a self-catering suite in the "Pigeonnier" for guest staying 3 nights or more. *Directions:* Chalus is located 35 km southeast of Limoges. Take the N21 southeast from Limoges. At Chalus, turn west following D901 toward Rochechouart. 2.4 km after leaving Chalus, you will a sign for Les Ourgeaux on the right side of the road.

LES OURGEAUX (Gîte de France)
Hosts: Vanessa & John McKeand
Pageas, 87230 Chalus, France
tel: 55.78.50.97 fax: 55.78.54.76
3 rooms, with private bathrooms
Single: 290F, Double: 320-3705F
Table d'Hôte: 115F per person
Credit cards: MC, VS @ 2% surcharge
Open all year
No smoking, no children under 7
Fluent English spoken
Region: Limousin, Michelin Map 233

Set in the midst of rolling, vineyard-covered hills, the Girard's gracious home offers a wonderful Bed and Breakfast experience. Formerly a hunting lodge built in 1700, the house is surrounded by grounds and majestic old pine and cedar trees. The ambiance of the Girard's home is one of home-like comfort enhanced by a certain refined elegance. Charming hosts Monsieur and Madame Girard are an attractive couple who delight in making visitors feel right at home. Inviting bedrooms attest to Michelle's flair for decoration, showcasing family antique furniture and harmonious wallpapers, curtains and bedspreads. Details such as bathroom soaps, good bedside lighting, and sweet-smelling floral print sheets add touches of personalized luxury. Bountiful breakfasts are served at a long table in the Girard's pretty dining room and include a large bowl of fresh fruits, and four varieties of homemade preserves. There is a terrace facing the park where breakfast is served out of doors in good weather. *Directions:* Chamboeuf is located 18 kilometers southwest of Dijon. Take N74, following signs for Gevrey Chambertin. Turn right in the village of Gevrey onto D31 in the direction of Quemigny Poisot and Chamboeuf. In the village of Chamboeuf, drive to the church and turn left to arrive at the Girard's private car park.

LE RELAIS DE CHASSE (Gîte de France)
Hosts: Monsieur & Madame Girard
21220 Chamboeuf, France
tel: 80.51.81.60 fax: 80 34 15 96
4 rooms, with private bathrooms
Double: 320-350F, Triple: 450F
No Table d'Hôte
Open all year
Very little English spoken
Region: Burgundy, Michelin Map 243

Monsieur and Madame Petit live in an atmospheric 200-year-old cottage covered by thick ivy, tucked away in a tiny country hamlet. Simone is a warm-hearted hostess who offers personal and caring hospitality. She loves plants and nature, and her home is entered through a greenhouse-like hallway festooned with vines and hanging plants. It is easy to feel comfortable and at home in the main sitting room where a cozy fireplace is surrounded by inviting couches and chairs. A bouquet of garden flowers dresses the dining room table where guests gather for breakfast and evening meals. Madame Petit is a creative cook whose breakfasts include several varieties of homemade breads, coffee cake and fruit in addition to the usual continental fare. Table d'Hôte dinners are relaxed, convivial meals featuring traditional yet healthful country cuisine. Small, charmingly decorated bedrooms offer a high level of comfort with good lighting, bathroom heaters and ample storage space. *Directions:* La Chapelaude is located approximately 10 kilometers northwest of Montluçon. Leave Montluçon on D943 towards Culan then 8 kilometers later, before reaching the town of La Chapelaude, turn right at a service station and follow a country lane to the hamlet of Montroir. The Petit's ivy-covered cottage is one of the first houses on the left.

PETIT SIMONE (Gîte de France)
Hosts: Monsieur & Madame Petit
Montroir
03380 La Chapelaude, France
tel: 70.06.40.40 New telephone 1993
3 rooms, with private bathrooms
Double: 180F
Table d'Hôte: 50F per person
Open all year
Very little English spoken
Region: Berry, Michelin Map 238

Madame Eliane Colombet is an interesting and artistic hostess who specializes in making pottery. Her lovely old manor home dates from 1800 and is of stone and plaster construction with red brick decoration. The house is set in an acre of shaded grounds, traversed by the peaceful stream La Chalaronne. Madame offers guest accommodation in a home-like cottage that adjoins her larger house; thus guests are afforded the complete privacy and independence of their own entrance and fully equipped kitchenette. A small, somewhat sparsely furnished salon has a cozy fireplace surrounded by comfortable seating and is decorated with examples of Madame's pottery artwork. Upstairs, the two bedrooms are furnished mostly in antiques and are tastefully decorated with floral print curtains and complementary wallpapers. A shared shower and WC are located on the ground floor. *Directions:* La Chapelle du Chatelard is located approximately 40 kilometers north of Lyon. Take N83 towards Strasbourg and Bourg en Bresse. At Villars les Dombes leave town on D80 towards Beaumont and La Chapelle du Chatelard. Six kilometers after Beaumont, but before the village of La Chapelle du Chatelard, look for a sign for Les Grands Verchères and turn right into Madame Colombet's driveway.

LES GRANDES VERCHÈRES (Gîte de France)
Hostess: Madame Eliane Colombet
01240 La Chapelle du Chatelard, France
tel: 74.42.85.71
2-bedroom apartment, share one shower/WC
Double: 400F, Triple: 540F
No Table d'Hôte
Open all year
Very little English spoken, German spoken
Region: Burgundy, Michelin Map 244

The Jura region is an unspoiled paradise with many lakes, forests, spectacular gorges and rolling, green hills—truly a nature-lover's dream. The entire area, preserved in its natural state, is like one big park . Charezier is a small village in the quiet countryside of central Jura near the large lake Vouglans where young Jacqueline and Guy Devenat offer guest accommodation in their spacious, newly remodeled farmhouse. Furnishings are simple and modest, and all is spotlessly clean and well-equipped. Travellers seeking reasonable prices and a relaxed, familial atmosphere will be most at home here, as living quarters are shared with the Devenats and their two children. Breakfast is informal and is enjoyed in the typical family kitchen. Guy and Jacqueline are friendly and helpful hosts who also put their comfortable living room and television at their guest's disposal. *Directions:* Charezier is located approximately 28 kilometers southeast of Lons le Saunier. From Lons, take N78 in the direction of Geneva (Genève) for about 22 kilometers, then turn left onto D27 towards Lake Chalain (Lac du Chalain). After about 4 kilometers, long before reaching the lake, look for a Chambres d'Hôtes sign directing you to turn left to Charezier where the Devenat's contemporary house is easily visible on the left.

CHEZ DEVENAT (Gîte de France)
Hosts: Jacqueline & Guy Devenat
Charezier
39130 Clairvaux les Lacs, France
tel 84.48.35.79
3 rooms, with private bathrooms
Double: 160F, Triple: 180F
No Table d'Hôte
Open all year
No English spoken
Region: Jura, Michelin Map 243

Set in the green rolling hills and pasture lands of the countryside between the Auvergne and Burgundy regions, the picture-perfect Ferme Auberge de Lavaux combines all the elements for a comfortable and memorable French farm stay. Paul and Paulette Gelin's farm complex is 150 years old and forms a pretty, tidy ensemble of warm-toned regional stone; carefully renovated to preserve its historic charm. The rustic dining room, originally a stable building, has a cozy atmosphere with exposed stone walls, beams and rafters, and a large stone fireplace. Delicious farm-fresh meals are enjoyed here at long wooden tables adorned with field-flower bouquets. Guest bedrooms are located across the courtyard in a stone annex with a flower-bedecked balcony. Recently remodeled, the bedrooms are all fresh and clean; furnished in antique reproduction furniture and equipped with modern bathrooms. *Directions:* Chatenay is located approximately 55 kilometers west of Macon. Travel on N79 for about 24 kilometers in the direction of Charolles, turning left onto D987 and continuing past Matour to the hamlet of Chevannes where you will turn right onto D300 towards Chatenay. From this point on the route is well-marked with homemade signs for the Ferme Auberge. Follow signs and country roads for about 3 kilometers, through the hamlet of Chatenay, to the Gelin's well-marked driveway.

FERME AUBERGE DE LAVAUX (Gîte de France)
Hosts: Paulette & Paul Gelin
Chatenay, 71800 La Clayette, France
tel: 85.28.08.48
4 rooms, with private bathrooms
Double: 240–260F
Table d'Hôte: 80-90F per person
Open Easter to November 15
Restaurant
Very little English spoken
Region: Burgundy, Michelin Map 243

The picturesque medieval town of Beaune is in the heart of the Côte d'Or wine producing district of France. Well known for its gourmet cuisine and fine wines, the region is a popular destination for foreign and French tourists alike, so it is a pleasure to find a good lodging value. Chez Deschamps offers modern comfort, a high level of cleanliness and the independence of hôtel accommodation combined with the warm, personalized atmosphere of a Bed and Breakfast. Bedrooms are all fresh and new, with thick carpeting, ample closet space, good lighting and spotless private bathrooms. Hostess Marie-Claire Deschamps is a friendly, energetic housewife who thoughtfully provides guests with soap, tissues and even cotton-wool balls, and is happy to help guests plan sightseeing expeditions in the region. Guest accommodation is found in a house completely separate from the Deschamps home and guests have their own home-like breakfast nook and sitting room with full bookshelves and a television. *Directions:* Chorey les Beaune is located about 5 kilometers northeast of Beaune. Take N74 toward Dijon, turning right towards Chorey les Beaune after about 1 kilometer. Just as you enter the village, take the first left and look for a Chambres d'Hôtes sign on the gatepost of the fourth house on the left. The contemporary stucco house in front is the guest house.

CHEZ DESCHAMPS (Gîte de France)
Hosts: Monsieur & Madame Deschamps
15, rue d'Aloxe-Corton
Chorey les Beaune, 21200 Beaune, France
tel: 80.24.08.13 fax: 80.24.08.01
5 rooms, with private bathrooms
Double: 240F
No Table d'Hôte
Open February 1 through December 1
No English spoken
Region: Burgundy, Michelin Map 243

Paul and Paulette Hennebel abandoned their successful yet hectic careers in the Paris fashion world 16 years ago to build their dream house in this unspoiled region of central France. Their quaint stone house is surrounded by rolling hills, small lakes and dark pine forests. The Hennebels took great care to build their home in an old style utilizing authentic regional stone and heavy wood beams. Inside they have created a warm, home-like feeling with Scandinavian natural wood furniture, pretty woven textured fabrics, a large fireplace, full bookshelves and many fresh wildflower bouquets. A well thought-out floor plan allows guests to enter through a separate entrance giving access to the two upstairs guest rooms. Furnishings and decor in the bedrooms are fresh and comfortable with much use of natural wood paneling and earth tone colors. The Hennebels are a charming, friendly couple who now cultivate bees and produce honey, bee pollen, honey spice bread and even a delicious liqueur said to have magic properties. *Directions:* Cieux is located about 30 kilometers northeast of Limoges. Take N147 to D711 to Cieux. Continue through the village of Cieux on D711 in the direction of St-Junien, then turn right following signs for Circuit des Monts de Blond and Boscartus to the right. The Hennebel's driveway is a bit farther on the right and is marked with a small yellow sign saying Miel des Monts de Blond.

CHEZ HENNEBEL (Gîte de France)
Hosts: Paulette & Paul Hennebel
Les Hauts de Boscartus
87520 Cieux, France
tel: 55.03.30.63
2 rooms, both w/shower & sink, share WC
Single: 170F, Double: 220F, Triple: 295F
Table d'Hôte: 100F per person
Open all year
Very little English spoken
Region: Limousin, Michelin Map 233

Madame Bruère has raised five children in her large, turn-of-the-century home and is now happy to fill her spare bedrooms with Bed and Breakfast travellers. The three-storey stone house is located in a small town convenient to shops and a train station. Madame has some lovely antiques on display throughout her home, particularly in the dining/breakfast room that is completely furnished in Henry IV style, including table, chairs and sideboard. Large windows let in sunlight and garden flowers lend a fresh, summery feeling to the inn. A highly polished, wide wooden stairway leads up to the guest bedrooms, that are located on the second and third floors. Rooms are comfortable, not luxurious, and adequately furnished with family antiques. A stay here under Madame Bruère's motherly wing is rather like making a visit to Grandmother's house; indeed Madame informed us that she already has ten grandchildren. *Directions:* Cinq Mars la Pile is located approximately 22 kilometers west of Tours on the north bank of the Loire. Take N152 in the direction of Langeais and, once in the village of Cinq Mars la Pile, follow signs for Gare SNCF (train station) and Chambres d'Hôtes. The Bruère home is a three-storey house built in 1912.

LA MEULIERE (Gîte de France)
Hosts: Monsieur & Madame Bruère
10, rue de la Gare
37130 Cinq Mars la Pile, France
tel: 47.96.53.63 fax: 47.48.37.13
*5 rooms, 3 with private bathrooms ***
**Other rooms share 1 bath/WC*
Double: 220F, Triple: 260F
No Table d'Hôte
Open all year
No English spoken
Region: Loire Valley, Michelin Map 232

For a stately 18th-century chateau with sophisticated charm, the Chateau de Barry, is a real winner—especially if you appreciate lovely decor. Here you will find large elegant lounges and seven exceptionally attractive bedrooms. Each is beautifully furnished in antiques and elegant fabrics color coordinating with pretty wall papers. What a surprise to learn that all the sewing for the handsome draperies was done by Madame Bouet who previously was a designer in Paris. Françoise Bouet is not only a most talented seamstress, but also a gourmet cook who with previous arrangements will prepare dinner, exquisitely served with fine china and beautiful linens. Chateau Barry is not the family home of the Bouets, but bought by them when Madame Bouet returned from the Orient. The home beautifully reflects his 35 years in the Far East—many artifacts and furniture of fine quality that he collected during his travels are seen throughout the house, especially in the lounge that overlooks the pool. *Directions:* Clairac is located 125 km southeast of Bordeaux. Take the A62/E72 southeast from Bordeaux for about 100 km. Take the Aiguillon exit and follow signs to Aiguillon. Go north on D666 and take the Clairac turnoff. Go across the river, make a jog to the left and follow the road toward Grateloup. When the road splits, go straight and follow Chateau de Barry signs .

CHATEAU DE BARRY
Hosts: Monsieur & Madame René Bouet
47320 Clairac, France
tel: 53.84.35.49 fax: 53.84.35.06
7 rooms, with private bathrooms
Double: 500-750F
Table d'Hôte: 300F per person, with wine
Credit cards: None
Open From May to October
Some English spoken
Region: Lot & Garonne, Michelin Map 234

Monsieur and Madame Élie's modest, half-timbered cottage is a former cider press-house located on a pretty country lane in the Norman countryside. The guest rooms are located in a separate wing where apples were once crushed in a huge vat. Furnishings are contemporary, but historic atmosphere is provided by the heavy old ceiling beams that were left intact during the renovation process. Each private bathroom is very clean and well-equipped with plenty of towels. Breakfast is served either in the Élie's homey family room where decor is provided by family photos and knick-knacks, or outside on the small terrace. This small, home-like Bed and Breakfast is ideal for travellers seeking quiet, comfortable accommodations in beautiful pastoral surroundings. *Directions:* Clarbec is approximately 38 kilometers east of Caen. The easiest route is to turn off N175 approximately 3 kilometers out of Pont L'Éveque onto the bridge that crosses the autoroute. You are now on D280 that will lead you to Clarbec where you should turn onto D285 towards St-Hymer. After crossing three little bridges, turn right and look for a sign indicating Chambres d'Hôtes on a gate in front of the Élie's half-timbered cottage.

PRESSOIR DU LIEU HUBERT (*Gîte de France*)
Hosts: Monsieur & Madame Guy Élie
Lieu Hubert, Chemin de la Galoche
14130 Clarbec, France
tel: 31.64.90.89
2 rooms, with private bathrooms
Double: 200F
No Table d'Hôte
Open all year
No English spoken
Region: Normandy, Michelin Map 231

A half-timbered exterior, overflowing window boxes and a wheelbarrow full of flowers in the front yard of this 250-year-old farmhouse only hint at the country charm found inside. Madame Anfrey is an energetic farmwife who, when not bustling about making sure her guests feel at home, helps her husband tend their cows and poultry. Madame's artistic nature is evident in the very cozy and pleasantly cluttered feeling she has achieved throughout her farm cottage. The guest bedrooms are all charmingly decorated with a variety of antiques, dried flower arrangements and old paintings. Breakfast is served at a round table in the main room supervised by an old grandfather clock in the corner. The low, beamed ceilings, hanging copper pots, country antiques and cozy fire on rainy days make this a tempting spot to linger over cafe au lait, tea or hot chocolate served in country pottery. We were sad indeed to leave this quaint, friendly Bed and Breakfast. *Directions:* Conteville is located approximately 60 kilometers west of Rouen via A13 to the Beuzeville exit, then N175 to N178 to Foulbec, then D312 to Conteville. There are several Chambres d'Hôtes advertised by roadside signs in the vicinity of Conteville, so be sure to follow those that indicate Le Clos Potier. The route involves several turns, but is very well signposted, and you will find the farmhouse tucked away on a country road behind a white fence.

LA FERME DU PRESSOIR (Gîte de France)
Hosts: Odile & Pierre Anfrey
Conteville, 27210 Beuzeville, France
tel: 32.57.60.79
3 rooms, 2 with private bath/WC
Double: 200F
Table d'Hôte: 100F per person
Open all year
Very little English spoken
Region: Normandy, Michelin Map 231

La Butte de L'Epine is an absolute jewel. Although the long, low stone and stucco building with steeply pitched tile roof reflects the local style of architecture from the 17th Century, the building is not old. It was designed and built by Michel Bodet who cleverly incorporated all the best of past and present into this beautiful home. But Michel shouldn't have all the credit. Even though the building oozes with charm, it is the interior that makes this home so very, very special. Michel's wife, Claudette, combines a love of flowers with an artistic flair for decorating. The home abounds with exquisite large floral arrangements that set to perfection the patina of many country antiques. The large living/dining room looks out to a manicured garden and beyond to a small woods. A private guest entrance leads to two cozy guest rooms tucked up under the eves. Both rooms are intimately charming, but my absolute favorite is the corner room with windows on two walls. The delicate green wallpaper with a tiny rose pattern covers the sloping walls and ceiling, pink bedspreads, and pretty pink floral material for the drapes and table cloth create a decorator-perfect scheme. You cannot help but be enchanted with the perfection of every detail including pink candy and pink flowers by the bedside: an oasis to return to after a day of chateaux excursions in the Loire Valley. *Directions:* From Bourgueil, take D749 north for 12 km to Gizeux. Turn right (east) on D15 and continue to Continvoir. At the church, turn left on D64. La Butte de l'Epine is less than a kilometer on your right.

LA BUTTE DE L'EPINE (Gîte de France)
Hosts: Claudette & Michel Bodet
37340 Continvoir, France
tel: 47.96.62.25
2 rooms with private bathrooms
Double 260-280F
No Table d'Hôte
Open all year except Christmas
No English spoken
Region: Loire Valley, Michelin Map 232

Usually the places to stay that we suggest are quite old, filled with historical ambiance. Not so with La Rabouillère—it is new. It was designed by the owner, Jean Marie, who actually built it himself on weekends. The building looks old, a typical brick and timber building with steeply pitched roof. There is a storybook quality to this beautiful Bed and Breakfast, it simply oozes with charm. One enters into a large living room where guests gather before the open fire in the winter. Antiques abound, and with the beamed ceiling and timber and exposed brick walls, the mood is certainly old world. This is where Martine serves breakfast on chilly mornings, although when the days are balmy, guests frequently prefer to eat outside. Martine has lovingly decorated each bedroom. The fabrics have a Laura-Ashley look, and each room has antique accent pieces. The rooms are all named after flowers. I think my favorite is Les Jonquilles room, just lovely with soft yellows used throughout. Each of the bathrooms is spacious, and offers special amenities such as built in hair dryers. The setting too is superb: a 7 hectare wooded estate with a small pond in front. And, for those who are chateau sightseeing, La Rabouillère is right in the heart of the chateau country. *Directions:* Go south from Blois on D 765 for about 9 km to Cour-Cheverny. Then take D102 toward Contres. About 6 km beyond Cheverny, turn left following the La Rabouillère signs to the B&B.

LA RABOUILLÈRE (Gîte de France)
Hostess: Martine Thimonnier
Chemin de Marçon
41700 Contres, France
tel: 54.79.05.14
5 rooms, with private bathrooms
Double 350-500F, Triple 600F
No Table d'Hôte
Open March to November 30
Some English spoken
Region: Loire Valley, Michelin Map 238

Renaud Gizardin inherited the Moulin de Marsaquet from his grandparents a picturesque, 200-year-old stone mill hugging the edge of a pretty lake. Today he lives here with his young wife, Valerie, their adorable little girl, Camille, several friendly dogs, and a cat (plus, a menagerie of other "friends"—horses, ducks, chickens, cows, etc). They have converted three bedrooms in their home into a Bed and Breakfast. There is nothing fancy about their operation, but a sense of gentle goodness permeates their home. When the weather is warm, dinner is served outside family-style on a picnic table; the hearty wholesome meals are prepared totally from ingredients from the farm (including the "foie gras" that Renaud makes himself). The prune liqueur served at the end of the meal is made by Valerie's grandfather. A narrow staircase leads up to the bedrooms: my favorite is the corner room, sweetly old-fashioned with pretty pink floral wall paper, natural wooden floors, fresh flowers on the small desk, antique headboard on the double bed, armoire, and a good-sized, sparkling clean bathroom. Casement windows on two walls open out to the farm, making the this room especially bright and cheerful. This farm is about as far from the bustle of civilization as you can get. During the day stretch out under a tree, hike or row your way to the middle of the pond and watch the wild ducks. *Directions:* From Limoges take D704 south to St-Yrieix. Then east for 10 km to Coussssac Bonneval where you look for the Chambre d'Hôtes signs directing you to the B&B, about 3 km from town.

MOULIN DE MARASGUET (Gîte de France)
Hosts: Valerie & Renaud Gizardin
87500 Coussac-Bonneval, France
tel: 55.75.28.29
3 rooms, with private bathrooms
Double 190F
Table d'Hôte 80F per person, includes wine
Open all year
Good English spoken
Region: Limousin, Michelin Map 239

The Chauveaus are antique dealers who have seasoned their expertise and good taste with a touch of whimsy to create wonderfully imaginative decor and furnishings in their 250-year-old home. Do not expect to see the same antique pieces on a second visit, however, as Monsieur Chauveau is fond of pointing out that all furniture is for sale and therefore subject to change. We stayed in a charming attic room with beautiful exposed support beams and an adjoining immaculate bathroom thoughtfully stocked with ample toiletries and luxurious fluffy towels. Floor level windows overlook the prettily landscaped swimming pool. The most outstanding bedroom (also the most expensive) is a corner room decorated in tones of lavender, green and yellow with windows (even from the enormous bathroom) that look out over the vineyards. The Chauveaus pay great attention to detail and serve an elegant breakfast complete with gold-trimmed china, silver service and a white linen tablecloth. Contented appetites are assured after beginning the day with an artful display of exotic fruits, warmed croissants, fresh bread, homemade preserves, rich cheese and country butter. *Directions:* Cravant les Coteaux is located 8 kilometers east of Chinon. Take D21 through Cravant les Coteaux in the direction of Panzoult. Two kilometers after leaving Cravant, look for a sign advertising Pallus, Bernard Chaveau and then take the next driveway on the right.

DOMAINE DE PALLUS (Gîte de France)
Hosts: Barbara & Bernard Chauveau
Pallus, Cravant les Coteaux
37500 Chinon, France
tel: 47.93.08.94 fax 47.98.43.00
3 rooms ,with private bathrooms
Double: 450-500F
No Table d'Hôte
Open all year
Fluent English, German spoken by Madame
Region: Loire Valley, Michelin Map 232

Crillon le Brave, a walled hilltop village, is comprised of a pretty small church and a cluster of weathered stone houses. One of these houses, the Clos St-Vincent, has been completely renovated and is now a delightful Bed and Breakfast. Guests enter through large iron gates into a spacious parking area in front of a typical tan stone building with brown shutters and tiled roof. A large swimming pool on the terrace captures a sweeping view of the surrounding countryside. There is a very attractive lounge for guests with white-washed walls, tiled floors, a snug nook with a few comfortable chairs for reading, and a large wooden table for dining. The five bedrooms are all very similar in decor with tiled floors, small table and chairs, and color-coordinated, Provençal-style fabrics used as dust ruffles, chair cushions and drapes. The feeling is very fresh, uncluttered, and pretty. *Directions:* Carpentras is located 24 km northeast of Avignon. From Carpentras take D 974 NE toward Bedoin. After about 10 km, follow the road signs to Crillon le Brave. As the road climbs the hill toward the old village, you will see the sign for Clos St-. Vincent. Turn right at the sign and continue on a small road for about 200 meters. Turn left and continue up the hill. The Clos St-Vincent is the second driveway on the left.

CLOS ST-VINCENT (Gîte de France)
Hostess: Françoise Vazquez
Les Vergers
84110 Crillon le Brave, France
tel: 90.65.93.36
5 rooms, with private bath/WC
Plus 1 small house for 4 persons
Double: 380-700, Triple: 500-760F
Table d'Hôte: 130F per person, includes wine
Credit cards: None
Open March to November 15
No English spoken
Region: Provence, Michelin Maps 245, 246

The Ricquart's comfortable home in a former mill enjoys a quiet, pastoral setting in the hilly countryside of Provence. They are an interesting, welltravelled couple who purchased the mill when it was virtually in ruins and completely remodeled it into the attractive home it is today. Monsieur is a former officer in the French Air Force, so they have resided in such exotic locales as Egypt, Israel, Morocco and Germany. Art and artifacts from their overseas journeys complement the contemporary furnishings and decor of the guest bedrooms. The bedrooms have a high level of comfort and privacy; the bathrooms are clean and modern and there is an independent entrance for guests. The Ricquart's warm, friendly welcome, reasonable prices and tranquil setting make the Moulin d'Antelon a delightful base from which to explore the historic towns and vividly colored landscapes of northern Provence. A large swimming pool has recently been completed. *Directions:* Crillon le Brave is located approximately 9 kilometers northeast of Carpentras. Take D974 following signs for Le Mont Ventoux par Bedoin. After travelling about 12 km, 1 km PAST the turnoff for Crillon-le-Brave, look for the Riquart's driveway on the left. Look carefully, as the house sits below the level of the road. The driveway is marked with a large sign: Chambres d'Hôtes, Bed and Breakfast.

MOULIN D'ANTELON (Gîte de France)
Hosts: Bernard & Marie-Luce Ricquart
Crillon le Brave, 84410 Bedoin, France
tel: 90.62.44.89 fax: 90.62.44.89
2 rooms, with private bathrooms
Double: 250F, Triple: 350F
No Table d'Hôte
Open all year
Good English spoken
Region: Provence, Michelin Maps 245, 246

It is not often that one can actually reside in an historical monument, but you can do just that at Le Prieure Saint Michel. When Anne and Pierre Chahine bought the property, it had been sadly neglected. But happily for the lucky traveller, the complex has been authentically restored and is truly a masterpiece. The granary is now used for various exhibitions and concerts, the giant press where the monks produced the Calvadoras brandy is still intact, and the lovely little chapel is now an art galley featuring the sketches of one of France's great artists, Edgar Chahine, who just happens to be the father of your congenial host. Equally outstanding are the splendid, meticulously tended gardens. There is an "antique" rose garden featuring an incredible variety of old-fashioned roses. In contrast there is the "new" rose garden, the Iris garden, the herbal gardens, and on and on. Each is laid out as they would have been in the days of old. Two ponds with ducks and swans complete the idyllic scene. In summer, the grounds are open to the public, but guests are assured of their privacy with their own intimate little garden. Each of the bedrooms is handsomely decorated.—even the least expensive of the bedrooms, is a real delight. *Directions:* Take D916 west from Vimoutiers toward Argentan. Just a few kilometers after leaving Vimoutiers, turn right at the sign for Crouttes. Go through town following signs for Le Prieure St. Michel.

LE PRIEURE SAINT MICHEL (*Gîte de France*)
Hosts: Anne & Pierre Chahine
61120 Crouttes, Vimoutiers, France
tel: 33.39.15.15 fax: 33.36.15.16
5 rooms, with private bathrooms
Double from 550F to 1,300F (suite)
No Table d'Hôte
Open all year
Fluent English spoken
Region: Normandy, Michelin Map 231

Madame de Saint-Père lives in a marvelous old house in the village of Dangu. She speaks fluent English and takes great pleasure in helping her guests plan sightseeing excursions in the surrounding countryside. Her house dates from around 1700, yet her two guest bedrooms are comfortable in size (not always the case in old houses) and are reached by a stairway that is independent of the rest of the house. The decor is an artfully conceived melange of antiques, old etchings and pleasing color schemes. In one of the rooms the bed is found behind a pretty flowered curtain; an intimate, delightfully French touch. Downstairs there is a cozy salon with a fireplace where guests are invited to relax with an aperitif before enjoying a lively Table d'Hôte dinner with Madame de Saint-Père. Breakfast is often served under a canopy on the terrace, that has a peaceful view over Madame's well-tended garden leading down to the shady banks of the river Ept. A strategically placed bench provides a tranquil spot for an afternoon of reading or quiet contemplation. *Directions:* Dangu is located 60 kilometers northwest of Paris via A15, changing to N14 to Bordeaux St-Clair, then D146 to Dangu. In Dangu, look for a Chambres d'Hôtes sign directing you to a cream-colored house with green shutters, located just next to the bridge over the stream.

LES OMBELLES (Gîte de France)
Hostess: Madame Poulain de Saint-Père
4, rue de Gue, 27720 Dangu, France
tel: 32.55.04.95 fax: 42.67.29.02
2 rooms, one with private bathroom
Double: 260F
Table d'Hôte: 110F per person
Open all year
Fluent English spoken
Region: Normandy, Michelin Map 231

Window boxes full of multi-colored flowers decorate the pretty, welcoming facade of Colette Geiger's chalet-style house. She is a friendly, motherly hostess who keeps her home and guest rooms in spotless condition, with pretty, feminine touches such as lace-trimmed pillowcases and sheets. Furnishings are antique reproductions and rooms are small, but very comfortable. Guests are encouraged to relax in the sitting room that is cozy and inviting and has a stone fireplace flanked by leather chairs and picture windows looking out over distant hills. Chez Geiger is found in a beautiful valley dotted with small villages and fields of cherry trees. This is a region of kirsch production and each town has its own distillery where the water of life is made from locally grown cherries. *Directions:* Dieffenbach au Val is located approximately 30 kilometers northwest of Colmar. Take N83 towards Strasbourg, turning left at Selestat onto N59 towards St-Die. After 3 kilometers, turn right onto D424 towards Ville. At the village of St-Maurice turn left following signs for Dieffenbach. Take the next left and then look for a Chambres d'Hôtes sign marking the Geiger's chalet-style house, that is set back from the road behind a front garden.

CHEZ GEIGER (Gîte de France)
Hostess: Madame Colette Geiger
19, Route de Neuve Eglise
67220 Dieffenbach au Val, France
tel: 88.85.60.48
3 rooms, with private bathrooms
Double: 190F
No Table d'Hôte
Open all year
No English spoken, fluent German
Region: Alsace, Michelin Map 242

Les Charmettes is a historic stone house dating from 1781, located on the banks of the tranquil Orleans canal. Hostess Madame Sicot is exceedingly proud of her home that has been in her family for the last 100 years, and is in the process of restoring it to its former beauty. She has a certain flair for decoration and has created a lovely country-home feeling with attractive color schemes, pretty wallpapers, polished antiques and objets d'art. Two charming and intimate guest bedrooms are found in the former attic servant's quarters at the top of a steep old wooden staircase. The three first-floor bedrooms are more easily accessible and are elegantly decorated with lovely old furniture and collectibles. A peaceful back garden bordering the canal offers a quiet refuge after a day of travel or sightseeing, and is also a pleasant spot to enjoy Madame Sicot's traditional continental breakfast. *Directions:* Donnery is located approximately 10 kilometers east of Orléans. To find Les Charmettes in Donnery, take N460 from Orleans in the direction of Chateauneuf sur Loire and Montargis, turning left on to D921 toward Fay aux Loges. Go through Fay aux Loges, turn left when you see the flower shop on your left. Cross the canal and turn left at the sign of Donnery and D709. Les Charmettes is the first house on your left as you enter Donnery. There is a large garden bordering on the canal in the rear and enclosed courtyard in the front. Drive through the narrow gate into the parking area in the court yard.

LES CHARMETTES (Gîte de France)
Hosts: Monsieur & Madame Sicot
45450 Donnery, France
tel: 38.59.22.50
5 rooms, 3 with private bathrooms
Double: 250F
Table d'Hôte: 100F per person, includes wine
Open all year
Some English spoken
Region: Loire Valley, Michelin Map 238

If you want to experience a Bed and Breakfast at a simple, real working farm, Le Temple might be a good choice. In days gone-by, this was the farm of the Templers, the knights of the religious order who went to the crusades, and, if you look carefully, in one wing of the courtyard in front of the house, you can still see the gothic windows of a 12th-century church. Inside, you will not find "decorator perfect" rooms nor antique decor, but you will experience genuine country hospitality from Chantal and Michel Le Varlet who have opened 4 bedrooms in their old stone farmhouse to guests. After entering into the home from the courtyard, there is a simple parlor where in the evening dinner is served family-style at one large table. Here guests can also read or watch television, but during the day, the choice place to relax is in the enormous walled garden in the rear. There are four guest rooms reached by a hallway with plastic wall paper. Although the decor is not outstanding, they are immaculately clean and each has a nice bathroom (and the price is very good for those on a budget). Chantal is a very good cook, and in the evenings prepares simple but delicious traditional meals using fresh produce from the farm. *Directions:* Take the "Dormans" exit from the A4 and turn right on the RD 380 toward Dormans. Stay on this road, and in a few minutes (before you reach Passy-Grigny) you will see the Gîte sign for Le Temple on your right.

LE TEMPLE (Gîte de France)
Hosts: Chantal & Michel Le Varlet
Passy-Grigny, 51700 Dormans, France
tel: 26.52.90.01 fax: 26.52.18.86
4 rooms, with private bathrooms
Single: 255F, Double 275F, Triple 370F
Table d'Hôte 105F per person, without wine
Open all year
Some English spoken
Region: Champagne, Michelin Map 237

Dating from 1846, Madame Lefloch's ivy-covered manor house is a home-like Bed and Breakfast, a good choice for families. Madame is a friendly, very down-toearth hostess who is happy to share her Brittany crêpe recipes and has prepared a guest book filled with brochures, maps and information on local sights and activities. Her entry salon is sparsely furnished with country antiques and fresh flower arrangements from her garden. She loves the feeling of a cozy fire, and at the slightest hint of a chill in the air sets a warm blaze in the old stone fireplace. The adjoining breakfast room is light and airy, with a charming wooden floor and more old furniture. On warm mornings guests may also elect to enjoy their breakfast on the sunny terrace overlooking the front lawn. The guest bedrooms are furnished in a mix of antiques and more contemporary pieces, with some leftover familial touches such as large cartoon drawings on a bedroom wall. *Directions:* Pouldavid is located just south of Douarnenez, that is about 22 kilometers northwest of Quimper via D765. Just outside of Douarnenez there is a roundabout; continue on D765 towards Audierne. After the traffic light, look for a Chambres d'Hôtes sign directing you to turn to the right. Continue following signs to the Lefloch manor house.

MANOIR DE KERVENT (Gîte de France)
Hostess: Madame Lefloch
Pouldavid, 29100 Douarnenez, France
tel: 98.92.04.90
4 rooms, without private bathrooms
Double: 190F, Triple: 250F
No Table d'Hôte,
Crêpe dinners & some cooking facilities
Open all year
Very little English spoken
Region: Brittany, Michelin Map 230

Hélène and Vincent Malo are a young couple who welcome guests to their farm with enthusiasm and warmth. They have 5 independent guest rooms in a former outbuilding. Proud of their Norman heritage, Hélène and Vincent took great care while remodeling to retain the charm of the original building. Inside, a freshness and simple charm is felt throughout the bedrooms, all of which are equipped with a basic sink and shower. The furnishings consist of light pine beds, writing tables and chairs. Lighting is good, and pretty touches such as watercolors by regional artists, lace bonnets and fresh flowers brighten the somewhat sparse decor. Dinners and breakfasts are served in the Malo's airy dining room looking out through picture windows to the front garden. Guests who dine at the Malo's are treated to a homemade pear aperitif, homemade apple cider and deliciously light meals featuring farm and garden produce, all complemented by lively conversation. The Malos are a friendly, accommodating couple who speak enough English to get by very well with their English-speaking guests. *Directions:* Écrainville is located about 25 kilometers northeast of Le Havre via D925 to Goderville, then D139 to Écrainville. In Écrainville take the first right following the sign for Fongueusemare. The Malo's home is 2 kilometers on the right.

LA FORGE VIMBERT (Gîte de France)
Hosts: Hélène & Vincent Malo
76110 Écrainville, France
tel: 35.27.17.97
5 rooms, all with sink/shower, all share 2 WC
Double: 185F (2 nights 320F)
Table d'Hôte: 60F per person, includes wine
Open March 1 through January 1
Good English spoken
Region: Normandy, Michelin Map 231

Dominating the unspoiled medieval village of Entrecasteaux is the Chateau d'Entrecasteaux, a handsome 11th-century castle that is open to the public as a museum, and, for a lucky few who make reservations in advance, as a Bed and Breakfast. The castle was purchased in the mid-1970's by Ian McGarvie-Munn, a dashing Scotsman whose zest for living and international escapades filled his days with a novel-worthy set of adventures. He was also an exceptionally talented artist and it seems he bequeathed his love of the arts along with his castle to his hospitable son, Lachlan. Lachlan is a patron of the arts and attracts world class exhibits that are beautifully presented in the spacious, sun-lit rooms on the first two floors of the castle that serve as an art gallery, museum and gift shop. One of the guest rooms (a suite brimming with antiques, including an ornate bed, and with a giant marble bathroom) is actually on display during the day as part of the museum. A private staircase leads to the third level where there are two more extremely large guest rooms, light and airy, with high arched windows that offer pretty views of the old town. *Directions:* Entrecasteaux is located approximately 25 km northeast of Brignoles. From Brignoles, take D562 northeast toward Carcès; 3 km beyond Carcès turn north on D31 to Entrecasteaux. The castle is in the middle of the town.

CHATEAU D'ENTRECASTEAUX
Host: Mr Lachlan McGarvie-Munn
83570 Entrecasteaux, France
tel: 94.04.43.95 fax: 94.04.48.46
3 rooms, with private bathrooms
Single: 750F, Double: 750-1500F
No Table d'Hôte
Open all year
Fluent English, Spanish & German spoken
Region: Côte d'Azur, Michelin Map 245

Isabelle and Patrick Blanc are an attractive and extremely energetic young couple who designed and built their rustic-style Auberge d'Anais (named after their adorable little girl) as a complement to their wine-growing activities. They love to meet people and entertain, and foster an informal, friendly atmosphere where guests feel right at home and friends and family always feel comfortable dropping by. Their property is set on a vineyard-covered hillside, surrounded by woods and valleys, and ablaze with the graceful yellow jenet flowers in the spring and summer months. Three guest rooms open out onto an upstairs terrace that overlooks the crystal blue swimming pool, a welcome refuge in this hot, dry climate. Rooms are spartanly furnished, but very comfortable and clean, with cool tile floors and modern baths or showers. Family-style dinners featuring fresh products from the Blanc's nearby farm are served downstairs in the spacious dining room furnished in country antiques. *Directions:* The village of Entrechaux is located approximately 16 kilometers north of Carpentras via D938 past Malaucene turning right towards St-Marcellin les Vaison and then taking the left fork towards Faucon. Two kilometers later look for a driveway on the left marked with a Chambres d'Hôtes sign as well as a small homemade sign for L'Auberge d'Anais.

AUBERGE D'ANAIS (*Gîte de France*)
Hosts: Isabelle & Patrick Blanc
Quartier Peyreras,
84340 Entrechaux, France
tel: 90.36.20.06 or 90.46.02.07
5 rooms, without private bathrooms
Double: 280F
Table d'Hôte: 85F per person, without wine
Open January 1 through November 1
No English spoken
Region: Provence, Michelin Maps 245, 246

Les Patrus, a simple 17th-century farmhouse set in the Champenoise countryside, is conveniently close to Paris and within an easy drive of Euro Disneyland. The stucco-covered stone buildings form a square, completely enclosing a central courtyard. The Royol family (Mary Ann, Marc, and their two pretty daughters, Fannie and Julie), live in the beautifully renovated stables—the original home is now exclusively for guests. Downstairs is a most inviting dining room with a long antique table that comfortably seats 12. One wall is dominated by a fireplace that in winter cozily warms the room. On the mantel is a collection of antique coffee pots, and on the wall, a display of antique hand scales. A handsome, very old, wooden stair case circles up to the five attractive bedrooms. My favorite is the "Poitou" room that looks out over the tiled roofs to rolling fields and a tranquil pond. If travelling with children, the "Auvergne" suite with two bedrooms sharing a bathroom would be perfect. Mry Ann runs Les Patrus with warmth and efficiency—she has a gift of making her guests feel genuinely "at home". An added bonus is her fluent English—not surprising as her father (a native of Texas) returned to France after World War II to marry his French sweetheart. *Directions:* From the A4, take the La Ferte exit and head south on D933. Just south of Viels Maisson, look for a small road to your right toward L'Epine aux Bois. You will see Less Patrus 500 meters on your right.

LES PATRUS (Gîte de France)
Hosts: Mary Ann & Marc Royol
02450 L'Epine aux Bois, France
tel: 23.69.85.85
5 rooms, with private bathrooms
Double 260-330F, family suite 615F
Table d'Hôte: 95-120F per person, without wine
Open all year
Credit cards: VS
Fluent English spoken
Region: Champagne, Michelin Map 237

Although not officially a Bed and Breakfast, the beautiful, ivy-covered Hôtel le Prieuré can quite justifiably be included in our guide as it is the private home of Marie Jose and Jean Pierre Treillou. This small inn has an enviable location, only a 30-minute drive from the Pari's Charles de Gaulle airport, and not only does it have much more charm than the airport hotels, the rooms are also less expensive. As the name implies, Le Prieure is adjacent to a beautiful old stone church with lovely stained glass windows. One side of the hôtel fronts the street, the other onto a lovely little garden, fragrant with the smell of roses. Madame Treillou has a knack with flowers and garden is a jewel. From the garden, one enters into the central hallway. To the right is a pretty parlor, filled with antiques, and to the left, a most inviting, cozy dining room with antiques tables set before the large fireplace. This is where breakfast is served each morning. There are only 11 rooms, each similar in furnishings, but with varying color schemes. Previously Madame and Monsieur Treillou were antique dealers, that accounts for their use of so many appealing pieces of furniture. *Directions:* Take the AI north from Paris. After you pass Charles de Gaulle airport, take exit **7**, marked Survillers/S. Witz and follow D922 signposted to Ermenonville. As you come into town, turn right following N330 toward Meaux. Before you leave Ermenonville, you will see a church on your left and next to it Hôtel Prieuré.

HÔTEL LE PRIEURÉ
Hosts: Marie Jose & Jean Pierre Treillou
Chevet de l'Eglise
60950 Ermenonville, France
tel: 44.54.00.44 fax: 44.54.02.21
11 rooms, with private bathrooms
Double 550-650F
No Table d'Hôte,
Open all year
Region:Île de France, Michelin Map 237

A stay with the friendly Chaix family on their working farm offers a real taste of rural life in France. Sheep, goats, dogs, cats, chickens and roosters fill the farmyard, but Marcel Chaix's principal occupation is irrigating his soybean, sunflower, wheat and corn crops. A relaxed, very fun-loving family, Marcel, Madeleine and their four daughters extend a sincere, open-armed welcome. Guest accommodations are found in renovated farm buildings away from the Chaixe's main house, so quiet and privacy are assured. Bedrooms are very clean and basic with contemporary furnishings, although some have exposed stone walls that add historic atmosphere. For travellers seeking simple comfort and warm hospitality in a countryside setting, La Mare is a perfect stopping place. *Directions:* Étoile is located approximately 9 km south of Valence. If arriving from Lyon via autoroute A7, exit at the south Valence exit (Valence Sud), and then follow signs for Gap on D111. At the entry to the village of Étoile, turn left towards Montmeyran. Follow signs advertising Chambres d'Hôtes to arrive at the Chaix farm about 3 km later.

LA MARE (Gîte de France)
Hosts: Marcel, Madeleine & Nathalie Chaix
Quartier la Mare
26800 Étoile sur Rhône, France
tel: 75.59.33.79
8 rooms, 5 with private bathrooms
Double: 195F
Table d'Hôte: 70F per person
Open all year
Very little English, spoken by daughters
Region: Rhône Valley, Michelin Maps 244, 246

Any doubts that the Mas Poli is very old are quickly dispelled when the personable Christiane Poli shows you the signs of the revolution, a cross and a fleur de lys, carved into the wall of the front of the house. When Robert and Christiane bought the house 15 years ago it was almost in total ruin: no running water, no heat, holes in the roof. The characterful old pump still stands in the entry hall, a reminder of the past, as does the old stone horse trough in the living room that used to be the stables but is now a charming, comfortable room where meals are served on chilly days. Madame Poli has tastefully renovated and decorated all the rooms, maintaining their old world charm while making them comfortable for her guests. Although the rooms are small, they are meticulously tidy and each decorated with a smattering of antiques and pretty fabrics. For a budget priced place to stay, the Mas Poli offers great value without sacrificing charm. *Directions:* Eyragues is located 12 km south of Avignon. In Éyragues go to the center of the village and follow signs north toward Chateaurenard. Before leaving town, you come to a Shell station and a pharmacy. Take the road to the right of the pharmacy and go straight, past 2 stop signs and after about 1.5 km the Mas Poli is on your left.

MAS POLI (Gîte de France)
Hosts: Christiane & Robert Poli
Chemin des Prés
13630 Eyragues, France
tel: 90.94.19.71
3 rooms, none with private bathroom
Double: 200 F
No Table d'Hôte
Open from April to September
No English spoken (but understood)
Region: Provence, Michelin Maps 245, 246

Le Domaine de Mestré, a former agricultural estate belonging to the Fontevraud Abbey, dates back to the 12th Century. Its origins are even older—stones in the courtyard show traces of an ancient Roman road that once ran through the property. You enter through gates into a courtyard. Immediately to your left is a pretty tithe barn that has been converted into an attractive boutique featuring beautifully packaged soaps and bath oils (sold under the trade name of "Martin de Candre"). These are manufactured right on the property by three generations of the Dauge family. Because all their products are completely natural, without any artificial coloring, fragrances or chemicals, they are very popular—some even exported to the United States. Across the courtyard from the boutique, the 12th-century chapel has been converted into the dining room, attractively decorated with yellow walls and small tables set with yellow linens. The bedrooms are in two separate stone buildings that also face onto the courtyard. Although not deluxe, all of the bedrooms are attractive and most have antique furniture and feature Laura Ashley fabrics. The gracious Dauge family is very personally involved in the operation of their Bed and Breakfast and strive to make each guest feel welcome in their home. *Directions:* From Montsoreau take D947 toward Fontevraud l'Abbaye. Soon after leaving Montsoreau, (before reaching Fontevraud-l'Abbaye), you will see the sign where you turn right for Le Domaine de Mestré.

LE DOMAINE DE MESTRÉ
Hosts: Rosine & Dominique Dauge
49590 Fontevraud l'Abbaye, France
tel: 41.51.75.87
12 rooms, with private bathrooms
Double 350F
Table d'Hôte 130F per person, without wine
Open all year
Very good English spoken by son-in-law
Region: Loire Valley, Michelin Map 232

The road seems to end at the tiny mountain hamlet of Freissinières, and one has the feeling of being at the edge of civilization. The village is extremely quiet, and is located on the boundary of the Parc National des Écrins (literally translated, Jewel Box National Park). The Relais des Vaudois is a rustic inn run mainly by Madame Moutier. Copious family-style lunches and dinners are served in the charming restaurant that has low, vaulted ceilings and is decorated with country antiques, old farm implements and dried flower arrangements. Bedrooms are very basic, but all are adequately furnished and have private shower and WC. The majority of the rooms have French doors that open onto a sunny front balcony overlooking the village. The Relais des Vaudois is a simple country inn rather than a family home, and is thus recommended mainly as a base for hikers or as an atmospheric lunch stop. *Directions:* Freissinières is located 20 kilometers southwest of Briançon. Take N94 in the direction of Gap. Just before entering the village of La Rôche de Rame, turn right onto D38 to Freissinières, following the road up a lovely valley into the hamlet. Continue through on the narrow street to the T intersection at the end of the village. The Relais des Vaudois is on the right and easy to find.

LE RELAIS DES VAUDOIS (*Gîte de France*)
Hosts: Monsieur & Madame Moutier
Freissinières
05310 La Rôche de Rame, France
tel: 92.20.93.01
12 rooms, all with private shower
Single: 202F, Double: 224F
Table d'Hôte: 64F per person
Open all year
No English spoken
Region: French Alps, Michelin Map 244

If you are looking for a chateau whose decor is primly perfect, the Chateau de Garrevaques would not be your cup of tea. But, if you are looking for a warm welcome, this home truly has heart. Since the 15th Century, the chateau has been in the family of the charming Mme Barrande who was persuaded by her daughter, Marie-Christine, to open her home as a Bed and Breakfast. (In fact, the creative Marie-Christine originated the concept of chateaux in France inviting paying guests.) Although their jobs dictate they must travel, when in town Marie-Christine (a purser for Air France) and Marie-Christine's husband, Claude Combes (a commercial pilot), live at the chateau. The whole family exudes genuine hospitality. If you have heard the French are aloof, a visit to Chateau de Garrevaques will quickly dispel that myth—even the cat (Fish) and the dog (Chips) are super friendly. Stay here and become friends with a French family. Dinner is great fun—filled with tales of the chateau (ask about the baby born in prison during the revolution who later retrieved his heritage or the faithful gardener who rescued the castle from destruction by the Nazis). Directions. From Toulouse take D1 southeast for 53 km to Revel. Turn northeast on D 79F for 5 km to Garrevaques.

CHATEAU DE GARREVAQUES
Hosts: Andrée Barande & Marie Christine Combe
81700 Garrevaques, France
tel: 63.75.04.54 fax: 63.70.26.44
12 rooms, 8 with private bathrooms
2-two bedroom suites each share a bathroom
Double: 650F, Triple: 900F
Table d'Hôte: 170F per person
Credit cards: AX, VS
Open March 15-November 30 *
* groups accepted in winter
Good English spoken
Region: Tarn, Michelin Map 235

It is a short walk through grassy fields to the sea from this wonderful 17th-century manor house. Francois and Agnes Lemarie are a friendly young couple who, along with their four adorable children aged 1 to 11, enjoy welcoming Bed and Breakfast guests to their working farm. A strong sense of the past prevails inside the old stone walls of the Lemarie's home, in the adjoining 15th-century chapel, converted to a salon for discussion, dreaming and listening to music, and in the large stone dovecote in the courtyard. The circular room with hundreds of former pigeon niches provides a unique ambiance for guests to enjoy picnics or light meals. Guest bedrooms are basic, and furnishings vary from very simple to family antiques. Dried flower bouquets warm the somewhat cool stone rooms. Breakfast is served in the Lemarie's dining room reminiscent of days gone by, with its walk-in stone fireplace and hanging copper kettle, heavy beamed ceiling and old farm furniture. *Directions:* Géfosse is located approximately 30 kilometers northwest of Bayeux. Take N13 west just past St-Germain du Pert, then D514 north towards Grandcamp Maisy. Turn left onto D199A to Géfosse. There are roadside signs for more than one Chambres d'Hôtes so be sure to follow those marked L'Hermerel. It will be the second driveway on the right.

FERME DE L'HERMEREL (*Gîte de France*)
Hosts: Agnes & Francois Lemarie
14230 Géfosse
Fontenay, France
tel: 31.22.64.12
4 rooms, with private bathrooms
Double: 220-250F
Table d'Hôte: 75F per person
Open March 15 to November 15
Some English spoken
Region: Normandy, Michelin Map 231

The Verjus family's historic farm inn is found in a lovely pastoral setting; on a hill, overlooking green pastures and hills. The only sounds disturbing the rural quiet are cow and sheep bells and a variety of lovely bird songs. The farmhouse is full of historic character, with vaulted ceilings and an old fireplace in the cozy dining room. Built in 1100 and enlarged in the 1700's, the inn combines clean, modern comfort with a traditional ambiance. Home-style dinners usually begin with a regional aperitif called a macvin, that is a potent combination of white wine and whisky, followed by several courses of delicious dishes made with fresh farm ingredients. Guest bedrooms are newly installed and offer good lighting and spotless private showers and WCs. Fresh light pine furniture and pretty floral print curtains create an appropriately rustic country atmosphere. *Directions:* Geruge is located approximately 10 kilometers south of Lons le Saunier, capital of the Jura department of France. From Lons, follow designated scenic route D117 through the village of Macornay, and continue up the winding road to Geruge, always following signs for the direction of St-Julien. Once in Geruge, look for signs directing you to the left for Ferme Auberge La Grange Rouge that is located just outside of the village.

LA GRANGE ROUGE (Gîte de France)
Hosts: Anne-Marie & Henri Verjus
Geruge
39570 Lons le Saunier, France
tel: 84.47.00.44
5 rooms, with private bathrooms
Single: 170F, Double: 200F, Triple: 250F
Ferme Auberge: 70F per person
Open all year
No English spoken
Region: Jura, Michelin Map 243

Young hosts Isabelle and Pierre Breton run a delightful ferme auberge restaurant with rooms in a lovely setting of rolling hills and pasture lands. Dating from 1770, their large farmhouse of regional gray stone is one of the oldest houses in the Cantal region and is filled with historic ambiance, especially in the guest dining room that has exposed stone walls, a large open-hearthed fireplace and a rarely seen type of stone alcove, originally used as a sink area and preparation kitchen. Country antique furniture and dried flower bouquets complete the rustic scene where guests enjoy delicious, traditional meals featuring farm-fresh meat products. Bedrooms are furnished simply, yet contain charming accents such as brass beds and old armoires. Located in the former attic, the rooms are small and intimate with sloping, beamed ceilings and dormer windows that let in the pure Auvergne air and look out over the unspoiled countryside. *Directions:* Giou de Mamou is located approximately 8 kilometers east of Aurillac. Take N122 in the direction of Vic sur Cere and Murat. About 5 kilometers out of Auillac, look for a sign to the left indicating the hamlet of Giou de Mamou via D58. Follow signs indicating Chambres et Tables d'Hôtes Barathe that lead down a country lane to the Breton's charming establishment.

FERME DE BARATHE (*Gîte de France*)
Hosts: Isabelle & Pierre Breton
15130 Giou de Mamou, France
tel: 71.64.61.72
5 rooms, with private bathrooms
Double 300F *
*rate includes breakfast & dinner
Table d'Hôte: included in room rate
Open all year
Some English spoken
Region: Auvergne, Michelin Map 239

For friends or a large family who are looking for an inexpensive abode while exploring Provence, Les Martins makes a very attractive choice. (It would help if one of one of your group understands a little French since the Perons do not speak English). The main house where the family lives is a typical old mas (farmhouse). The guest rooms are located in an annex located a short stroll up a little lane. Here you will find another characterful building with exposed stone exterior, windows framed with brown shutters and a roof of heavy tile. The four bedrooms share a pleasant lounge area that is attractively decorated by a large antique wooden table surrounded by country-style chairs. Adding to the rustic, country ambiance of the room are some antique farm instruments artfully displayed on the walls. Doors that open on to a sunny terrace are also shared by all. The bedrooms are basic in decor and ambiance, but for the price, certainly adequate. *Directions:* Gordes is located about 38 km east of Avignon. Although the address is Gordes, Les Martins is actually located much closer to the tiny village of Les Beaumettes if you can find it on your map. From the N100, take the 103 north toward Gordes. In about 2 km there is a Gîte sign on the left side of the road. Turn left and in a few minutes you will see Les Martins on your left.

LES MARTINS (Gîte de France)
Hosts: Denise & Claude Peron
84220 Gordes, France
tel: 90.72.24.15
4 rooms, 3 with private bathrooms
Double: 200F, Triple: 250F
Table d'Hôte: 80F per person
Open February to November 15
No English spoken
Region: Provence, Michelin Maps 245, 246

When the Konings family (whose home was Holland) asked a realtor to find a place for them to retire in Provence, they expected the search to take many years. Amazingly, the perfect property, a very old stone farmhouse with great potential charm, was found almost immediately. So, even though the timing was a bit sooner than anticipated, they bought the farmhouse and restored it into an absolute dream. The six guest rooms are in a cluster of weathered stone buildings that form a small courtyard. The name of each room gives a clue as to its original use such as The Old Kitchen, The Hayloft, The Wine Press, etc. Arja Konings has exquisite taste and each room is decorated using country antiques and Provençal fabrics. Most conveniently, the Koning's son, Gerald, (who was born in the United States) is a talented chef. He oversees the small restaurant that is delightfully appealing with massive beamed ceiling, tiled floor, exposed stone walls and country-style antique furnishings. The dining room opens onto a terrace that overlooks the swimming pool. *Directions:* Gordes is located about 38 km northeast of Avignon. From Gordes, head east the D2 for about 2 km. Turn right (south) on D156. In just a few minutes you will see La Ferme de la Huppe on your right.

LA FERME DE LA HUPPE
Hosts: Family Konings: Mr. Bert, & Ms Arja
Route D156
84220 Gordes, France
tel: 90.72.12.25 fax: 90.72.01.83
6 rooms, with private bathrooms
Double: 500F
Gourmet restaurant
Credit cards: MC, VS
Closed January to March 15
Fluent English spoken
Region: Provence, Michelin Maps 245, 246

The Moulin de Fresquet is truly a jewel, offering not only the charm of an old mill, but also beautiful antiques and great warmth of welcome. The hearth of the old stone mill dates back to the 17th Century. The mill stream still flows right beneath the house. In fact from room 4, you can look out the casement window and watch and listen to the gurgling waters. Many places to stay in this price range are pleasant, but lacking in style, not so with Moulin de Fresquet. The family room where guests gather for dinner, is filled with beautiful antiques that Gerard inherited from his Grandmother. The ambiance is one of rustic beauty with handsome stone walls accented by family portraits and 200-year-old tapestries, heavy beamed ceiling, bouquets of fresh flowers, a massive stone fireplace and the patina of fine antiques. A narrow staircase leads to the lower lever where there are five bedrooms. The bedrooms are attractive with stone walls and color coordinated draperies and bed spreads. Bedroom number 5 is the most expensive, but very large and with doors leading to the terrace. Claude, so pretty with sparkling brown eyes, is a wonderful cook and the dinner in the evening must not be missed. You will love this marvelous mill and its location, so near Gramat and Rocamadour, that is such an oasis of quiet. *Directions:* From Gramat take N140 south toward Figeac. Just 500 meters after leaving town, take the small lane on the left signposted to Moulin de Fresquet. You will see the mill on your right.

MOULIN DE FRESQUET (Gîte de France)
Hosts: Claude & Gerard Ramelot
46500 Gramat, France
tel: 65.38.70.60
5 rooms, with private bathrooms
Double: 230-320F
Table d'Hôte: 95F per person
A little English spoken
Open all year
Region: Dordogne, Michelin Maps 235, 239

For a tranquil little hideaway while exploring the beautiful area of Provence, the Domaine du Bois Vert is truly a gem. Although only a few years old, the clever owners, Jean Peter and Veronique Richard, have tastefully achieved the ambiance of an old farm house by incorporating a typical rosy-tan stuccoed exterior, light blue wooden shutters and a heavy tiled roof. The mood of antiquity continues within where dark beamed ceilings, tiled floors, dark wooden doors, and white walls enhance a few carefully chosen country-style Provençal pieces of furniture. There are only two bedrooms, but each is immaculately tidy and prettily decorated. The bedroom to the back of the house is especially enticing with windows looking out onto the oak trees. Meals are not served on a regular basis, but Veronique treats guests who stay a week to a dinner featuring typical regional specialties. *Directions:* Grans is located approximately 40 km east of Arles and 6 km from Salon de Provence. From Grans, go south for on D19 (signposted to Lançon-Provence). About 1 km after you pass Grans, turn left on a small road where you will see a Gîte sign. In a few minutes turn left again at another Gîte sign and take the lane to the Domaine du Bois Vert.

DOMAINE DU BOIS VERT (Gîte de France)
Hosts: Veronique & Jean Peter Richard
Quartier Montauban,
13450 Grans, France
tel: 90.55.82.98
2 rooms, with private bathrooms
Double: 220-265F, Triple 310-340F
No Table d'Hôte
Credit cards: None
Open all year
Good English spoken
Region: Provence, Michelin Maps 245, 246

Jacqueline and Auguste Bahuaud recently purchased a fabulous home dating from the mid-1800's that they have, with much love and labor, meticulously restored to its original splendor. Throughout the home, everything is fresh, new and beautifully decorated. The bedrooms are especially outstanding: each has its own personality, each is very inviting. My particular favorite is the "blue room" that has a prime corner location, affording windows on two walls looking out to the rear garden. One of the very nicest aspects of Chez Bahuaud is its setting: the park-like grounds stretch behind the house with terraced lawns shaded by mature trees. A romantic path through the garden leads down to Grez-Neuville: a real gem of a small village nestled on the banks of the Mayenne River. There are many boats along the Mayenne that can be rented by the day or week for exploring the picturesque countryside. Your hosts, Jacqueline and Auguste, are gracious hosts who warmly open their home and hearts to their guests. *Directions:* From Angers, take N162 north for about 17 km and take a right on to the Grez-Neuville exit. Go into the village and find the old church. As you go down toward the river, you will see on your left a beautiful old stone church, and just adjacent to it, the Chambre d'Hôtes sign on the gate of the Bahuaud's home.

LA CROIX D'ETAIN (Gîte de France)
Hosts: Jacqueline & Auguste Bahuaud
2, rue de l'Ecluse
49220 Grez-Neuville, France
tel: 41.95.68.49
4 rooms, with private bathrooms
Double 320-350F
Table d'Hôte: 100F per person, wine not included
Open Easter to November
Some English spoken
Region: Loire Valley, Michelin Map 232

Le Vieux Cognet has a prime position, directly on the edge of the Loire River. In fact, if you walk down to the river's edge, you can see the towers of the cathedral. The approach, to this small Bed and Breakfast does not display its potential: all you see is a house sitting directly on the road. But, once you pull into the driveway, the superb setting is revealed. The cottage-like dove gray home with gray roof is right on the banks of the Loire River. In early summer, a mass of roses laces the exterior. Each of the bedrooms has a fabulous, unobstructed view of the water. All of the rooms are individually decorated. The furnishings are fresh and new and have color coordinated drapes and spreads. There are three guest rooms on the lower level, each with a bathroom ensuite. Upstairs are three more bedrooms. If you don't mind a tiny room and want a real bargain, tucked up under the eaves with a bathroom across the hall is a room just big enough to squeeze in one double bed, that is rented for 280F per night. Each morning breakfast is served either outside when the weather is warm, or else in a cozy beamed-ceiling dining room just off the terrace. Francois is a good cook and serves fresh baked bread, home-made jams, and just-out-of-the oven cakes each morning. *Directions:* From Blois, follow N152 southwest along the banks of the Loire. Watch carefully for the Chambre d'Hôte sign on the side of the road where you make a sharp left turn into the driveway.

LE VIEUX COGNET (Gîte de France)
Hostess: Françoise Cosson
4 Levee des Grouëts
41000 Blois, France
tel: 54.56.05.34
6 rooms, with private bathrooms
Double from 280-350F
No Table d'Hôte
Open April to October 15
Some English spoken
Region: Loire Valley, Michelin Map 238

The Paulous are a friendly, well-travelled couple who have filled their 300-year-old cottage with antiques and artifacts from their many voyages. A low, stone doorway leads into the main room of their house that they have transformed into a very cozy dining room/kitchen area. This welcoming room has a low, beamed ceiling, stone walls, walk-in fireplace and country antique furniture and is an inviting spot to linger with Monsieur and Madame over breakfast that, on warm mornings, is enjoyed with good conversation on the sunny courtyard terrace. Madame Paulou is also happy to bring breakfast to your room on a tray. The Paulous offer a charming, twin-bedded guest room that has an entrance completely independent of the rest of the house. Furnishings are tasteful, clean and fresh, accented by an interesting carved chest and artwork from their son's travels in Korea. This is a real jewel of a Bed and Breakfast, made even more delightful by the warm welcome extended by the Paulous. *Directions:* Loyan, referenced by the larger, neighboring town of Guidel, is located approximately 10 kilometers east of Lorient or 58 kilometers southeast of Quimper. Leave Guidel on D162 in the direction of Ploemeur. This country road has many twists and turns, so be sure to continue following signs to Ploemeur. Just after passing the sign at the entry of the tiny hamlet of Loyan, turn into the first driveway on the left.

CHEZ PAULOU (Gîte de France)
Hosts: Monsieur & Madame Paulou
Route de Ploemeur, Loyan
56520 Guidel, France
tel: 97.86.34.85
1 room, with private bathroom
Single: 180F, Double: 195F
No Table d'Hôte
Open all year
Very little English spoken
Region: Brittany, Michelin Map 230

A romantic, enchanted quality pervades the lovely old Moulin de la Dive, a former flour mill covered with ivy and surrounded by magical wooded grounds. Originally built by a noble family in the 14th Century, the mill was burned by the Protestants in 1569 and rebuilt in the early 17th Century, only to be burned again during the French Revolution. Annick Vanverts and her husband are extremely warm and solicitous hosts who relocated here from Paris, seeking a more natural existence away from the fast pace and pollution of the big city. Guests have a private entrance through an old arched doorway and up a marble staircase to the two upstairs bedrooms, each uniquely decorated. Seville is furnished entirely in Spanish antiques, and Nohant reflects the graceful style of 18th-century France and is named after the home of French novelist Georges Sand. All the rooms have spotless, modern bathrooms and large windows that let in the pure country air. Breakfast is enjoyed either in the Vanvert's charming, country-elegant salon or outside in the lush garden. *Directions:* Guron is located approximately 30 kilometers southwest of Poitiers. Take N10 in the direction of Angoulême for about 25 kilometers past the village of Les Minieres, then turn left onto D29 towards the town of Auche. Two kilometers later look for a Chambres d'Hôtes sign marking the Vanvert's gate on the right.

LE MOULIN DE LA DIVE (*Gite de France*)
Hosts: Monsieur & Madame Vanverts
Guron, 86700 Payre, France
tel: 49.42.40.97
2 rooms, with private bathrooms
Double: 340-360F
No Table d'Hôte
Open July & August
Very little English spoken
Region: Atlantic Coast, Michelin Map 233

In the lovely Périgord region of France, tucked along the banks of a small river, you will find the quaint Le Moulin de la Crouzille. This storybook-perfect, vine-covered old mill abounds with character: it is constructed of mellow-toned, honey-colored stone that is highlighted by casement windows and pretty white shutters. The steeply pitched roof (a jumble of characterful angles) appears even more whimsical with perky little dormer windows peeking out. Stone steps lead up to the front door that opens directly into a homey living room where comfortable chairs and a sofa are grouped around a large open fireplace. To the left of the fireplace, a door opens to a terrace where dinner is usually served in the summer. There are two bedrooms, each with its own bathroom "down the hall." One of the bedrooms is especially appealing with a painted. four-poster bed. The owners, Diana and John Armitage, were born in England, but now make France their home. Guests are welcomed as friends and dine with the family. Diana is a super cook and personally prepares the meals. *Directions:* From Périgueux take D5 east towards HAUTEFORT. Two and a half kilometers after passing through the village of Tourtoitac, turn left at a small crossroads sign-posted La Palue and La Crouzille. Le Moulin is the first lane on your right (30 km E of Périgueux).

LE MOULIN DE LA CROUZILLE
Hosts: Diana & John Armitage
Tourtoirac
24390 Hautefort, France
tel: 53.51.11.94
2 rooms, with private bathrooms
Double 500 F
Table d'Hôte: 150F per person, without wine
Open all year except Christmas
Fluent English spoken
Region: Périgord, Michelin Map 233

A stay at Chez Boch is like a visit to an aunt in the country, offering a chance to relax in a home-like atmosphere, looked after by solicitous hostess Frieda Boch. Her contemporary chalet-style house is found in a suburb of Heiligenstein and is furnished with an assortment of knickknacks, prints and souvenirs that comprise an eclectic collection of memorabilia. Bedrooms are comfortable and somewhat basic, furnished in a mix of antique and reproduction furniture. An adjoining annex has a sitting room with a television, refrigerator and sink for guest's use. Breakfast is also served here on a cheerful enclosed porch, bordered by bright red geraniums. Frieda serves a particularly delicious and substantial morning buffet consisting of a large selection of coffee cakes and breads, several varieties of cheeses and cold cuts, four kinds of preserves, honey and the usual choice of hot coffee, tea or chocolate. *Directions:* Heiligenstein is located approximately 28 kilometers southwest of Strasbourg. Take N422 past the turnoff to Obernai and just before the town of Barr look for the turnoff to Heiligenstein to the right. Once in Heiligenstein, go through town following the directions for Obernai. The Boch house is on the left on the road out of town and is marked with a Chambres d'Hôtes sign.

CHEZ BOCH (Gîte de France)
Hostess: Madame Frieda Boch
144, rue Principale
67140 Heiligenstein, France
tel: 88.08.97.30
4 rooms, with private bathrooms
Double: 200-220F
No Table d'Hôte
Open all year
No English spoken, fluent German spoken
Region: Alsace, Michelin Map 242

The old manor house of Le Petit Pey is set on pretty grounds and tended with care by energetic hostess Annie de Bosredon, a very charming, refined, yet down-to-earth hostess who takes great pleasure in opening her home to guests. Le Petit Pey is a regional stone building with windows and French doors framed by white shutters. The oldest part dates from the 1600's, while the newer wing was added in about 1760. Madame de Bosredon's aristocratic drawing room combines comfort with elegance and is filled with valuable antiques, artifacts and fresh-cut garden roses. Bedrooms are furnished in family antiques, and each has its own country charm. The drawing room and bedrooms are actually in a separate wing of the house, so guests are afforded privacy and the luxury of being at home in the lovely salon. There are plenty of historic walled towns in the region as well as the interesting towns of Issigeac and Bergerac. *Directions:* Issigeac is approximately 60 kilometers south of Périgueux via 21 through Bergerac. About 11 kilometers after Bergerac, turn left onto D14 towards Issigeac, then at Issigeac take D21 south towards Castillonnes. Two kilometers later at Monmarves, look for a sign reading Domaine du Petit Pey and turn into the green gate.

LE PETIT PEY (Gîte de France)
Hostess: Madame Annie de Bosredon
Monmarvès
24560 Issigeac, France
tel. 53.53.99.99 or 53.58.70.61
2 rooms, with private bathrooms
Double: 310F
No Table d'Hôte
Open all year
Good English spoken
Region: Périgord, Michelin Map 235

The Château du Plessis is a lovely, aristocratic country home, truly one of France's most exceptional private chateaux-hôtels and a personal favorite; one of the few establishments that we are including in both our guidebooks to France. Madame Benoist's family have lived here since well before the revolution, but the antiques throughout the home are later acquisitions of her great, great, great grandfather, as the furnishings original to the house were burned on the front lawn by the revolutionaries in 1793. Furnishings throughout the home are elegant, yet the Benoists establish an atmosphere of homey comfort. Artistic fresh flower arrangements abound and one can see Madame's cutting garden from the French doors in the salon that open onto the lush grounds. In the evening the large oval table in the dining room provides an opportunity to enjoy the company of other guests and the country-fresh cuisine of Madame Benoist. The Benoists are a handsome couple who take great pride in their home and the welcome they extend to their guests. *Directions:* To reach La Jaille-Yvon travel north of Angers on N162 and at the town of Le Lion d'Angers clock the odometer eleven kilometers further north to an intersection, Carrefour Fleur de Lys. Turn east and travel 2 1/2 kilometers to La Jaille-Yvon—the Château du Plessis is on its southern edge.

CHÂTEAU DU PLESSIS
Hosts: Monsieur & Madame Paul Benoist
49990 La Jaille-Yvon, France
tel: 41.95.12.75   fax: 41.95.14.41
8 rooms, with private bathrooms
Double: 700F
Table d'Hôte: 270F per person
Open March 1 to November 1
Credit cards: all major
Very good English spoken
Region: Loire Valley, Michelin Map 232

Young Jacques and Valerie Advenier are charming hosts who are dedicated to the restoration of Jacque's family chateau and preserving a peaceful and refined ambiance. Their enchanting home is found in an area rich in history; the region of France that was once home to the ruling Bourbon family. A fascinating collection of ancient fortresses and castles can be visited throughout the surrounding countryside. During the day, Jacques and Valerie open their gracious oak-paneled dining room to the public and offer tea, coffee and homemade pastries. The lovely room, set with round tables covered with pretty floral print tablecloths, is also where guests enjoy leisurely breakfasts and candlelit dinners. A beautiful wide stone stairway leads upstairs to the inviting guest bedrooms, all of that Jacques has lovingly restored and decorated with impeccable taste and attention to detail, including direct dial phones in each room. Furnished in fine antiques, lovely fabrics, rugs and artwork, each room is a delightful haven for travellers. *Directions:* Jaligny is located approximately 40 kilometers north of Vichy. Travel via D906 or N209 to D907 to Lapalisse then leave town on D480 to Jaligny, Dompierre. Go through the town of Jaligny, leaving on D989 towards the town of le Donjon. Not quite 2 kilometers out of town, look for a sign to the right for Le Lonzat. A lovely tree-lined drive curves around to the entrance.

CHATEAU DE LONZAT (Gîte de France)
Hosts: Valerie & Jacques Advenier
03220 Jaligny sur Besbre, France
tel: 70.34.73.39 fax: 70.34.81.31
5 rooms, with private bathrooms
Double: 370-726F, Triple: 636-848F
Table d'Hôte: 130F per person
Open March 1 through December 31
Some English spoken
Region: Berry, Michelin Map 238

The Chaffois cottage is found in a beautiful mountain setting where grassy hillsides are broken only by delicate wildflowers and grazing horses. Bernard and Mireille Chaffois are an attractive, friendly couple who, in addition to offering Bed and Breakfast accommodation also grow lavender to make perfume and raise goats to produce fresh homemade goat cheese. Their charming home dates from 1600 and is simply, yet comfortably furnished. Guest bedrooms are located upstairs and have an independent guest entrance and a spacious sitting area. In the mornings guests wake to fresh country bread and plenty of hot cafe au lait served in large pottery pitchers. This traditional French country fare is served in the historical dining room that features vaulted stone ceilings. *Directions:* Jansac is located approximately 60 kilometers southeast of Valence. If arriving via autoroute from Lyon, exit at Valence Sud (south exit of Valence) and follow directions for Crest on D111. Continue past the large town of Die about 15 kilometers to the village of Récoubeau. Go through town and then turn right following signs for Jansac: the road winds up into the mountains to this tiny hamlet. The Chaffois's home is impossible to miss because part of the house forms an arch over the road and is marked with a sign.

CHEZ CHAFFOIS (*Gîte de France*)
Hosts: Mireille & Bernard Chaffois
26310 Récoubeau-Jansac, France
tel: 75.21.30.46
5 rooms, 1 with private bathroom
Double: 200-240F
Table d'Hôte: 70F
Open all year
Very little English spoken
Region: Alps, Michelin Maps 245, 246

Twelve years ago Christel Hofstadt came on holiday from Germany and fell in love with the absolute tranquillity surrounding the Mas Soupetrière. Although the stone farm building was in complete disrepair, she could not resist buying it. The house has been completely renovated and is open as a delightful Bed and Breakfast. The facade of the house is very attractive: a combination of honey-colored stone interspersed with light tan stuccoed walls, heavy tiled roof and light gray-blue shutters. Christel has excellent taste and the decor is fresh and pretty: country antiques, provençal-style fabrics, white plastered walls, and oriental carpets. Meals are usually served outside on a pretty terrace in front of the house (a hearty dinner, featuring the specialties of Provence and wine, is included in the room rate). An added bonus is the swimming pool located in a field near the house. Apartments are also available, but we prefer the main house. *Directions:* Gordes is located 38 km northeast of Avignon. From N100, take D60 north toward Joucas. Before Joucas, turn right (east) on the D2. Turn left at the second road (marked D 102) and take the very first lane to your right. In a few minutes you will see the Bed and Breakfast on your left.

MAS DE LA SOUPÉTRIÈRE (Gîte de France)
Hostess: Madame Christel Hofstadt
Joucas
84220 Gordes, France
tel: 90.05.78.81 fax: 90.05.76.33
3 rooms, with private bathrooms
*Single: 640F, Double: 820F ***
* rate includes breakfast & dinner
Table d'Hôte included in room rate
Open all year
Fluent English spoken
Region: Provence, Michelin Maps 245, 246

A winding country road leads to the Rénévot's modest farmhouse in this typically Breton region of farmlands dotted with white stone houses. The Rénévots raise dairy cows and poultry on their farm that has been in Monsieur's family for several generations. The original stone farmhouse has been transformed into a comfortable apartment for stays of a week or more. Next door, the Rénévots now live in a newer house where they offer an upstairs and downstairs bedroom to Bed and Breakfast guests. Decor is simple and home-like and bedrooms are small. The house does not have an historic ambiance, but the welcome provided by Madame Rénévot is very warm and sincere. She enjoys opening her parlor to guests and is happy to give advice on planning sightseeing tours in the area. The scenic Brittany coast is only minutes away, as is the picturesque town of Quimper. If you seek a true slice of French country farm life, a stay at the Rénévot's will not disappoint. *Directions:* Le Juch is located approximately 20 kilometers northwest of Quimper. Take D765 towards Douarnenez then after approximately 16 kilometers look for a sign to the right for Le Juch. Just after entering the village, you will see a cemetery on the left: take the next right in the direction of Guengat, then turn at the second right that is marked Route Tar-ar and leads to the Rénévot's white cottage.

KERSANTEC (Gîte de France)
Hosts: Yvette & René Rénévot
29100 Le Juch, France
tel: 98.74.71.36
2 rooms, each with private bath, share WC
Double: 200F
No Table d'Hôte
Open all year
No English spoken
Region: Brittany, Michelin Map 230

Madame and Monsieur Chatel, and their two sons, delight in welcoming guests into their pretty Norman farmhouse. The Chatels restored this 200-year-old farmhouse over a period of several years and now have a comfortable, independent wing for their guests. A Dutch door leads to the downstairs foyer where the Chatels have placed a wealth of local sightseeing and restaurant information on an antique table. The three bedrooms are all fresh and clean, with the downstairs room being particularly charming as it contains an antique bed and armoire. Morning baguettes are enjoyed outdoors on the guest terrace or in the delightful living/dining room with its beamed ceilings, pretty antique furniture and collection of old plates. The original walk-in stone fireplace provides a cozy blaze on cool mornings and evenings. The Chatels have been welcoming Bed and Breakfast guests since 1983 and are solicitous hosts, always ready with advice on the many local sights and excursions. *Directions:* Jumièges is located approximately 23 kilometers west of Rouen via D982, then D143. In Jumièges look for a green and yellow Chambres d'Hôtes sign directing you to leave town on a small country road and continue for about 1 kilometer to the Chatel's low, stone farmhouse with a Gîtes de France sign outside.

CHEZ CHATEL (Gîte de France)
Hosts: Monsieur & Madame Chatel
rue de Quesney
76480 Jumièges, France
tel: 35.37.24.98
3 rooms, all with sink/WC, 2 share shower
Double: 185F
No Table d'Hôte
Open all year
No English spoken
Region: Normandy, Michelin Map 231

It is tempting not to share the discovery of the Mas du Bas Claux—it is just too perfect. Judy (who is English) and Jan (who is Dutch) bought this beautiful piece of property (located just outside the charming medieval village of Lacoste) when Jan took early retirement from the DuPont Company. It took several years of dedicated labor, but what had been a neglected 18th-century stone farmhouse is now a beautiful home. Jan is a keen gardener and, when the house was redesigned, the setting was also restructured so that what had been a sloping field is now a dramatic, beautifully-manicured, grassy terrace with a romantic outlook over the vineyards and beyond to the beckoning hills. Also in the garden there is a delightful swimming pool, a lovely place to relax after a day of sightseeing. It is not the beauty of the house or garden, however, that make this place so perfect: it is the warmth of the owners, Judy and Jan, who are perfect hosts. They are not listed in any of the official Bed and Breakfast organizations because they wish to remain small and exclusive, maintaining the size and quality to treat each and everyone as a friend and pampered guest. *Directions:* Lacoste is located 45 km east of Avignon. Take the D108 east from Lacoste. After 1 km, watch for a sign on the left side of the road for Mas du Bas Claux.

MAS DU BAS CLAUX
Hosts: Judy & Jan van Horck
84480 Lacoste, France
tel: 90.75.90.49 fax: 90.75.90.49
2 rooms, with private bathrooms
Double: 400F
No Table d'Hôte
Credit cards: None
Open all year
Fluent English spoken
Region: Provence, Michelin Maps 245, 246

In the heart of a picturesque hill town at the foot of a castle once home to the infamous Marquis de Sade, Monsieur Court de Gebelin offers exquisite accommodation in his charming 17th-century home. Monsieur has spent several years lovingly restoring and improving his house to achieve a harmonious mix of historic surroundings with the latest in modern conveniences. Bedrooms are furnished in understated good taste and feature subdued lighting and luxurious private baths. Each room is unique in its design and decor, with the high level of comfort and attention to detail remaining uniform throughout. As an added luxury for guests, Monsieur has installed a small, jewel-like swimming pool beside the upstairs terrace where guests are invited to relax after a day of sightseeing, or simply to escape summer's midday heat. The sincere, warm welcome offered by Monsieur Court de Gebelin and his mother complete the perfection of the unforgettable Relais du Procureur. *Directions:* From Avignon to Cavaillon take N100 towards Apt, turning right at the village of Lumières following signs for Lacoste. Once in the village, keep to your right, the route to the Relais du Procureur is well marked, although the narrow old streets can be difficult to navigate in a large car.

RELAIS DU PROCUREUR (Gîte de France)
Host: Antoine Court de Gebelin
Rue Basse
84710 Lacoste, France
tel: 90.75.82.28 fax: 90.75.86.94
Book by phone only, major credit cards OK
6 rooms, with private bathrooms
Double: 500-650F
No Table d'Hôte
Open all year
Very good English spoken
Region: Provence, Michelin Maps 245, 246

Monsieur and Madame Rebiffe take great pleasure in welcoming Bed and Breakfast guests into their 300-year-old farmhouse. The house is characteristically long and low, built of pretty, regional stone and situated in a scenic region where Monsieur Rebiffe enjoys guiding horse drawn carriage trips. Madame is fond of cooking regional Table d'Hôte dinners including specialties such as pork with wild mushroom or chestnut sauces, garlic soup and black cherry cobbler. She lived in Washington and New York in the mid-1940's and retains a fair fluency in English through her love of literature. Guests have a private entrance into a cozy sitting room with exposed stone walls, old fireplace, comfy couch, easy chairs and a bookcase full of English and French classics. Upstairs, the bedrooms have pretty views over the surrounding countryside and are comfortably furnished with a mixture of family furniture. *Directions:* Ladignac le Long is located approximately 35 kilometers south of Limoges. Take D704 towards St-Yriex la Perche, turning right about 5 kilometers after the village of St-Maurice les Brosses onto D15 to Nexon. Before the castle at the entrance to Nexon, turn left to Ladignac le Long. Go through Ladignac and follow signs for the hamlet of Mazerollas. In 4 km, at the little intersection of Mazerollas, turn left towards Bourdoulet. The Rebiffe farm is 300 meters on the right marked with a Chambres d'Hôtes sign.

CHEZ REBIFFE (Gîte de France)
Hosts: Monsieur & Madame Rebiffe
Mazerollas
87500 Ladignac le Long, France
tel: 55.09.35.92
2 rooms share one bath/WC
Double: 155F, Triple: 225F
Table d'Hôte: 75F per person
Open all year
Good English spoken by Madame Rebiffe
Region: Périgord, Michelin Map 233

Martine and Jean-Pierre Halope and their two young daughters live in their restored farmhouse in a tranquil countryside setting. The neat and tidy buildings are of light-colored regional stone and have a storybook farm feeling. Farm animals abound, as the Halopes raise horses, cows, chickens, geese, goats and dogs. Guests may sample farm produce and livestock at the family Table d'Hôte dinners served at a long wooden table in the breakfast/dining room. An old stone fireplace warms the room on cool mornings and evenings. The Halope's homey living room is also open to guests and is a pleasant spot to enjoy an aperitif or afternoon tea. The simple, yet charming guest bedrooms are offer peaceful views of the surrounding fields and nearby woods. All is fresh and newly renovated in the rooms, each decorated in a different pastel color scheme. Perfectly located for touring the castles of the Loire Valley, the Ferme de l'Êpeigne offers comfortable Bed and Breakfast accommodation in a busy family home. *Directions:* Langeais is located approximately 22 kilometers west of Tours on the north bank of the Loire. Take N152 to Langeais, then follow signs for the town of Hommes via D15. After 2 kilometers there is a Chambres d'Hôtes sign on the right indicating L'Êpeigne.

LA FERME DE L'ÉPEIGNE (Gîte de France)
Hosts: Martine & Jean-Pierre Halope
37130 Langeais, France
tel: 47.96.54.23 or 47.96.37.13
5 rooms, 3 w/pvt WC/shower, rest share
Double: 220-260F
Table d'Hôte 90-100F per person, includes wine
Open all year
A little English spoken
Region: Loire Valley, Michelin Map 232

The seaside town of Larmor Plage is a popular summer destination for sailors, wind surfers and sightseers. For travellers seeking this type of beach town ambiance, the Allanos offer very comfortable and clean accommodation in their suburban home. The front entry hall sets the tone of this genteel home with old pictures, antiques and fresh flower arrangements. A faux marble staircase leads upstairs to guest rooms that are comfortably furnished in antique reproductions. The downstairs guest bedroom has an independent French door entry that leads to a flagstone terrace and the Allano's tranquil lawn and garden. Furnished in family antiques, this is a pretty, though somewhat small, room. A possible drawback is the house's proximity to the often heavily trafficked road, yet the Allanos have a faithful returning clientele who enjoy their oasis of comfort in this summer resort community. *Directions:* Larmor Plage is located 5 kilometers south of L'Orient. Once in Larmor Plage, go through town and follow the route for Kerpape that will turn into the beach front road rue des Roseaux. Look for a small Chambres d'Hôtes sign on the gatepost of number 9 that will be on the left. The Allano's white house is not easily visible from the road.

VILLA LES CAMELIAS (*Gîte de France*)
Hosts: Monsieur & Madame Allano
9, rue des Roseaux
56260 Larmor Plage, France
tel: 97.65.50.67
4 rooms, with private bathrooms
Double: 230F
No Table d'Hôte
Open all year
Very little English spoken
Region: Brittany, Michelin Map 230

A narrow cobblestone alley leads to the entrance of La Taverne de la Dame du Plô, a convivial piano bar and gathering place in a brick and half-timbered house dating from the Middle Ages and full of historical flavor. Bernard Fevre artfully and lovingly restored the medieval house into a cellar piano bar and Bed and Breakfast. A separate entrance leads to the charming guest accommodation; small, intimate rooms tastefully decorated with dainty print wallpapers in soft color tones, furnished with choice country antique pieces. All have a tiny private shower and basin area and private WC. Breakfast can be enjoyed in the garden across the lane or in the adjoining dining room. There is also a small kitchen area for guest's use. *Directions:* Lavaur is located approximately 30 km east of Toulouse. Take D112 and enter the town of Lavaur, following signs for centre ville (the town centre). At the fountain, take La Grande rue (main street) straight on and follow it to the old part of town where it will narrow and its name will change to rue Père Colin. After the road veers to the right, look for a Chambres d'Hôtes sign on the right marking the Fevre's three-storey brick house on a corner. The cross street is rue Carlipa.

LA TAVERNE DE LA DAME DU PLÔ (Gîte de France)
Host: Monsieur Bernard Fevre
5, rue Père Colin
81500 Lavaur, France
tel: 63.41.38.77
4 rooms, with private bathrooms
Single: 170F, Double: 200F, Triple: 230F
No Table d'Hôte
Open all year
Good English spoken
Region: Tarn, Michelin Map 235

If you want to experience a stay in a typical French farmhouse, Montpeyroux (a handsome large two-storey home, softened by ivy and white shutters) makes an excellent choice. The ambiance within does not conform to any trendy decorating scheme—this is truly a family home with old-fashioned furnishings Yet, I was quite impressed: the bedrooms are all wall papered and have color coordinated draperies, cushions, and bedspreads—all beautifully sewn by Madame Sallier. Splurge and request the most expensive room—not only because it is the largest and the only one with a private bathroom, but also because it is just beautiful with genuine antiques set off by a color scheme of creams and greens. The farm also has its own swimming pool and tennis court—quite a surprise for such a simple farmhouse. *Directions:* Castres is located 71 km east of Toulouse. From Castres go southwest on N126 then D622 toward Revel. About 18 km after leaving Castres turn north on D12 to Lempaut. From Lempaut drive west on D46 for about 2 km. When you come to a large cemetery on your left, turn left on the small road just before the cemetery. The road loops around the cemetery. Follow this road until you see the Gîte sign and the large house on your right.

MONTPEYROUX
Hosts: Monsieur & Madame A. Sallier
Montpeyroux
81700 Lempaut, France
tel: 63.75.51.17
5 rooms, 1 with private bath/WC
Single: 200F, Double: 250-300F
Table d'Hôte: 80F per person
Credit cards: None
Open April to November
No English spoken
Region: Tarn, Michelin Map 235

Prefontaine is a stately, two-storey 18th-century manor in a beautiful, park-like setting. Do not be put off by the exterior that needs some loving care, because the interior is lovely. As you enter the front hall, there is a living room on your right that has a very lived in look with a modern sectional sofa in front of the fireplace. On the left is a most appealing dining, room, very cozy with pretty fabric on the walls, antique table set in front of a large open fireplace, and a beamed ceiling. Marie-France serves dinners here by the warmth of the fire in winter, but when the weather is balmy, breakfast and dinner are served on the rear terrace overlooking lovely gardens and a tranquil little pond. All of the bedrooms are outstanding in decor. Each is different, and has its own charm along with a large, beautifully appointed bathroom. The one I like best is "le Serment d'Amour," a dream with lovely blue and white wall paper and coordinating fabric used throughout, even in the bathroom. Marie France is warm and gracious, and since she used to be a flight attendant for TWA, speaks excellent English. *Directions:* Take the N23 east from Angers. About 2 km after you go through the village of La Chapelle, there is a small road on your left with a Chambres d'Hôtes sign. Turn left at the sign. Prefontaine is the first house on your right (total of about 23 km from Angers).

PREFONTAINE (Gîte de France)
Hostess: Marie-France O'Neill
49430 Lézigné, France
tel: 41.76.97.71
3 rooms, 2 suites, with private bathrooms
Double 350-400F, Suites 450-550 for 4
Table d'Hôte: 100F with wine
Open all year
Fluent English
Region: Loire Valley, Michelin Map 232

Cécile and Jan Balsem are energetic hosts who have renovated their 250-year-old farmhouse into a simple, yet very atmospheric home. Jan is originally from Holland and speaks fluent French, English, German and, of course, Dutch. In his spare time he is a hang-gliding enthusiast, and willingly escorts guests on sojourns to the local countryside. His warm, friendly wife Cécile is a talented watercolorist who also finds time to make homemade breads and preserves plus look after their children, an extensive vegetable garden and assorted farm animals. Bedrooms are high-ceilinged and spacious, furnished in family antiques and decorated with dainty wallpapers and fresh flower bouquets. The atmosphere of Chez Balsem is relaxed and no-frills; with renovation still in progress, but rough edges removed, it is easy to be captivated by the Balsem's open-hearted welcome and lovely hilltop location. *Directions:* Lhopital is located about 40 kilometers southwest of Geneva. Take autoroute A40 to exit number 10. Then turn south on D991 in the direction of Vovray. Stay on D991 and follow signs for Seyssel. Continue about 10 kilometers to the village of Lhopital and look for a Chambres d'Hôtes sign that directs you to the left up a steep, narrow road. The Balsem's stone house is on the left at the top of the road.

CHEZ BALSEM (Gîte de France)
Hosts: Cécile & Jan Balsem
01420 Lhopital, France
tel: 50.59.50.58
3 rooms, share 1 bath/WC
Double: 150F
Table d'Hôte: 75F per person, includes wine
Open all year
Very good English spoken
Region: Rhône/Alps, Michelin Map 244

Bed and Breakfast at the Domaine de Gradille means home-like, family accommodation in a countryside setting full of bucolic charm. A pretty footpath leads to a nearby lake, completely hidden by lush deciduous woods, where guests may swim in the refreshing water. Warm and friendly hosts Monsieur and Madame Soulié offer three guest rooms in their family farmhouse and two modern bedrooms, each with private bath and WC, in a recently remodeled adjoining building. Bedrooms exhibit a mixture of decor and taste, but are very comfortable and have personal touches such as bud vases of fresh flowers. Two of the rooms have lovely views over tranquil pastures and hills. Guests usually gather in the early evening on the terrace or in the tiny bar for a delicious sample of the Soulie's homemade fruit liqueurs. Table d'Hôte dinners are served en famille in the cozy dining room and feature several courses of carefully prepared dishes. *Directions:* Domaine de Gradille is located about 14 kilometers past Lisle sur Tarn, a total of approximately 50 kilometers northeast of Toulouse. Take N88 in the direction of Albi, turning left at Gaillac onto D999 in the direction of Montauban, then 4 kilometers outside of Gaillac, look for Chambres d'Hôtes signs directing you to a small road on the right. Take the first driveway on the right to the Soulié's white, two-storey tile-roofed farmhouse.

DOMAINE DE GRADILLE   (Gîte de France)
Hosts: Monsieur & Madame Soulié
81310 Lisle sur Tarn, France
tel: 63.41.01.57 fax: 63.57.03.66
5 rooms, 3 with private bathrooms
Double: 145-180F, Triple: 205-250F
Table d'Hôte: 70F per person
Open all year
Good English spoken, also Spanish
Region: Midi-Pyrénées, Michelin Map 235

The Chaumière de Kerisac is one of our most picturesque Bed and Breakfasts, offering comfortable accommodation in a lovely, country setting, complemented by cultivated hosts. The Cheilletz-Maignan's charming, thatch-roofed house has been in their family for many years, although it is only since Monsieur's retirement that they returned here on a full-time basis after their many years of living overseas in Morocco and Indochina. Breakfast is served in their cozy salon/dining room filled with family antiques and artifacts from their extensive travels. Low, beamed ceilings and an old stone fireplace enhance the evocative decor. Monsieur and Madame have many fascinating stories to share as does their talented daughter who is a bookbinder by trade. A small exterior stone stairway leads up to two of the guest bedrooms in this long, low stone house, while the third bedroom is completely independent and even has a small private garden. Rooms are pleasingly furnished in a mix of antique furniture and pretty floral wallpapers. Madame's attention to detail is evident in her thoughtful touches such as aspirin in the bathrooms and fresh flowers in every room. *Directions:* Locqueltas is about 10 kilometers north of Vannes via D767 then north on D767a to Locqueltas. From here, the way is well marked by Chambres d'Hôtes signs.

CHAUMIRE DE KERISAC (Gîte de France)
Hosts: Monsieur & Madame Cheilletz-Maignan
Locqueltas, D767
56390 Grandchamp, France
tel: 97.66.60.13 fax: 97.66.66.73
3 rooms, all with private bath/2 share WC
Double: 300F, Triple: 350F
No Table d'Hôte
Open all year
Good English spoken (mainly by daughter)
Region: Brittany, Michelin Map 230

A stay at the lovely Chateau de Longecourt is a wonderful opportunity to experience life in a French country castle. Surrounded on all sides by a tranquil moat, the castle has a delicate fairy-tale quality enhanced by its graceful towers and neo-classical Italian decoration. Inside, the elegant, gilt-trimmed salon, dining room, reception rooms and library are all furnished and decorated in authentic antiques from the Louis XV period. Bedrooms are also highly charming; generously furnished with beautiful antiques, Oriental rugs, paintings and objets d'art. Each room is unique, with intimate tower bedrooms featuring stone vaulted ceilings and others offering marble fireplaces and tall windows overlooking the peaceful grounds. The Chateau de Longecourt is as memorable for its exquisite surroundings as for the warm welcome extended by the Comtesse de Saint-Seine and her personable sons. They make an effort to pamper their guests with luxurious details such as bedtime chocolates and copious breakfasts served on heirloom china. *Directions:* Longecourt en Plaine is located approximately 15 kilometers southeast of Dijon, on the Burgundy canal. Leave Dijon on D968 following signs for Longecourt en Plaine. Once in the village, signs for Chateau de Longecourt point the way to the castle that is located near the church.

CHATEAU DE LONGECOURT
Hostess: Contesse de Saint Seine
Longecourt en Plaine
21110 Genlis, France
tel: 80.39.88.76
4 rooms, with private bathrooms
Double: 650F
Table d'Hôte: 250F
Open all year
Very little English spoken
Region: Burgundy, Michelin Map 243

Three hundred meters from Brittany's northern coastline, Madame Sillard's historic home is the former residence of French author Ernest Renan. Set in wooded grounds, this small manor house is furnished in lovely country antiques and offers Bed and Breakfast accommodation to fortunate travellers. A lace-curtained front door leads into the entry hall that is warmly decorated with an antique armoire, bookcase and dried flower arrangements. Madame Sillard is a charming, well-travelled hostess who has spent extended periods of time in the United States, thus speaks very good English. Her guest bedrooms are decorated with pretty fabrics and fresh flower bouquets while furnishings are a tasteful mix of antiques and some more contemporary pieces. Breakfast is served at a long wooden table in the country-elegant drawing room where two tabby cats often share the seat of a tapestry chair. *Directions:* Louannec is located approximately 70 kilometers northwest of St-Brieuc, 40 kilometers northwest of Guingamp. From Lannion (30 kilometers northwest of Guingamp), take D788 north in the direction of Perros Guirec. After 7 kilometers, turn right onto D6 to Louannec. Just before town, there will be a sign indicating Chambres d'Hôtes up a small lane to the right. A driveway on the left leads to Madame's pretty house, set back behind a garden.

ROSMAPAMON
Hostess: Madame A. Sillard
Louannec, 22700 Perros-Guirec, France
tel: 96.23.00.87
4 rooms, 2 with private bath/shower
Double 280-350F
No Table d Hôte
Open April through September
Fluent English spoken
Region: Brittany, Michelin Map 230

Every summer the Belières leave Paris and relocate to their family castle near Loubressac. The chateau dates from 1630 and is highly charming, filled with an assortment of country antiques and artifacts. The Belières have kept the building in more or less its original state, so a very authentic feeling of the past remains, including a musty odor of days gone by. Guests climb up a circular tower staircase to reach the second floor that is devoted entirely to Bed and Breakfast accommodation. All of the bedrooms are loaded with old fashioned, albeit faded, charm, decorated with old paintings, dainty, flowerprint wallpapers, brass or antique beds and dried flower arrangements. There are also apartment-style accommodations available for longer stays that are found in a very quaint adjoining stone building. A casual feeling of a holiday in the country tempts guests to spend entire afternoons relaxing in the walled garden or near the pool, soaking up the tranquil atmosphere. *Directions:* Loubressac is located approximately 45 kilometers northwest of Figeac. Take N140 towards Rocamadour, turning right at Le Bourg towards St-Cere. Leave St-Cere on D30 in the direction of Carennac and, after a small, old water tower on the right, look for a small sign, also on the right, that says Gramot with an arrow directing to a driveway on the left.

CHATEAU DE GAMOT (Gîte de France)
Hosts: Monsieur & Madame Belières
46130 Loubressac, France
tel: 65.38.58.50 or in Paris (1) 48.83.01.91
7 rooms, 3 w/pvt WC/bath, others share
Double: 260-350F, Triple: 350-400F
No Table d'Hôte
Open all year
Some English spoken
Region: Dordogne/Lot, Michelin Maps 235, 239

Michel Descorps resides in a long, low country house reminiscent of stable buildings. He did indeed once keep a full stable of horses here and is a former champion of the French four-in-hand competition. Inside, his ivy-covered ranch style home has a very British country cottage feeling: in fact, Monsieur avows himself to be quite an Anglophile. Laura Ashley wallpapers such as the pretty, yet understated, Scottish thistle pattern decorate the walls in his guest bedrooms, while Cecil Aldin prints brighten the hallways. Bathrooms are all newly renovated and extremely clean, modern and well-equipped. All the accommodations are fresh and very tasteful, with rustic antique furniture and old exposed support beams adding historic character to the rooms. Table d'Hôte dinners are available with advance notice and are served in the cozy dining room full of Cecil Aldin prints on a background of green striped wallpaper. In the morning, guests are pampered with breakfast in their rooms, on the garden terrace or in the dining room. *Directions:* Luynes is located approximately 10 kilometers west of Tours on the north bank of the Loire. Take N152 to Luynes, then turn onto D49 towards Pernay. Continue towards Pernay on D6 and at Le Maupas take the first right turn, after which the first driveway on the right is signposted Le Quart.

LE QUART (*Gîte de France*)
Hosts: Monsieur & Madame Michel Descorps
37230 Luynes, France
tel: 47.55.51.70 or 47.48.37.13
4 rooms, with private bathrooms
Double: 550-950F
Table d'Hôte: price varies
Open all year
Fluent English spoken
Region: Loire Valley, Michelin Map 232

The Marcs are friendly country folk in their 40's who have lived in their ivy-covered former stable house for 20 years, while converting it, bit by bit, to the comfortable, if modest home it is today. This is a working farm, where the Marcs raise cattle, sheep, chickens and the occasional goose. Their home is very clean and well-kept. They offer three guest rooms in the main house and an apartment located just across the pretty courtyard. The bedrooms are furnished simply but with taste—antique-style pieces decorate every room, all of which have private baths. The Marcs have made every effort to make their home comfortable and welcoming for guests and are ready to help in any way. Although the Marcs do not speak English, they overcome any language barriers with their warm welcome and farm-style hospitality. *Directions:* Mainneville is located about 75 kilometers northwest of Paris via A15 to Pontoise, then D915 through Gisors, and finally on D14 to Mainneville. In Mainneville, look for a green and yellow Chambres d'Hôtes sign directing you to the Marc's farm. Located just on the edge of town, the low, ivy-covered house is set back from the road with a lush green lawn and big trees in front. Pretty natural wood shutters flank all the doors and windows.

FERME DE SAINTE GENEVIÈVE (Gîte de France)
Hosts: Jeannine & Jean-Claude Marc
27150 Mainneville, France
tel: 32.55.51.26
4 rooms, with private bathrooms
Double: 200F
No Table d'Hôte
Open all year
Very little English spoken
Region: Normandy, Michelin Map 237

The Derepas' Bed and Breakfast, set in an imposing stone farmhouse, once the dependent farm of the manor house on the hill above, is recommended for travellers seeking a quiet, countryside setting. Françoise Derepas offers freshly remodeled rooms that are very clean and comfortable. All of the fixtures and flooring are new, so little of the building's historic character is visible from the inside, but the exterior boasts two old ruined towers that date from the last century. An effort has been made to preserve a historic feeling in the high-ceilinged dining room that is furnished with a large old oak armoire and table with rustic ladder-backed chairs. Breakfast is enjoyed either here, or, for a more leisurely morning, on the sunny back terrace overlooking a scenic view of the surrounding countryside. The five guest bedrooms are found upstairs and all have pretty arched windows and pleasant, if modest decor. *Directions:* Mancey is located approximately 6 kilometers west of Tournus. Leave Tournus on D14 in the direction of Charolles, continuing straight ahead on D215 towards Mancey. Just after the sign for the village of Mancey, but before actually entering the village centre, look for a gate on the left marked with a Chambres d'Hôtes sign. Go past the manor house on the hill, following an unpaved drive down the hill to the large stone farmhouse below.

CHEZ DEREPAS (Gîte de France)
Hostess: Madame Françoise Derepas
Dulphey, Mancey
71240 Sennecey le Grand, France
tel: 85.51.10.22
5 rooms, all with private shower, share 2 WC
Double: 190F, Triple: 220F
No Table d'Hôte
Open all year
Good English spoken
Region: Burgundy, Michelin Map 243

A real find, the Loisel's Georgian-style farmhouse is tastefully furnished with family antiques and pleasing color combinations. The two high-ceilinged guest bedrooms have been recently redecorated in pretty flower print wallpapers, complemented by carpets and upholstery in soft color tones. Bathrooms are scrupulously clean and well equipped. Downstairs in her dining room furnished in French country antiques, Madame Loisel serves delicious breakfasts and Table d'Hôte dinners featuring fresh farm produce. The imposing oak armoire and sideboard date from the time of her grandparent's marriage and add to the peaceful feeling of history and continuity that pervades Madame Loisel's lovely home. This pleasant B&B is enhanced by our energetic hostess who enjoys introducing her guests to regional dinner specialties and also teaches lace making and embroidery. *Directions:* Manneville la Goupil is located about 26 kilometers northeast of Le Havre via N15 to St-Romain de Coulbosc, then D10 to Manneville la Goupil. Across from the church you will see a green and yellow Chambres d'Hôtes sign that directs you to turn left onto a small road leading out of town. About 1.5 kilometers later, turn right at the white fence that has a Gîtes de France sign posted on it.

CHEZ LOISEL (Gîte de France)
Hosts: Nicole & Hubert Loisel
Manneville la Goupil
76110 Goderville, France
tel: 35.27.77.21
4 rooms, 3 with private bathroom
Double: 230F, Triple: 290F
Table d'Hôte: 100F, includes cider
Open all year
No English spoken
Region: Normandy, Michelin Map 231

We received a warm welcome at Monsieur and Madame Bouteiller's charming half-timbered farmhouse where they have made their home for the last 40 years. Monsieur explained that he was originally a city boy from Rouen, but always wanted to be a farmer. He has achieved his dream in this pastoral setting where he and his wife have raised seven children. Madame's Table d'Hôte dinners always include regional specialties such as creamed chicken, duck with peach sauce and, of course, one of several varieties of homemade apple tarts. These friendly meals are served in the light and cheerful entry salon with its long table decorated with a wildflower bouquet in an earthenware jug. An antique sideboard and old stone mantel displaying pewter candlesticks add to the country ambiance. The Bouteiller's two guest rooms are clean and well equipped with simple decor and furnishings, including wooden beds and armoires. *Directions:* Martainville is located approximately 58 kilometers from Rouen via A13 to the Beuzeville exit. In Beuzeville, turn left at the traffic light at the church. Follow signs for the town of Paignes via route D27. Approximately 3 kilometers later you will see a Chambres d'Hôtes sign directing you to turn right. A driveway on the left will then lead you to the Bouteiller's low, half-timbered farmhouse.

CHEZ BOUTEILLER (Gîte de France)
Hosts: Monsieur & Madame Jacques Bouteiller
Martainville, 27210 Beuzeville, France
tel: 32.57.82.23
2 rooms, with private bathrooms
Double: 180F, Triple: 210F
Table d'Hôte: 70F per person
Open all year
Some English spoken by Monsieur
Region: Normandy, Michelin Map 231

The small, out-of-the-way village of Maureilhan is a picturesque oasis of calm for travellers who like to get off the beaten track. A stay at the Fabre-Barthez's comfortable home is a convivial, relaxing experience, a wonderful change from the commercial, impersonal atmosphere of many hotels. Monsieur and Madame are friendly wine growers who produce rose and red wines in addition to welcoming Bed and Breakfast guests. They enjoy beginning an evening with a shared house aperitif, followed by a delicious four-course Table d'Hôte dinner and perhaps completed by a group sing-along. Meals are most often enjoyed in the small, tree-shaded garden where Madame grills savory meats over grapevine branches. Peaceful bedrooms are located upstairs and are accessible through French doors from an outdoor balcony overlooking the courtyard and garden. Furnishings and decor are home-like and comfortable, with charming touches such as brass beds, crocheted coverlets and embroidered tablecloths. *Directions:* Maureilhan is located approximately 8 kilometers west of Béziers. Take N112 in the direction of St-Pons until reaching the village of Maureilhan. Once in the village follow Chambres d'Hôtes signs to the second right turning, then right again under a stone archway to Fabre-Barthez's courtyard.

CHEZ FABRE-BARTHEZ (Gîte de France)
Hosts: Monsieur & Madame Fabre-Barthez
7, rue Jean Jaures
Maureilhan, 34370 Cazouls les Béziers, France
tel: 67.90.52.49
6 rooms, with private bathrooms
Double: 190F, Triple: 230F
Table d'Hôte: 75F per person
Open all year
A little English spoken
Region: Midi Pyrénées, Michelin Map 240

Le Moulin de Gennebrie is an old mill set in luxuriant countryside near Niort. The lush front garden of the ivy-covered building is filled with multicolored flowers and banana palms. Breakfast is often enjoyed by the stream in the cool, grassy back grounds, shaded by tall poplars and weeping willow trees. Quiet and peaceful, Le Moulin de Gennebrie is truly an oasis in time and space. The guest entry is like a museum; through a cellar-like room and past the old mill wheel that still turns and produces electricity. Up two flights of rickety stairs, all the while observing the inner workings of the mill, guests finally arrive at the large unfinished attic area off that the three charming and tastefully decorated bedrooms are found. Pretty print fabrics and family antiques furnish the rooms, all of that share bath and WC. As parts of the mill are still in their un-embellished original state, lodging here is recommended for travellers who seek character rather than up-to-date modern decor. Also, since no English at all is understood, this B&B would be preferable for those who want to practice their French. *Directions:* Melle is located approximately 24 kilometers southeast of Niort. Take D948 to Melle, turning right onto D950 towards Brioux sur Boutonne. About 1 kilometer after passing the hamlet of Charzay, turn right and continue towards Perigne. After travelling a very short distance, about 1 kilometer, look for signs for Le Moulin de Gennebrie on the right.

LE MOULIN DE GENNEBRIE (Gîte de France)
Hosts: Monsieur & Madame Merigeau
79500 Melle, France
tel: 49.07.11.96
3 rooms, all share 1 separate WC & shower
Double: 150F, Triple: 190F
No Table d'Hôte
Open May 1 to October 1
No English spoken
Region: Atlantic Coast, Michelin Map 233

Home-like Provençal charm abounds in the Derenty's contemporary villa located in northern Provence. They built their house in a typical regional style with a burnished tile roof and warm toned exterior walls, and an interior of cool tile floors and white plaster walls. Madame Derenty has decorated her guest bedrooms with curtains and bedspreads in the dainty and colorful prints typical of the Provence region and added pretty watercolors on the walls and some country antique furniture to create a fresh, feminine feeling throughout. A two-bedroom suite is offered in the main house, while an adjoining annex has two additional bedrooms, each with an independent entrance and private shower and WC. Breakfasts and Table d'Hôte dinners are usually enjoyed in the Derenty's quiet back garden and are friendly, family meals. A stay with the Derentys means modern comfort and fastidious attention to detail, as Madame Derenty is a solicitous hostess who makes sure her guest's every need is fulfilled. *Directions:* Mirabel aux Baronies is located approximately 7 kilometers south of Nyons via D538. Leave the village in the direction of Villedieu as directed by Chambres d'Hôtes signs, and 1 kilometer later the Derenty's driveway will be on the left.

LA FOURNACHE (*Gîte de France*)
Hostess: Madame Derenty-Maridor
Route de Villedieu
Mirabel aux Baronies
26110 Nyons, France
tel: 75.27.14.83
3 rooms, with private bathrooms
Double: 360F including breakfast & dinner
Open March to October
Some English spoken by husband
Region: Provence, Michelin Maps 245, 246

The 16th-century Manoir de Clénord is an absolute jewel—truly a superb manor in the heart of the Loire Valley, ideally situated for exploring the rich selection of chateaux in the region. In fact, the beautiful wooded estate actually flows right into the enormous Chambord forest. The interior exudes an ambiance of lived-in comfort with exquisite family heirlooms combined with flair and impeccable taste. There are two dining rooms: one a beautiful 18th-century room positioned to capture the manicured gardens; the other, a less formal room dating back to the 15th Century, is stunning with beamed ceiling, huge fireplace and a fabulous trestle table, mellowed with the patina of age. A dramatic wooden stair case leads to the upper level where the guest rooms are located. Each is individual in decor, exuding quiet elegance and exquisite taste. Handsome wall coverings color coordinate with fabrics used on the drapes and beds. The suites are especially elegant, but if you want a budget-conscious splurge, there is one small room, barely big enough for a double bed, that can be had for 360F a night, a tremendous bargain for such quality. In addition to the formal gardens and surrounding forest, there is a large, beautiful swimming pool and tennis court. The owner, Christiane Renauld, is a warm, gracious hostess. *Directions:* From Blois go 10 km on D 765 toward Cheverny and Romorantin. At Clénord, turn left at the sign for the Manoir de Clénord. The entrance is signposted on your left

MANOIR DE CLÉNORD (Gîte de France)
Hostess: Madame Christiane Renauld
Route de Clénord
41250 Mont Pres Chambord, France
tel: 54.70.41.62 fax: 54.70.33.99
3 doubles, 2 suites, with private bathrooms
Double: 550F, suites 700-950F (2 to 4 persons)
Table d'Hôte: 180F per person with wine
Credit cards: EC, MC, VS
Open all year, Good English spoken
Regions: Loire Valley, Michelin Map 238

An unprepossessing entrance through a small arched gateway leads to the modest Auberge des Noyers. The cozy restaurant has exposed stone walls, a large fireplace and intimate seating at six tables dressed with rose-colored tablecloths and napkins topped by white lace. Madame Galy serves old-fashioned cuisine utilizing fresh farm meats and vegetables while Monsieur attends mainly to his primary occupation as a wine-grower. Their regional red wine can be purchased or enjoyed with dinner specialties such as rabbit cooked over a wood fire and savory bean and meat stews. The bedrooms are all very basic and plain in their furnishings, with small, but adequate, bathroom facilities. Most rooms have their own French door providing access to an outdoor terrace. In order to keep the summer heat under control, the rooms are windowless with thick stucco walls, cool tile floors and heavy shutters over the French doors. A refreshing blue swimming pool offers a pleasant escape on hot days. *Directions:* Montbrun des Corbiéres is located about 35 kilometers east of Carcassonne. Take N113 towards Narbonne, turning left after about 20 kilometers towards Montbrun des Corbiéres. In the village, follow signs for Ferme Auberge.

FERME AUBERGE DES NOYERS (Gîte de France)
Hosts: Monsieur & Madame Galy
Montbrun des Corbières
11700 Capendu, France
tel: 68.43.94.01
5 rooms all with private shower/WC
Double: 190F, Triple: 260F
Table d'Hôte: 90-150F per person
Open Easter to October 15*
*also open weekends all year
Some English spoken
Region: Midi Pyrénées, Michelin Map 235

Montchavin is a picturesque mountain town of Alpine chalets and narrow, winding streets. In winter, skiers flock here for intimate lodging and dining near the major ski area of La Plagne. Monsieur and Madame Favre are a friendly, attractive young couple who run the convivial La Bovate restaurant and also offer guest accommodation. Guests enjoy regional dishes such as beef and cheese fondues in the rustic dining room built with dark wood paneling, beamed ceilings and a large stone fireplace. A pretty annex houses guest rooms that are clean and fresh, featuring natural wood walls and furniture. There is also an apartment and even a separate chalet with its own garden and terrace, fireplace and well-equipped kitchen. *Directions:* Montchavin is located about 100 kilometers east of Chambéry. From Chambéry follow directions for Albertville on N90. At Albertville, continue towards Moutiers, Bourg St-Maurice, then 1 kilometer after the village of Bellentre, look for a turnoff for Landry, Montchavin les Coches. Follow a winding road up a hillside, following signs for Montchavin. Enter the village of Montchavin le Plan through an archway and continue straight up the main street, veering to the right once the streets become twisty. The road will narrow and basically come to an end in a little square: look for La Bovate on the right.

LA BOVATE (Gîte de France)
Hosts: Fortuné & Michèle Favre
Montchavin, 73210 Bellentre, France
tel: 79.07.83.25
1 room, 5 apartments, 1 chalet, all w/private bath
Double: 260F, Triple: 320F
Table d'Hôte: moderately priced restaurant
Open Dec. 20 to Mar. 15 & June 28 to Sep. 6
Some English spoken
Region: French Alps, Michelin Map 244

The Chateau de Montmaur is a designated historic monument dating from the 14th Century. Found in a small village surrounded by tree-covered hills and mountains, the castle is built on a grand scale, with thick stone walls and two great halls. Authentic wood floors, fresco paintings and huge fireplaces all testify to the castle's colorful past as a fortress, a royal castle and even a headquarters for resistance fighters during World War II. The Laurens family is dedicated to breathing life into their historic home and have opened the large halls to public tours, weddings, classical music concerts, receptions and parties. Parts of the castle are still being restored and five intimate suites have recently been completed for Bed and Breakfast guests. The rooms are prettily decorated with elegant fabrics and wallpapers and each has private shower and WC as well as an independent entrance. Breakfast is served in the Lauren's charming salon/dining room that has a beamed ceiling and a lovely stone fireplace and is decorated with country antiques and fresh flower bouquets. *Directions:* Montmaur is located approximately 17 kilometers west of Gap. Take D994 towards Veynes, then about 4 kilometers after the town of Roche des Arnauds, turn to the right following signs for Montmaur. The castle gate is clearly marked at the entry to the village.

CHATEAU DE MONTMAUR (*Gîte de France*)
Hosts: Elyse & Raymond Raymond
Laurens
Montmaur, 05400 Veynes, France
tel: 92.58.11.42
5 Suites, with private shower/WC
Double: 400F, Triple: 480F
Table d'Hôte: 100F
Open all year
No English spoken
Region: French Alps, Michel Map 245

For a romantic, inexpensive hideaway filled with charm, La Pension de l'Abbaye can not be surpassed. You would never just "happen upon" upon this little jewel tucked into the ruins of a colorful 12th-century abbey. The two storey stone cottage has two very simple rooms: beamed ceilings, thick white-washed walls, casement windows, scrubbed wood and well worn tile floors, embroidered linen curtains, fresh bouquets of garden flowers. Artistic care was taken not to "over-renovate" or "over-decorate"—doing so would distract from the austere simplicity of this wonderful old stone building. Although the two rooms in the small cottage are rustic, the comfort is sophisticated: firm mattresses, plenty of hot water, big bars of soap, and some of largest towels we had in France. Odile is a fabulous cook, and prepares delicious meals using the freshest produce from the local farms and markets. During the winter months, Odile and her artist husband, Brian, live in New York where he displays his paintings. In the summer they return to France where Brian paints while Odile runs the small Bed and Breakfast. *Directions:* From Nouans-les-Fontaines take D760 toward Montrésor. In 5.5 km, when you reach the village of Villeloin-Coulangé, just after you pass the pharmacy on your left, turn left and continue to the bottom of the hill. Just after the small square on your right (before the bridge), turn right and pass through the towers of the Abbey and you will see the Gîtes de France sign straight ahead.

LA PENSION DE L'ABBAYE (*Gîte de France*)
Hostess: Odile Rousseau Wood
Rue de l'Abbaye
Villeloin-Coulangé, 37460 Montrésor, France
tel: 47.92.77.77 fax: 47.92.66.96 (France)
tel: (212) 255-5961 (New York-winter reservations)
2 rooms with private bathrooms
Double 295F, Table d'Hôte: 100F per person
Open end of May to October
Fluent English spoken
Region: Loire Valley, Michelin Map 238

With so many of the places in the Loire Valley extremely expensive, it is a pleasure to recommend the well-priced Manoir de la Salle, an attractive Bed & Breakfast tucked into the hillside above the river Cher. Terraced gardens buffer it from any street noise below and enhance the views from the patio. The grounds boast a tennis court, a rose garden, ponds and shaded lawns that tempt one to sit and relax after a day of sightseeing. The manor house was recently purchased by the Boussard family who are continuing with the same gracious welcome as the previous owners who also opened their home as a Bed and Breakfast. Guest rooms are found both in the tower and in the main building. They vary in size, but all have a private bathroom and are decorated with family furnishings and thoughtfully appointed. Guests are made to feel as if the manor is their home for the duration of their stay. Breakfast is served in the dining room where guests have the chance to meet and talk to fellow travellers. The Manoir de la Salle is located just to the south of Chaumont and east of Chenonceaux, an ideal base for touring the chateaux of the Loire Valley. *Directions:* From Montrichard travel D176 east for approximately three kilometers to the village of Bourre. The Manoir de la Salle is signposted just beyond the village of Bourre, above the road.

MANOIR DE LA SALLE
Hosts: Monsieur & Madame Boussard
69, route de Vierzon
Bourre, 41400 Montrichard, France
tel: 54.32.73.54
4 rooms, with private bathrooms all with private bath
Double: 450F to 650F
Table d'Hôte: check with owner
Open all year
Some English spoken by M. Boussard
Region: Loire Valley, Michelin Map 238

Descriptions of Places to Stay   139

I had seen photographs of the Chateau de Colliers, a handsome two-storey, buff-colored chateau with white trim and gray mansard roof, and knew that it would be beautiful. But upon arrival, I was in for a wonderful surprise—I had not realized that the back of the chateau is perched on a terrace overlooking the Loire river. What bliss in the morning to open wide the casement windows, hear the birds sing and see the river flow by below. And, for those who like to start the day with an early morning stroll or jog, a perfect path just below the terrace follows the river's edge. The chateau once belonged to the Marquis of Vaudreuil (Governor of Louisiana and French Canada until 1779). It has been in the same family since that time and thus the furnishings are authentic antiques, nothing contrived in a decorator-perfect way -a real family home. Each of the bedrooms is unique in decor, each is filled with antiques. If you arrange ahead for Table d'Hôte, you are in for a real treat. *Directions:* From Blois, cross the Loire river and take D 951 northeast toward Orleans. Before reaching the town of Muides sur Loire, you will see the chateau on your left.

CHATEAU DE COLLIERS (Gîte de France)
Hosts: Marie-France & Christian de Gelis
41500 Muides-sur-Loire, France
tel: 54.87.50.75 fax: 54.87.03.64
5 rooms with private bathrooms
Double 600-700F
Table de Hôte: 200F per person with wine
Open from March to November 30
Very good English spoken
Region: Loire Valley, Michelin Map 238

The Manoir de Montflambert, a 17th-century manor house hugging the edge of the forest of Reims, fronts onto a simple farmhouse courtyard. It is only after entering the home that one of its nicest aspects is revealed—behind the house is a large walled garden with a wide expanse of lawn bordered by carefully manicured beds of flowers. The grassy area stretches out to a quiet pond in a wooded glen. Inside, both the dining room and parlor take advantage of the garden view. The dining room is especially attractive with handsome dark paneling that, appropriately for the champagne regions, is banded by a design of intricately carved grapes. A large fireplace dominates one wall of the room where the evening meal is elegantly served by the glow of candlelight. An elegant 350 year-old staircase of polished wood winds up from the entry hall to the bedrooms, each with walls covered in a corduroy-like velour of a different hue. *Directions:* From Epernay, cross the river and take D1 east toward Ay and Mareuil where you take the turn off north to Mutigny. The Manoir de Montflambert is signposted with a Chambre d'Hôte sign and also the name "Rampacek."

MANOIR DE MONTFLAMBERT (Gîte de France)
Hostess: Madame Renee Rampacek
51160 Mutigny, Marne, France
tel: 26.52.33.21 fax: 26.52.31.15
5 rooms & 2 suites, with private bathrooms
Double from 350 F
Table d' Hôte, 160-300F per person
Open all year except January
No English spoken, but learning
Region: Champagne, Michelin Map 237

The Chateau le Goupillon is an imposing chateau found in a tranquil setting in the open countryside. Madame Calot is the independent, energetic hostess who has used her artistic talents to renovate her grand home, creating a home-like rather than elegant feeling in her guest rooms and public areas. Orange walls, a parquet floor and country antique furniture lend a warm, comfortable feeling to the dining room where breakfast is enjoyed. Bedrooms are large and airy, with high ceilings and bright, earth-toned color schemes. Hand-crafted macramé and weaving warm the walls. Furniture is a mix of antique and modern, but all is comfortable and spacious. Two adjoining bedrooms, one with double bed and one with two twins, form a suite that is perfect for families. Madame has even supplied toys in the children's room. Guests are welcome to relax in the downstairs salon, casually furnished with family antiques and inviting couches and chairs, or on the front terrace that looks out over a long expanse of green lawn bordered by tall trees. *Directions:* Neuillé is located 8 kilometers north of Saumur. Take N147 from Saumur to D767 in the direction of Vernantes le Lude. After passing a miniature golf course, turn left onto D129 towards Neuillé. Look for Chambres d'Hôtes signs that will lead directly to Madame Calot's driveway.

CHATEAU LE GOUPILLON (Gîte de France)
Hostess: Madame Calot
Neuillé, 49680 Vivy, France
tel: 41.52.51.89
2 rooms, 1 suite, with private bathrooms
Double: 280-390F
No Table d'Hôte
Open April 1 to November 1
No English spoken
Region: Loire Valley, Michelin Map 232

Madame Gourlaouen enjoys a tranquil location near the spectacular coastline and beaches of southern Brittany and the artist community of Pont Aven. This picturesque port town is the former home of many French impressionist painters, as well as Paul Gauguin. Madame Gourlaouen is a young, capable hostess who offers Bed and Breakfast as well as apartment accommodation in her pretty stone farmhouse. Dating from 1730, the long, low house is built from the golden-hued stones that are typical of the Concarneau, Pont Aven region. An independent entrance leads to the guest bedrooms that are furnished with antique reproductions. Rooms are small but charming and all have private WC and shower—a great bargain for the money. The intimate breakfast room is full of charm with a low, beamed ceiling, old stone hearth, country antiques and fresh garden flowers. *Directions:* Nevez is located approximately 30 kilometers southeast of Quimper. Leave the town of Pont Aven on D70 towards Concarneau, turning left just outside town following signs to Nevez. In the village of Nevez, continue past the church, then take the left fork in the road onto D77 towards Port Manech. After about 4 kilometers, just before entering Port Manech, look for a Chambres d'Hôtes sign directing you to turn right. Continue following signs, turning at the first left, and you will arrive at this sunny farmhouse 300 meters from the sea.

CHEZ GOURLAOUEN (Gîte de France)
Hostess: Madame Yveline Gourlaouen
Port Manech, 29920 Nevez, France
tel: 98.06.83.82
6 rooms, with private bathrooms
Single: 180F, Double: 201F
No Table d'Hôte
Open all year
Some English spoken
Region: Brittany, Michelin Map 230

A modest, contemporary home in a quiet, pastoral suburb of Niort is the setting for Bed and Breakfast accommodation Chez Boudreault. A spacious, well landscaped garden and lawn surround the home, with a refreshing swimming pool adding a touch of luxury. The bedroom is adequately furnished with somewhat basic, old-fashioned decor, but is highly comfortable and adjacent to a modern, private bathroom. Welcome details such as a large bath, double basins and good lighting are supplemented by thoughtfully supplied soap and fluffy towels. Breakfast is served in the family kitchen and is basic Continental fare. The Boudreaults are friendly hosts and have two teenage children who speak a very small amount of English. Chez Boudreault is recommended primarily as a convenient stopover as it is close to the main road, reasonably priced and provides a warm and personal family welcome. *Directions:* Chez Boudreault is in the village of Surimeau that is located approximately 3 kilometers north of Niort. Leave Niort on D743 in the direction of Parthenay. After travelling about 1 kilometer, look for a used car lot on the right and take the road opposite, on the left, that leads to Surimeau. The Bourdreault's house is the first on the right: 27, rue de Mineraie.

CHEZ BOUDREAULT (Gîte de France)
Hosts: Monsieur & Madame Boudreault
27, rue de Mineraie
Surimeau, 79000 Niort, France
tel: 49. 24.51.93
1 room with private bath
Single: 170F, Double: 200F
Table d'Hôte: 50F per person
Open all year
Very little English spoken
Region: Atlantic Coast, Michelin Map 233

The magical forested hills surrounding the village of Obersteinbach are dotted with ruins of ancient medieval fortresses: mystical remnants of the region's feudal past. Carved from the red sandstone rock formations and overgrown with vines and wildflowers, with ancient doors, walls and windows still easily visible, they offer a fascinating glimpse back to the 13th century. Maison Ullmann (the only 4 star B&B in Alsace) is a truly special place to stay and an ideal base for hikers; near many mountain paths leading through enchanted pine and deciduous forests. Local historian and nature lover Cristelle and her husband Jean are warm, relaxed hosts who enjoy introducing their guests to the wonders of the surrounding countryside and the region's rich past. Their garden is a medieval delight featuring herbs and roses. Bedrooms are furnished with charming simplicity and artistic flair, providing comfortable, home-like accommodation with a kitchenette in every room. *Directions:* Obersteinbach is located about 60 km north of Strasbourg, very near the German border. Travel north on N83 to Hagenau, continuing in the direction of Wissembourg until just outside of town where you will pick up D27 past Woerth to Lembach. Veer left onto D3 and continue to Niedersteinbach and Obersteinbach. Traverse the village on the main street (rue Principale) and look for Maison Ullmann on the left.

MAISON ULLMANN (Gîte de France)
Hosts: Jean & Cristelle Zerafa-Ullmann
49, rue Principale
67510 Obersteinbach, France
tel: 88.09.50.59 fax: 88.09.53.56
5 rooms, with private bathrooms
Double: 310-360F
Table d'Hôte: 65F per person (lunch or dinner)
Open all year except January
Good English spoken, also fluent German
Region: Alsace, Michelin Map 242

Madame Benech is a widow who lives on a peaceful farm in the hills of Auvergne where she offers Bed and Breakfast accommodation in her pretty stone farmhouse. Guest bedrooms are simply and comfortably equipped with old-fashioned furniture and neutral color schemes. Bathroom facilities are shared, but each room has its own basin. Breakfast is served downstairs in the inviting dining room at a long wooden table in front of a large open-hearthed fireplace. Charming touches are added by hanging copper pots, red geraniums at the windows and country antiques. Chez Benech is recommended for travellers who do not mind shared bath facilities and are seeking practical, very clean accommodation at reasonable prices. The Auvergne region is lovely and unspoiled, offering endless opportunities for hiking and exploring medieval castles and villages. *Directions:* Olmet is located approximately 14 kilometers east of Aurillac. Take N122 towards Vic sur Cere and Murat. At the small settlement of Comblat, turn right onto D57 to Olmet and Aris. Once in the hamlet of Olmet, look for a Chambres d'Hôtes sign directing you to turn right up a country lane. Madame Benech's two-storey white house is on the right, set back from the road behind a green field.

CHEZ BENECH
Hostess: Madame Benech
Olmet, 15800 Vic sur Cère, France
tel: 71.47.50.54
4 rooms, none with private bath
Double: 155F
Minimum stay 3 nights
No Table d'Hôte
Open June through September 15
Very little English spoken
Region: Auvergne, Michelin Map 239

The Chez Langlais is a hidden jewel. From the outside, the house that fronts the road looks non-descript and the neighborhood rather ho hum, but once you have entered through the white side gate into the back garden, the scene is magically changed. You are surrounded by a garden filled with flowers and fruit trees, and, the property, that looks so small from the front, actually stretches all the way out to a tiny river. Also, the home itself takes on a whole new dimension. Seen from the back, the white house with steeply sloping roof and gables is cozy as can be. White tables and chairs are set out under the trees, an oasis where guests gather after a day of busy sightseeing to relax and share their experiences. The living room, with its beamed ceiling and exposed stone walls, offers a cozy retreat in front of the fire for breakfast (unless the day is warm when guests usually eat outside). A narrow, very good-looking antique staircase leads upstairs to the bedrooms, each lovingly decorated by Martine, who made everything herself. The fabrics and wall covering are all color coordinated. My favorite is the "green room" with a darling floral print wallpaper, airy white curtains and a view out over the back garden. However, it is not the decor or the ambiance that makes a stay here such a delight. Martine and George Langlais truly love having visitors, pampering them as they would guests in their home. *Directions:* From the center of ONZAIN, take the D 58 west. Just after leaving town, watch for a Citroen shop on your right and, on your left, the Chambre d'Hôte sign.

CHEZ LANGLAIS (Gîte de France)
Hostess: Martine Langlais
46 rue de Meuves, 41150 Onzain, France
tel: 54.20.78.82 fax: 54.20.78.82
5 rooms, with private bathrooms
Double 320F
No Table d'Hôte
Open April to December
Very good English spoken
Region: Loire Valley, Michelin Map 238

The small village of Ordonnaz, tucked away in the hilly, forested countryside, is the peaceful setting for La Ferme Auberge Le Charveyron where the Laracine family offers home-like guest accommodation and delicious, farm-fresh meals. They make all their own pastries and breads and serve savory local specialties in their cozy rustic dining rooms or on a pretty outdoor terrace overlooking the surrounding hills. For travellers seeking a high level of privacy and comfort, a newly built annex offers three bedrooms, each with private shower and WC. *Directions:* Ordonnaz is located approximately 50 kilometers west of Aix les Bains. From Aix, loop around the southern end of the lake on N201 and N211 and pick up N504 following signs for Belley, Amberieu en Bugey and Bourg en Bresse. Continue about 9 kilometers past Belley to the small village of Pugieu. On the main street, look carefully for a turnoff to the left for Contrevoz. Follow this lovely country lane that winds up through trees and green pastures through Contrevoz and on to Ordonnaz. Once in the village, go to the central fountain and veer left. The Laracine's home is on the right and easily recognizable by the table umbrellas on the front terrace.

LA FERME AUBERGE LE CHARVEYRON (*Gîte de France*)
Hosts: Monsieur & Madame René Laracine
01510 Ordonnaz, France
tel: 74.40.90.20 fax: Gîte office 74.22.65.86
3 rooms with private bathrooms
Double: 200F
Table d'Hôte: 60-80F, without wine
Open all year
Very little English spoken
Region: French Alps, Michelin Map 244

The lovely Chauveau home enjoys an idyllic setting on a hillside overlooking the family vineyards and the distant River Vienne. The fine art of relaxing is easy to master in these luxurious and scenic surroundings where each day begins with fresh croissants and coffee or tea on the terrace overlooking the lush valley. Impeccable taste prevails in the furnishings and decor, creating an elegant country home ambiance. Madame Chauveau offers two bedrooms in her home as well as a two-bedroom poolside suite. The suite is very handsome with stone walls, slate tile floors and pretty country antique furniture. Sunny yellow print curtains and matching upholstery complete the pleasing ensemble. The Chauveau's pool and sunbathing terrace is only steps away; perfect for an early morning dip. Guest bedrooms in the main house are furnished in highly tasteful combinations of designer fabrics in floral motifs complemented by charming old paintings, antique chests and beds. A stay at Domaine de Beauséjour is truly an experience to be savored. *Directions:* Panzoult is located approximately 12 kilometers east of Chinon. Take D21 in the direction of L'Île Bouchard through the village of Panzoult. Two kilometers out of town there is a sign marking the driveway of Domaine de Beauséjour to the right—the pretty, light stone house on the edge of the woods.

DOMAINE DE BEAUSÉJOUR (Gîte de France)
Hosts: Marie-Claude & Gérard Chauveau
Panzoult, 37220 L'Île Bouchard, France
tel: 47.58.64.64 fax: 47 95 27 13
4 rooms, 2 with private bath/WC
Double: 400F, Triple: 500F
No Table d'Hôte
Open all year
Good English spoken
Region: Loire Valley, Michelin Map 232

The romantic L'Ormeraie, secreted on a tiny lane in a splendid non-touristy area of southwest France, is owned by the charming Michel de l'Ormeraie. It took him over 20 years to transform the neglected 17th-century farmhouse into the dream it is today—a picture perfect, mellow stone farmhouse accented with white shutters and climbing roses. There are five guest rooms: my choice is the Chambre du Parc, a spacious room, nicely decorated with antiques and with French doors opening onto the garden. But, the favorite place of all is the terrace where guests can relax and enjoy a scene of utter tranquillity looking out over the sloping pastures to forested hills. A path leads down from the terrace to a small circular swimming pool nestled on the lawn. Whereas many of the places we saw in France has a bit of a ramshackle look about them, Michel has managed to achieve an informality about his little farm yet maintain a beautifully groomed, carefully tended look both to his house and his lovely rose and flower gardens. *Directions:* Agen is located 140 km southeast of Bordeaux via the A62 / E72. From Agen go north on N21 to Villeneuve and take D676 northeast to Monflanquin. Then take D272 northeast 7 km to Laussou and turn right on the narrow road 161 toward Bonnenouvelle. L'Ormeraie is about 1.5 km down 161 on your right.

L'ORMERAIE   *(Gîte de France)*
Host: Michel de l'Ormeraie
47150 Paulhiac, France
tel: 53.36.45.96
5 rooms, with private bathrooms
Double: 275-500F, Triple: 585F
*Table d'Hôte: 140F per person ***
**(includes great Bordeaux wines)*
Credit cards: Visa
Open Easter to November 15
Very little English spoken
Region: Lot & Garonne, Michelin Map 235

Veal farmers Janine and Charles Lacaze have recently converted their historic barn into comfortable guest accommodation. A large arched doorway leads into a spacious guest kitchen and dining area with exposed stone walls and a stone fireplace. Upstairs, the five recently remodeled guest bedrooms are fresh and inviting with reproduction antique furniture and dainty floral print wallpapers. Janine is a scrupulous housekeeper who makes sure linens are fresh and rooms spotless. Skylight windows look out over the wooded hills and let in the pure country air. Breakfast is served in the Lacaze's farmhouse, a pretty stone structure dating from the early 1800's that has been in Charles' family for three generations. Fresh coffee and croissants are enjoyed at a long table in the low-ceilinged dining room before an arched stone fireplace. The charming scene is completed by hanging copper pots, exposed stone walls and a friendly collie dog asleep by the hearth. *Directions:* Pers is a very small village located about 25 kilometers west of Aurillac. Take N122 south towards Toulouse. After about 18 kilometers, turn right towards Pers. The road forks several times; keep following signs pointing to Pers. Go through the village and look for a Chambres d'Hôtes sign at the far edge, indicating a driveway on the left.

FERME DE VIESCAMP (*Gîte de France*)
Hosts: Janine & Charles Lacaze
15290 Pers, France
tel: 71.62.25.14
5 rooms, with private bathrooms
Double: 185F, Triple: 234F
No Table d'Hôte
Open April 15 to November 15
No English spoken, fluent Spanish spoken
Region: Auvergne, Michelin Map 239

Monsieur and Madame Colin open their lovely home in the quiet village of Plaissan to guests on a B&B basis. The house features restored tiled floors, hand-painted decoration, marbling, furniture, pictures and china to evoke the 1920's but with 1990's facilities and comfort. On the first floor is the dining room with a handsome table. There are four bedrooms, each with its private bathroom. The most expensive one is a suite with the bathroom dividing the room into two sleeping areas, however, I preferred the less expensive rooms: my favorite one faces the park and has a handsome antique bed. There is a small garden tucked along side the B&B where a lovely breakfast is served under the trees when the weather is warm. Although no table d'Hôte is offered, a small kitchen and dining room are for the use of guests, as is the secure, covered parking in the huge adjoining barn. Although this home offers simple accommodation, it is inviting, pleasantly furnished and efficiently managed. *Directions:* Plaissan is located 42 km west of Montpellier. Drive southwest from Montpellier on the A9 for 21 km. Then take the Sete exit and go north on D2 via Poussan. As you drive into town, turn right at the Gîte sign (rue des Prunus) and go 3 blocks. The house is located on the left side of the street, on the corner of des Prunus and rue de L'Aire, across the street from the park.

CHEZ COLIN (Gîte de France)
Hosts: Monsieur & Madame Colin
Rue des Prunus (1, rue de L'Aire)
34230 Plaissan, France
tel: 67.96.81.16
4 rooms, with private bathrooms
Double: 185-280F
No Table d'Hôte, restaurant nearby
Credit cards: None accepted
Open all year
No English spoken
Region: Midi Pyrénées, Michelin Map 240

Several years ago Even O'Neill gave up a high-powered role in the business world in order to take on that of host in his family's 15th-century manor house hôtel. His deep love for his heritage shows in every aspect of his solicitous management of the Manoir de Vaumadeuc. All the rooms have been renovated and redecorated under Even's direction, ushering in a new era of freshness and elegant style to the ancient medieval surroundings. In spite of the thick stone walls and huge walk-in fireplaces, the feeling throughout is light, airy and very comfortable. The guest rooms in the main house are very large with high ceilings and fireplaces. Lovely floral fabrics, paintings and antiques lend a luxurious, yet personalized atmosphere. There are also two cottage style bedrooms located in the carriage house that are smaller and thus cozier than those in the manoir. Delicious dinners are graciously served in the intimate restaurant by personable Even and his wife Carol. Located twelve miles from Brittany's coast in the Hunaudaye Forest, the manoir reflects an ambiance of beauty, gentility and peace. *Directions:* From Plancoët, take D768 towards Lamballe. 2 km later, go left on D28 for about 7 km to the village of Pléven. Go through the village and you will see the Manoir de Vaumadeuc on the right.

MANOIR DE VAUMADEUC
Hosts: Carol & Even O'Neill
Pléven 22130 Plancoët, France
tel: 96.84.46.17 fax: 96.84.40.16
14 rooms/suites, all with pvt bath
Double: 490-950F
Restaurant, rates from 185F per person
Open March 15-January 5
Good English spoken
Region: Brittany, Michelin Map 230

Les Tilleuls resembles typical English Bed and Breakfast—this is not surprising, as the owners, Cas and Don Hamilton, were born in England. They moved to the Dordogne a few years ago and bought Les Tilleuls, formerly the summer home of the bishops of Périgueux. You enter the house by a covered front porch, cheerfully decorated with pots of geraniums and hanging plants. It is here that dinner is served in the summer. On cooler evenings, guests dine family style at a large table in the living room that has a very relaxed, homey ambiance. Cas and Don both enjoy cooking and together they prepare exceptionally delicious meals enhanced by herbs from their garden. A wide staircase curves to the upper levels where the bedrooms are located down hallways slanted with the character of time. My favorite is the bright and cheerful "Sweet Pea Room" with blue carpet, an antique white iron bed, a light pine chest, barely pink walls and cheerful sweet pea floral drapes and matching cushions on the window seat. It has its own bathroom just across the hall. Les Tilleuls is not fancy, nor is it meant to be. This is a homey, old-fashioned, Bed and Breakfast offering the best commodity of all: outstanding warmth of welcome. *Directions:* From Périgueux take N89 toward Brive. at Niversac take D710 toward Les Eyzies. Left in Les Versannes, signposted Rouffignac. Go through Rouffignac toward Montignac-Lascaux. Plazac is 6 km from Rouffignac.

LES TILLEULS
Hosts: Cas & Don Hamilton
24580 Plazac, France
tel: 53.50.80.65
5 rooms, 2 with private bathrooms
Double 180-250F
Table d'Hôte 75F per person, with wine
Open April to October
Fluent English spoken
Region: Dordogne, Michelin Map 233

The Manoir de Kergrec'h, located on the coast of Brittany, is a superb 17th-century manor, impressively large, yet ever so inviting—especially in early summer when a profusion of old-fashioned pink roses lace and soften the stern gray stone exterior. The most outstanding attribute of the Manoir de Kergrec'h is its splendid setting in an enormous park that stretches to the sea, an absolute paradise for walking. When you enter into the large front hallway, to the right is a very formal, very fancy, somewhat intimidating living room. To the left is a handsome dining room with beautiful parquet floors in a herringbone pattern, and a massive fireplace that soars almost to the ceiling. A spiral stone staircase, worn with the footsteps of time, winds up through the tower to the bedrooms that are most attractively decorated with color coordinated fabrics and absolutely gorgeous antique furniture. All the bedrooms are appealing, but my particular favorite was located on the top floor. It is a real gem, especially cozy with gabled windows and decorated in a delicate floral print wallpaper in tones of rose and green. All of the bedrooms have large, modern, bathrooms. *Directions:* From Treguier, take D8 7 km north to Plougrescant. Turn right just beyond the quaint old church and continue a short distance and you will see the manoir on your right.

MANOIR DE KERGREC'H
Vicomte & Vicomtesse Stephane de Roquefeuil
22820 Plougrescant, France
tel: 96.92.56.06 or 96.92.59.13
4 rooms, with private bathrooms
Double 510F, Suite from 650F
Table d'Hôte from 180F per person
Open all year
No English spoken
Region: Brittany, Michelin Map 230

L'Estel, located in the heart of Provence, is a small B&B that might well appeal to you, especially if your are travelling with small children and would like to practice your high school French. The handsome, most gracious young owner, Pierre-Jean Turion, showed us around the inn while his pretty wife was in the kitchen caring for the children who will be the 5th generation to live in this 200-year old farm house. The farmhouse is located right on the main road, but a high stone fence creates a nucleus of privacy for the pretty walled garden where breakfast is served each morning. Pierre-Jean said that the wall is going to be extended and a swimming pool tucked onto the property. A central room, bright and cheerful with lots of sunlight streaming through large windows, is attractively decorated by antique groupings of tables and chairs. Upstairs are 5 absolutely immaculate bedrooms. Several of them have small lofts where, if you are travelling with children, they would love to sleep. Jacqueline, upon prior notice, cooks dinner for her guests. *Directions:* Pont du Gard is located 25 km west of Avignon. From Remoulins take D 981 following signs to Uzes. After about 3 km you will see the Gîte sign on your right, drive in and park. L'Estel is located on the main road D981.

L'ESTEL (Gîte de France)
Hosts: Jacqueline & Pierre-Jean Turion
La Begude de Vers
30210 Pont due Gard, France
tel: 66.37.18.11
5 rooms, with private bathrooms
Double: 290F
Table d'Hôte: 70F per person, includes wine
Credit cards: None accepted
Open all year
No English spoken
Region: Provence, Michelin Maps 245, 246

Conveniently located for sightseeing in the interior of Brittany, the Chateau de Pontgamp offers guests luxurious accommodation in an old Breton manor home. Monsieur Pourdieu is your gracious host who happily shares his extensive knowledge of the region, helps plan walking tours and even offers lessons in the traditional Breton method of cooking crepes. Perched on a hillside above the town of Pontgamp, the Pourdieu home is furnished with many elegant antiques, and offers almost every comfort imaginable for guests including televisions, private baths and writing desks. Decor is very attractive; soft toned wallpapers and carpets in harmonious colors. *Directions:* The village of Pontgamp adjoins the village of Plouguenast and is located approximately 38 kilometers south of St-Brieuc. If approaching from the north, drive through Plouguenast and turn left at the first street after the bridge over the river. At this point you can see the Chateau de Pontgamp on the hill above. The driveway is on the left.

CHATEAU DE PONTGAMP (Gîte de France)
Host: Monsieur Pourdieu
Pontgamp
22150 Plouguenast, France
tel: 96.28.71.99
2 Suites, both with private bath
Double: 250-300F, Triple: 380F
No Table d'Hôte
Open all year
A little English spoken
Region: Brittany, Michelin Map 230

Drive down a country lane past a field of sunflowers to arrive in the tiny hamlet of La Galeze, where friendly hosts Denise and Pierre Billat extend a warm welcome to their peaceful country home. The front garden is a glorious profusion of colorful flowers, blackberry brambles and sweet-smelling herbs; bordered by a hedge that conceals a large garden full of healthy vegetables. Nearby woods and countryside offer many footpaths for long walks or bike rides. Adjoining the main house is an inviting stone room once used for distilling cognac, now renovated into a cozy guest salon. There is also a dining room where Denise and Pierre share delicious and convivial home-cooked meals with their guests. Guest rooms vary in size; the ground-floor bedrooms are spacious and have private baths, while the attic rooms are smaller, with shared bath facilities. All the rooms are tastefully decorated in a simple country style with details such as lace curtains and flowering plants adding Denise's personal, feminine touch. *Directions:* Pouillac is located approximately 50 kilometers northeast of Bordeaux. Take N10 north in the direction of Angoulême just past the town of Montlieu la Garde to Pouillac. Go through the village and turn left, following directions for the hamlet of La Galèze. One kilometer later look for a Chambres d'Hôtes sign on the right indicating a short driveway to the Billat's picturesque home.

LA THÉBAÏDE (Gîte de France)
Hosts: Denise & Pierre Billat
La Galèze - Pouillac
17210 Montlieu la Garde, France
tel: 46.04.65.17
4 rooms, with private bathrooms
Double: 220F
Table d'Hôte: 80 per person
Open all year
No English spoken
Region: Atlantic Coast, Michelin Map 233

The Van der Elst manor house is a large, tile-roofed white home set amidst sand dunes and coastal pine trees. Only 5 kilometers from the shore, it is close to wind surfing, swimming and fishing. Reasonable prices and an adequate level of comfort make this a good base from which to explore the surrounding region. The Van der Elst's son Alexandre, a poet, novelist and playwright, is host to Bed and Breakfast guests. The atmosphere at the Domaine de l'Estarac is relaxed and informal, and guests often include artists and visiting scholars. An adjoining wing houses a small theater where plays and music are performed. There is a patio, but no indoor lounge or common areas for guests, so breakfast is served in the rooms or outdoors. Bedrooms vary in their furnishings and decor; some have lovely antiques while others contain more contemporary pieces. The Domaine, built in 1800, is showing its age both inside and out, yet is a good bargain, especially for travellers who appreciate its casual, theatrical flavor. *Directions:* PRAT de Cest is located approximately 8 kilometers south of Narbonne via N9 in the direction of Pèrpignan. Just after the town of Prat de Cest look for a sign for Estarac at which you turn to the left. Continue about 800 meters down a dirt road to the Van der Elst's driveway.

DOMAINE DE L'ESTARAC (*Gîte de France*)
Host: Monsieur Alexandre Van der Elst
Vanderlist, Prat de Cest
11100 Narbonne, France
tel: 68.41.57.31
5 rooms, with private bathrooms
Double: 155F, Triple: 200F
No Table d'Hôte
Open all year
Good English spoken
Region: Midi Pyrénées Michelin Map 240

This particularly scenic section of Normandy is called Norman Switzerland due to its green, forested hills and valleys. Claude and Monique Chesnel live here in a pretty stone house, next door to which they have created an extremely pleasant room for Bed and Breakfast guests. Almost a suite, this spacious room can sleep up to four persons and is very comfortably furnished with a divan, double bed, antique armoire, wooden table and chairs. Decor is very attractive with soft carpets and harmonious colors. Located on the ground floor, the room is entered through wide French doors that lend a light, airy feeling. The bathroom is sparkling clean and extremely well equipped. For the traveller seeking great comfort in independent, peaceful surroundings, the Chesnels offer the perfect haven. *Directions:* Préaux Bocage is located approximately 16 kilometers southwest of Caen via D8, turning left after 6 kilometers onto D36 and continuing through St-Honorine du Fay, until the turnoff for D171 to the left (look carefully: the sign faces the other direction). About 2 kilometers later, turn right onto D139 towards Goupillières. One kilometer down this road, look for a hard-to-find, homemade sign on a tree indicating Chambres d'Hôtes to the left (if you arrive at the church, you've missed this sign; go back). The next sign directs you to the right down a dead-end lane, at the bottom of which you will see the Chesnel's white gate.

LA CRÊTE AUX OISEAUX (*Gîte de France*)
Hosts: Monique & Claude Chesnel
La Crete - Préaux Bocage
14210 Evrecy, France
tel: 31.79.63.52
1 room, with private shower
Double: 270F
No Table d'Hôte
Open all year
Some English spoken
Region: Normandy, Michelin Map 231

Monsieur and Madame Line are an attractive, hospitable couple who take great pleasure in welcoming guests to their charming home in the countryside. The Lines enjoy inviting their guests to share an aperitif in their airy glassed-in verandah looking out over their peaceful back garden and tennis court. An independent entrance leads upstairs to the three pretty bedrooms that are furnished with highly polished antique beds, chests and armoires and complementing designer wallpapers, upholstery and curtains. Breakfast is a special treat at the Lines,' as they serve a copious meal complete with a special goat cheese from their nearby farm. The country breakfast room is indeed a pleasant place to linger, with its old tiled floor and stone fireplace, country antiques and pewter collection. This is a Bed and Breakfast that tops our list; including all the elements of comfort, reasonable price, charming decor, atmosphere and an open-hearted welcome. *Directions:* Pussigny is located about 22 kilometers north of Chatellerault. Take N10 north in the direction of Tours, turn left at the village of Port de Piles in the direction of Marigny, then, just after crossing the River Vienne, turn left again in the direction of Pussigny. Just after entering the village limits, look for a Chambres d'Hôtes sign and the Line's warm stone house on the left.

LE CLOS SAINT-CLAIR (*Gîte de France*)
Hosts: Monsieur & Madame Line
Pussigny, 37800 Ste Maure de Touraine, France
tel: 47.65.01.27 fax: 47.65.04.21
4 rooms, with private bathrooms
(Two on ground floor suitable for handicapped)
Double: 250F, Triple: 310F
Table d'Hôte: 90F per person (except Sunday)
Open all year
Very little English spoken
Region: Loire Valley, Michelin Map 232

A circular drive, soft green lawn and brightly painted blue door welcome guests into the imposing home of Monsieur and Madame Rogoff. The Rogoffs are a farming family who have raised three children here in this pleasant manor house. Decor is home-like rather than elegant, with bright touches such as colorful lamps and fresh flower bouquets. Madame enjoys crafts and her handiwork is evident in the crocheted bedspreads and dried flower wreaths that add personality to the bedrooms. The downstairs bedroom is very spacious with a private bath/WC located across the hall. Upstairs, a very pretty room with country antique furniture shares a WC in the hall but has a private adjoining bath. Breakfast is served at a long table in Madame's sunny country kitchen where a fire warms the hearth on cool mornings. The front garden offers a peaceful retreat after a day of sightseeing in nearby Bayeux, well known for its collection of beautiful tapestries—the most famous of which depicts the Battle of Hastings. *Directions:* Ranchy is located 2 kilometers southwest of Bayeux via D5 towards le Molay Littry, turning left after 1 kilometer onto D169 to Ranchy. There is a sign for another Chambres d'Hôtes just before entering the village of Ranchy, so be sure to continue into town where you will see a second Chambres d'Hôtes sign directing you to the Rogoff's gate.

CHEZ ROGOFF (*Gîte de France*)
Hosts: Monsieur & Madame Rogoff
Ranchy 14400 Bayeux, France
tel: 31.92.36.42
2 rooms, both w/private bath, one shares WC
Double: 180F
No Table d'Hôte
Open all year
No English spoken
Region: Normandy, Michelin Map 231

If you are looking for a wonderful castle, absolutely brimming with character, tucked far from the maddening crowds, the Chateau de Regagnac is your dream come true. The road to the castle winds through a forest and finally deadends at the Chateau de Regagnac. Go through the gates and into the courtyard that extends to a bluff and offers a sensational view out to forested hills. Chateau de Regagnac is totally furnished in family antiques—although the decor is stunning, there is a homey ambiance—nothing seems stiff or formal. Some of the bedrooms are in the main part of the castle and others in across the courtyard, but it does not matter which you reserve, they are all beautiful. Serge Pardoux is a great collector: don't miss seeing his stunning collection of lead soldiers. Mme Pardoux is a superb cook, and with advance reservation, will prepare a gourmet meal for you—the price is not inexpensive, but the meal will be memorable. Serge Pardoux is the epitome of graciousness who says "once a person walks through the gates, he is becomes a friend, a guest in my home." *Directions:* Bergerac is located about 87 km east of Bordeaux via the D936. Head east from Bergerac on D660 for 27 km to Beaumont. Then take D25 east to Cadouin and turn right on D2 toward Monpazier; then take the 3rd small road on the left and follow signs to Regagnac.

CHATEAU DE REGAGNAC
Hosts: Monsieur & Madame Serge Pardoux
Regagnac, 24440 Beaumont, France
tel: 53.63.27.02
5 rooms, with private bathrooms
Double: 600F
Table d'Hôte: 500F per person, prior notice
Credit cards: None accepted
Open all year
Fluent English spoken
Region: Périgord, Michelin Map 235

Monsieur and Madame Vandel recently purchased the magnificent Chateau de Reignac, once a residence of famous French general, La Fayette, and have lovingly refurbished and redecorated it in highly authentic 17th-century style. The Vandels are antique dealers and part of the castle houses their wellstocked showroom where guests are welcome to browse among their many treasures. Perfection is a key word at Chateau de Reignac and Madame and Monsieur, along with their daughter and two sons, are friendly hosts who attend to the smallest details with indefatigable energy. All of the beautifully preserved and furnished public rooms are open to guests and contain museum-quality decor including crystal chandeliers and original carved wood ceilings. Guest breakfasts are served in the oldest part of the castle; the former soldier's quarters, dating from the 11th Century. Bedrooms are all elegant works of art, displaying period furniture and artifacts, and wallpapers that are copies of old designs. Even the bathrooms provide a taste of the past, as each contains an old-fashioned claw foot bathtub. *Directions:* Reignac sur Indre is located approximately 22 kilometers southeast of Tours. Take N143 towards Loches, turning left after about 20 kilometers onto D58 to Reignac. Once in the village, look for the castle gate across from the church.

CHATEAU DE REIGNAC (*Gîte de France*)
Hosts: Monsieur & Madame Vandel
37310 Reignac sur Indre, France
tel: 47.94.14.10
7 rooms, with private bathrooms
Single: 300F, Double: 600F, Triple: 900F
No Table d'Hôte
Open all year
Some English spoken
Region: Loire Valley, Michelin Map 232

Madame Le Platre's elegant town home enjoys a central, picturesque location on La Place des Religieuses in the small town of Richelieu. This entire town is classified as an historical monument and is the former site of Cardinal Richelieu's magnificent castle and estate. Madame Le Platre is a local history buff who is happy to share her extensive knowledge with her guests and help them plan sightseeing excursions. Her own home dates from 1638 and is like a modest museum with its antique furnishings, decor and collections. All of her inviting bedrooms are decorated in a refined, old-fashioned style. Madame also offers an adorable little apartment across the rear courtyard where guests have a small downstairs sitting area and two bedrooms. The larger bedroom has a beautiful dark red tile floor and is furnished with impressive old paintings and antique furniture, while the smaller bedroom is furnished in a very cute manner with a blue checked cloth forming a canopy over the bed. On warm mornings breakfast can be enjoyed in the tranquil courtyard at an outdoor table. *Directions:* Richelieu is located approximately 35 kilometers northwest of Chatellerault. Take A10 to the St-Maure de la Touraine exit, then follow signs for Richelieu. You will enter the town via La Place des Religieuses and Madame Le Platre's house is number 24.

HÔTEL DES RELIGIEUSES (Gîte de France)
Hostess: Madame Marie Josèphe Le Platre
1, rue Jarry, 37120 Richelieu, France
tel: 47.58.10.42
4 rooms, with private bathrooms
Double: 260F, Triple: 360F
No Table d'Hôte
Open all year
No English spoken
Region: Loire Valley, Michelin Map 232

Le Moulin des Chézeaux is a picture-perfect 14th-century flour mill, painted white with delft-blue shutters, and red geraniums spilling from boxes at every window. Adding to the storybook ambiance is a small lake (with ducks, of course) and a stream. Inside, the enchantment continues. In any one of the three guest rooms you will feel as if you are living in a stage setting—superb fabrics, antique furniture, fresh flowers everywhere and the finest of linens. The creation of this elegant little B&B was the handiwork of Ren Rijpstra, a talented interior designer, and Willem Prinsloo, a successful business consultant. Their genuine warmth of welcome combined with a boundless desire to pamper their guests makes one feel like royalty. Ren, is not only a clever decorator, but a fabulous chef—be sure to reserve for dinner. A few steps away, Ren and Willem have beautifully restored and decorated a 3 bedroom, 2 bath, 300-year-old stone cottage (for weekly rentals). Note: no smoking, no children under 10. *Directions:* Rivarennes is located 76 km east of Poitiers. From Poitiers take N151 east. Just west of St-Gaultier, exit north on D46 toward Migne. Turn right at the first road, then left at the second road that immediately splits. Follow the right hand lane down to the mill.

LE MOULIN DES CHÉZEAUX   (*Gîte de France*)
Hosts: Ren Rijpstra & Willem Prinsloo
Rivarennes
36800 St-Gaultier, France
tel: 54.47.01.84 fax: 54.47.10.93
3 rooms, with private bathrooms
Double: 325-350, House: 3,000F-4,000F/week
Table d'Hôte: from 130F per person
Credit cards: None
Open January to December
Fluent English spoken
Region: Limousin, Michelin Map 238

Les Salles is recommended for travellers seeking basic, modern comfort and a high degree of cleanliness rather than historic ambiance. Conveniently located near the scenic river canyons Gorges du Tarn, the Meljac's newly built house of light-toned regional stone is surrounded by Monsieur's family vineyards. They produce a red table wine that accompanies their Table d'Hôte dinners featuring fresh garden vegetables. The home-like guest dining room is furnished in rustic reproduction furniture accented by bright red tablecloths and has French doors that lead out to a peaceful front terrace. Simple, family-style meals and hospitality are offered at Les Salles. The bedrooms are furnished mainly in rattan furniture and are somewhat stark in their decor, with cool white walls and tile floors. A refreshing swimming pool is a welcome addition in the summer months. *Directions:* Rivière sur Tarn is located approximately 50 kilometers southeast of Rodez. Take D911 to Millau, turning off onto N9 towards the well-known canyons of Gorges du Tarn. After about 8 kilometers, turn right at Aguessac onto D107 and go through the town of Rivière sur Tarn, continuing towards Rivière sur Tarn village. Look for a Chambres d'Hôtes emblem indicating the Meljac's driveway to the left.

LES SALLES (Gîte de France)
Hosts: Monsieur & Madame Jean Meljac
12640 Rivière sur Tarn, France
tel: 65.59.85.78
5 rooms, all w/pvt. shower/sink*
* All share hallway WCs
Double: 190F, Triple: 230F
Table d'Hôte: 70F per person
Open all year
Very little English spoken
Region: Tarn, Michelin Map 240

A cool oasis in this sometimes hot, dry climate, the Aboujoid's Bed and Breakfast offers a lovely azure pool that looks out over a spectacular view of the peaceful valley below. Young, friendly hosts Monsieur and Madame Aboujoid offer accommodation in their recently completed pool pavilion whose guest rooms open directly onto the pool's flagstone terrace. The Aboujoid's summer house is located a few steps away and has an inviting kitchen and dining room area where guests share breakfast, and if desired, Table d'Hôte dinners. This is an idyllic setting, perfect for travellers who would like to spend some time relaxing by the pool rather than rushing off on all day sightseeing excursions. Bedrooms are small and very simply furnished in a functional, basic style; each with private shower, sink and WC. *Directions:* Chez Aboujoid is actually located in the small hamlet of Roquemaure. The nearest large town is St-Sulpice that is located about 30 kilometers northeast of Toulouse. Take N88 in the direction of Albi for about 25 kilometers to St-Sulpice. Turn left onto D630 in the direction of Montauban and continue to the village of Bessières, where you will turn right towards Mirepoix. Follow signs and arrows that direct you up a hill, then onto an unpaved country road to the Aboujoid's stone and tile-roofed house on the right.

LE PENDUT (Gîte de France)
Hosts: Monsieur & Madame Aboujoid
Roquemaure
81800 Rabastens, France
tel: 63.41.90.07 or 61.84.10.23
2 rooms, with private bathrooms
Single: 210F, Double: 240F, Triple: 260F
Table d'Hôte: 80F per person
Open June 1 through October 1
No English spoken
Region: Tarn, Michelin Map 235

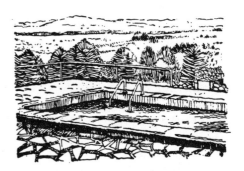

A stay at La Bergerie is for travellers seeking inexpensive accommodation in an authentic French farm atmosphere. The facade of this three-storey farmhouse is softened by large Easter lilies that grow under the front windows, and the small front lawn is dotted with hens and roosters strutting about looking for grain under a white lilac tree. We arrived on a Saturday afternoon, when Madame LeFrancois was busily preparing a dinner of fresh trout and farm vegetables for expected evening guests. She and her husband are an energetic couple who serve Ferme Auberge dinners on weekends, offering seating at five tables in their cozy dining room decorated by a large old fireplace, antiques and many flowers and plants. On weekdays, Bed and Breakfast guests can share family-style meals at the long table in Madame's farm kitchen. The two guest bedrooms are spacious and furnished with family antiques and home-like knick-knacks. No English is spoken here, but Monsieur and Madame Le François (and their five children) offer an authentic slice of life and simple farm hospitality. *Directions:* St-Arnoult is approximately 30 kilometers west of Rouen via D982. Just outside the town of Caudebec en Caux, still on D982 going towards Lillebonne, look for sign for a Ferme Auberge to the right. Continue following signs that will lead you to this three-storey white farmhouse.

LA BERGERIE (Gîte de France)
Hosts: Chantel & Lucien LeFrançois
Route de la Bergerie
St-Arnoult, 76490 Caudebec en Caux, France
tel: 35.56.75.84
2 rooms, 1 with private bath, share WC
Double: 170F, Triple: 255F
Table d'Hôte: 75F per person (Gourmet 135F)
Open all year
A little English spoken
Region: Normandy, Michelin Map 231

At the edge of the small town of St-Chartier, near the castle of 19th-century French novelist Georges Sand, Ralph Metz offers home-like Bed and Breakfast accommodation at Le Chalet. A medium-sized stone building dating from 1890, his house is shaped like an Alpine chalet; hence its unusual name. Monsieur Metz spent 22 years living and working overseas in Madagascar and Africa, and has filled his home with interesting artifacts from his life on the dark continent. A fascinating collection of black and white photographs depicting African tribal life are displayed throughout his home and some especially lovely photos line the winding Italian staircase that leads up to the guest bedrooms. Rooms vary in size and decor, and contain basic, contemporary furnishings, with neutral color schemes creating a somewhat masculine atmosphere. Informal breakfasts are shared in Monsieur's modern kitchen or enjoyed on the sunny back terrace. *Directions:* St-Chartier is located approximately 30 kilometers southeast of Chateauroux. Travel south on D943 towards La Chatre, turning left onto D918 to St-Chartier after about 25 kilometers. Once in the village of St-Chartier, take D69 towards Verneuil and look for a Chambres d'Hôtes sign indicating a driveway on the left that enters the tree-shaded front yard of Le Chalet.

LE CHALET (*Gîte de France*)
Host: Monsieur Ralph Metz
Route de Verneuil
36400 St-Chartier, France
tel: 54.31.05.76
4 rooms, 2 w/pvt WC/shower others share
Single: 200F, Double: 230F
No Table d'Hôte
Open all year
A little English spoken
Region: Berry, Michelin Map 238

St-Clar's market square is a pretty ensemble of stone arcaded buildings dating from the 17th Century. This intimate place is a designated historic monument and is also the site of the old town hall: hence its name, Place de la Mairie. Nicole and Jean-Francois are an interesting, artistic young couple who live in a partially restored section of the buildings on the square and offer charming Bed and Breakfast accommodation to travellers. To reach their home, one enters through an arched stone doorway into a wide hallway, formerly horse stables, and ascends a stairway to the second floor. All the guest bedrooms are separate from the Cournot's living quarters. Madame has decorated the rooms in a charming, attractive style utilizing cheerful Laura Ashley wallpapers and bright, fresh color schemes. Guests are welcome to relax in the Cournot's lovely salon that has exquisite 100-year-old gold leaf wallpaper still intact and a marble fireplace flanked by comfortable leather chairs and couch. Breakfast is served en famille in the cozy kitchen with a blue and white tile floor and rustic country antique furnishings. One of the large guest rooms is especially well-suited for families and even had its own kitchen. *Directions:* St-Clar is located about 40 km south of Agen. Take N21 towards Auch, turning left at Lectoure onto D7 to St-Clar. In St-Clar, follow signs for Place de la Mairie.

CHEZ COURNOT (Gîte de France)
Hosts: Nicole & Jean-Francois Cournot
Place de la Mairie
32380 St-Clar, France
tel: 62.66.47.31
3 rooms share separated WC & shower
Double:190F
Table d'Hôte: 95F per person
Reduced prices for 3 night reserved stays
Open all year
Some English spoken
Region: Tarn, Michelin Map 235

Originally La Villa Medicis, which has three springs on the property, was used as a spa by Queen Maria of Medicis who would come here with her court "for the waters." Today, the handsome two-storey home, beautifully located in a thickly wooded oasis just east of Blois, has been transformed into a most delightful Bed and Breakfast. Downstairs, the dining room and living areas are nicely decorated and have a wonderful, homey ambiance. Indeed, this is a real home, as the Baron and Baronne have three sons and a daughter. The bedrooms are especially lovely, with the decor reflecting a country ambiance using lovely fabrics and antique beds and chests. All rooms look out into the garden and trees, and are all named for flowers. My favorite was the "Marguerite room" a charming room with soft yellow walls and charming floral drapes. Veronique de Caix is a superb hostess, a "natural," who truly looks forward to welcoming guests and showering them with attention. She loves to cook and many guests return just for her fabulous meals. *Directions:* From Blois take the RN 152 east toward Orleans. In 3.5 km turn right at St-Denis (Macé) at the Chambres d'Hôtes sign. Continue following the signs to La Villa Medicis.

LA VILLA MEDICS (Gîte de France)
Baron & Baronne de Caix de Rembures
Macé
41000 St-. Denis-sur-Loire, Blois, France
tel: 54.74.46.38 fax: 54.78.20.27
6 rooms, 1 suite, with private bathrooms
Double 350-450F
Table d'Hôte: 200F per person with wine
Open all year
Good English spoken
Region: Loire Valley, Michelin Map 238

If you want to open the door of your room and be face to face with a field of cabernet sauvignon grapes, then you might want to join Françoise and Ivo Leemann at their home in the famous Médoc region of France. After retirement, they bought a pretty mini-chateau built of honey-colored stone accented by white shutters in the very old wine town of Saint Estèphe. There are two rooms located in a separate building, but be sure to request the room in the main house with a private entrance—this is the only accommodation with a vineyard view. This bedroom does not have much old word ambiance, but is spacious and modern with tiled floor and sort of a South Pacific motif with grass cloth wallpaper, rattan furniture, a barrel for a night table and Tahitian prints on the walls. Françoise and Ivo genuinely enjoy receiving guests into their home, and since they speak such good English, can help plan your wine tasting adventures in the area. Françoise prepares breakfast for guests each morning with juice, coffee/tea, honey, home made marmalades and French bread and croissants. *Directions:* Take 215 north from Bordeaux. Exit at St-Laurent and take road to Pauillac, then north on D2 following signs to St-Estèphe. Turn left at the foot of the hill below the village toward Chateau Phelan Segur winery. The house has no sign, but is across the street from an ivy covered pharmacy.

CHEZ LEEMANN (Gîte de France)
Hosts: Françoise & Ivo Leemann
P.O. Box 07, Au Bourg
33180 St-Estèphe, France
tel: 56.59.72.94 fax 56.59.39.58
3 rooms with private bathroom
Double 300-450F
Table d'Hôte 100F per person
Open all year
Fluent English
Region: Médoc, Michelin Map 233

The Gay family has recently constructed a wing of rooms for Bed and Breakfast guests that is a perfect stopping place for travellers seeking modern convenience over historical ambiance. Bedrooms are functional and attractive, all with shuttered French doors opening onto a covered outdoor hallway. The dimensions are small, but rooms are very comfortable, with great attention to detail such as soundproofing, good lighting, electrical plugs and spotless bathrooms. The Gays have also built a fully equipped kitchen at the end of the guest wing that is completely at guest's disposal. There is parking in the courtyard and a barbecue under an apricot tree, also for guest use. St-Georges d'Orques is well known for the red wine produced in the region, and the Gay's home is located a bit out of town in a quiet setting of hills and vineyards. Monsieur and Madame have three sons who all speak English and are willing to help guests in any way they can. *Directions:* St-Georges d'Orques is located approximately 8 kilometers west of Montpellier. Take N109 in the direction of Lodève, turning left at Juvignac onto D27e towards St-Georges d'Orques. Once you are in the village, you will find Chambres d'Hôtes signs leading the way to the Gay's house on the edge of town.

RÉSIDENCE SÉRENIS (Gîte de France)
Hosts: Monsieur & Madame Gay
2, Chemin de Bouisson
34680 St-Georges d'Orques, France
tel: 67.75.07.67
6 rooms, with private bathrooms
Double: 205F
No Table d'Hôte, but kitchen available
Open all year
Good English spoken by sons
Region: Provence, Michelin Map 240

Set in the mystical marshlands of coastal Normandy, La Ferme de la Rivière is an imposing fortified farmhouse dating from the 16th Century. The main entry leads directly into an old tower and up a well-worn spiral staircase to the dining room. The friendly Marie family serve Ferme Auberge dinners as well as guest breakfasts in this warm, inviting room with its atmospheric stone floors, walk-in fireplace and country furniture. Bedrooms are found upstairs—most have enchanting views over the surrounding fields and marshes. Two of the bedrooms are quite large, share a bath and WC, and can be rented as a suite. The two smaller bedrooms have an intimate charm all their own, and each has a private shower and WC. All of the bedrooms are simply furnished, mostly in family antiques. La Ferme de la Rivière is a rare find, offering charming, comfortable accommodations, delicious country cuisine, peaceful scenery and a warm family welcome. *Directions:* St-Germain du Pert is located 28 kilometers west of Bayeux via N13. Approximately 6 kilometers before Isigny sur Mer, turn left onto D199 which leads to St-Germain du Pert. Continue through the very small village, then turn left onto D124 following signs for Ferme Auberge de la Rivière. One kilometer later turn right at the Marie's gate which is marked with a sign.

LA FERME DE LA RIVIÈRE (Gîte de France)
Hosts: Paulette & Hervé Marie
14230 St-Germain du Pert, France
tel: 31.22.72.92
4 rooms, 2 share bath, separate WC
2 rooms with private bath/WC
Double: 180F, Triple: 230F
Table d'Hôte: 75F per person
Open Easter to October 30
Very little English spoken
Region: Normandy, Michelin Map 231

The pretty old complex of La Croix de la Voulte is built of white, regional stone and dates from the 15th and 17th Centuries. All the guest bedrooms are found in an independent wing, and are newly renovated with much attention to detail. A high level of comfort prevails; each room has a private bathroom, soft carpets cover the stone floors and luxurious bedding assures a good night's sleep. Each room has a private entry and special character all its own. The largest bedroom is very regal with a massive old stone fireplace, king-sized four poster bed, old armoire and tapestry chairs. Another is more feminine in decor, with rich rose-colored wallpaper, matching curtains and complementing bedspreads. Low, beamed ceilings, light stone walls and lovely antique furniture add historical character to all the bedrooms. The tranquil courtyard is a pleasant outdoor location to enjoy a leisurely breakfast, although guests may also elect to pamper themselves by being served in their rooms. There is a refreshing pool available for guests' use on warm summer days. *Directions:* St-Lambert des Levées is located about 3 kilometers west of Saumur on the north bank of the Loire. Take D229 in the direction of St-Martin de la Place, pass the Saumur train station and continue 3 kilometers until you see a Chambres d'Hôtes sign directing you to turn into a driveway on the right.

LA CROIX DE LA VOULTE (Gîte de France)
Hosts: Monsieur & Madame Minder
St-Lambert des Levées
49400 Saumur, France
tel: 41.38.46.66
4 rooms, with private bathrooms
Double: 380-450F, Triple: 570F
Open all year
No Table d'Hôte
Fluent English spoken
Region: Loire Valley, Michelin Map 232

La Pastourelle is a low, stone farmhouse whose construction is typical of the Brittany region. A pleasing construction is formed by gray stones of varying sizes mortared together in a seemingly haphazard manner: in fact it is easy to pick out one large boulder that was simply left in place and incorporated into the front wall of the house. The Lédés and their two young sons live in a separate wing of their pretty farmhouse, offering guests an independent entry, salon, dining room and five guest bedrooms. A charming, country ambiance is felt throughout, created by Madame's collection of lovely antiques and special touches such as wildflower bouquets. The bedrooms are spotlessly clean and tastefully decorated in dainty flower-print wallpaper, softly colored carpets and crocheted bedspreads. Delicious Table d'Hôte dinners are served downstairs in the cozy dining room and often include local fish or grilled meats and regional specialties such as crepes or galettes. *Directions:* St-Lormel is located approximately 66 kilometers northwest of Rennes, near the town of Plancoet. From Plancoet, travel north on D768 for 1 kilometer, then turn left onto D19 towards St-Lormel. Before reaching the village, look for Chambres d'Hôtes signs indicating La Pastourelle that will lead to the Lédé's Breton farmhouse.

LA PASTOURELLE (*Gîte de France*)
Hostess: Madame Lédé
St-Lormel, 22130 Plancoet, France
tel: 96.84.03.77
5 rooms, with private bathrooms
Double: 205F, Triple: 255
Demi-pension: 160F per person
Open March through November
Very little English spoken
Region: Brittany, Michelin Map 230

The Chateau de Vergières' magic begins as you approach by way of a tree-lined lane ending at the stately, three-storey manor whose pastel facade is accented by white shuttered windows and heavy tiled roof. The rather formal exterior belies the warmth of welcome one finds within. For many years the chateau has been in the family of Marie-Andrée who has opened her heart and home to guests from all over the world. She is ably assisted by her gracious husband, Jean Pincedé. Inside as well as outside, the chateau reflects the patina of age displaying an ambiance of homey comfort. Quality country antiques are everywhere, yet nothing is contrived, cutely redone or decorator perfect. The dining room is especially outstanding with its beamed ceiling, fabulous antique armories, side board and long wooden table surrounded by French Provençal-style wooden chairs. Be sure to plan ahead so you can have the fun of sharing a meal here with your fellow guests. *Directions:* Vergières is located approximately 25 km southeast of Arles. From St-. Martin de Crau take D24 south toward La Dynamite and after 3 km watch for a small sign on the left side of the road to the Chateau de Vergières. Turn left at the sign. Continue for 4.3 km to the lane leading to the chateau.

CHATEAU DE VERGIÈRES
Hostess: Marie-Andrée Pincedé
Vergières, La Dynamite
13310 Saint Martin de Crau, France
tel: 90.47.17.16 fax: 90.47.38.30
6 rooms, with private bathrooms
Single: 800F, Double: 800F
Table d'Hôte: 250F per person
Credit cards: all major
Open March to October
Very good English spoken
Region: Provence, Michelin Maps 240, 245, 246

Michel and Josette Garret are former prize-winning dairy farmers who extend a warm, sincere welcome to their farm in the pastoral region north of Bordeaux. Their farmhouse is built in the typical regional style: long and low, of pretty warm-toned stone. They have completely renovated the interior; preserving the heavy beamed ceilings, exposing the light stone walls and adding cool tile floors and modern conveniences. Sharing an avid interest in local history and regional antiques, they have filled their home with lovely old pieces such as a huge Bordeaux armoire, a Louis XIV mantelpiece and a cherry wood grandfather clock. Bedrooms are prettily furnished and enhanced by French doors leading out to bucolic pasture lands. Since our last visit, an additional bedroom with private bathroom and WC has been added in a converted outbuilding. *Directions:* St-Martin de Laye is located approximately 30 kilometers northeast of Bordeaux. Leave Bordeaux on N89 to Libourne, then take D910 to St-Denis de Pile, where you will turn left over the bridge onto D22 towards Bonzac. Before arriving in St Martin de Laye, take the turn marked Gaudart Buisson. Turn left at the second driveway, and continue past the first farmhouse on the left to the Garret's house at the end of the driveway.

CHEZ GARRET (*Gîte de France*)
Hosts: Josette & Michel Garret
St Martin de Laye
33910 St Denis de Pile, France
tel: 57.49.41.37 fax: 57 49 41 37
3 rooms, with private bathrooms
Single: 170F, Double: 210-230F
Table d'Hôte: 80F per person
Open Easter through October 31
No English spoken
Region: Atlantic Coast, Michelin Map 233

Claudine and Christian Pinier are a most endearing young couple—you cannot help liking them. When we first met, they had an adorable, curly headed little girl and another baby on the way. Although she is a busy mother, Claudine runs her Bed and Breakfast with quiet efficiency and professionalism. The two-storey white stone house, located just across the street from the Loire, has belonged to Christian's family for over 150 years. Behind the house there is a garden where Claudine grows fresh vegetables for her home-cooked dinners, and beyond it stretch acres of apple and pear orchards that have been cultivated by Chritian's family for many generations. Inside, the house is basic: a central hallway when you enter that opens to a dining room on the left that also has a lounge area with sofa and chairs for guests. There are four bedrooms upstairs, each with its own bathroom. Ask for the corner bedroom in the back—I think this is by far the prettiest. It has a sweet floral print wallpaper, antique bed and beautiful armoire. Plus, with windows on two sides, it is very bright and cheerful. For those of you who do not expect everything to be decorator perfect and would enjoy sharing the family home of an exceptionally gracious, hardworking, young couple, the Piniers will certainly take good care of you. *Directions:* From Saumur, take D952 west along the Loire for 25 km. About 1 km after leaving St-Mathurin-sur-Loire, you will see the Pinier's home on your right.

CHEZ PINIER (Gîte de France)
Hosts: Claudine & Christian Pinier
118, rue du Roi Rene
49250 St-Mathurin-sur-Loire, France
tel: 41.57.02.00 fax: 41.57.31.90
4 rooms with private bathrooms
Double 225F-290F
Table d'Hôte: 90F per person, with wine
Good English spoken
Open all year
Region: Loire Valley, Michelin Map 232

The 16th-century "Prince of Poets," Ronsard, wrote some of his greatest love sonnets to Marie at the Manoir du Port-Guyet. However, the characterful old stone house had fallen into sad disrepair when it was purchased by Madame Valluet Deholin who has lovingly restored its original simple elegance. The house, built in the 15th Century as a hunting lodge for the Abbaye de Bourgueil, was never meant to be a fancy home. Madame Valluet Dehoin has taken great care to maintain the original ambiance. The patina of fine-quality antique furniture contrasts beautifully with the original walls and floors. Massive fireplaces attest to days long ago when hunters gathered before the open fire to warm themselves after a day of hunting. Although the walls are very thick, the home is sunny and cheerful as light streams in through tall casement windows. There are just three bedrooms, each individually decorated and authentically furnished in antiques. Your charming hostess, Madame Valluet Deholin, welcomes guests as friends in her home. *Directions:* From Bourgueil take D35 west to Saint Nicolas. About 700 meters beyond the church, turn left at a small street signposted Port Guyet. Almost immediately there is a road to the left. Do NOT take this, but continue down the hill for about 300 meters to where the road splits. Turn left here and you will see the gates to the Manoir du Port-Guyet immediately on your right with a brown and white sign saying "Historical Monument". Note: since our visit a sign has been put on the main road (D35) directing you to "Manoir du Port Guyet."

MANOIR DU PORT-GUYET (Gîte de France)
Hostess: Madame Geneviève Valluet Deholin
37140 St-Nicolas de Bourgueil, France
tel: 47.97.82.20 fax: 47.97.98.98
3 rooms with private bathrooms
Double 550-750F
Table d'Hôte 200F per person, includes wine
Very good English spoken
Region: Loire Valley, Michelin Map 232

Monsieur and Madame Lawrence are an interesting, well-travelled couple who enjoy a healthy, outdoor lifestyle in the Provençal region. Their lovely, golden-toned stone house is set on a tranquil hillside overlooking a breathtaking vista of vineyards and green hills. Guests have a separate entrance through French doors off a shady terrace. The guest bedroom has a mezzanine area for a third person, and is very tastefully decorated with a mixture of contemporary and antique furniture, Oriental rugs and a subtle color scheme. Some unusual and fascinating pieces such as a carved wooden chest from Monsieur and Madame's travels in Bali provide attractive accents to the room's decor. A spotless and well-equipped bathroom completes the comfortable accommodation. *Directions:* St-Pantaléon is located approximately 40 kilometers east of Avignon. Take N100 in the direction of Apt, turning left at the village of Coustellet towards Gordes. After passing the hamlet of Les Imberts, turn right, following signs for St Pantaléon, until coming to a crossroads. Continue straight through, avoiding the right turn into the village. Fifty meters farther, turn up the first small road on the left, and the first driveway on the right leads to the Lawrence home.

VILLA LA LEBRE (*Gîte de France*)
Hosts: Monsieur & Madame Lawrence
Pres de St-Pantaléon
84220 Gordes, France
tel: 90.72.20.74
1 room with private bath/WC
Double: 200F, Triple: 250F
No Table d'Hôte
Open all year
Good English spoken
Region: Provence, Michelin Maps 245, 246

Charles Henry de Valbray, affectionately known to family members as Charlie, has recently begun restoration and decoration of the Chateau de Saint Paterne, which has been in his family for over a century, but neglected and abandoned for the past 30 years. Henry IV used to rendezvous with his mistress here at Saint Paterne; his crest and the her initials can still be seen on the ceiling beam of one of the bedchambers. The magnificent bridal suite was Chorale's grandmother's room. It is large, overlooks the garden and in the morning the light plays on the yellow walls to cast a soft warm glow. The theme of the handsome Duck room reflects its name, and there is a single room for a child next to the bath. A ground floor room decorated in blue and white fabric and has a private entry and patio. All the rooms have direct dial phones and are individually decorated with family antiques and lovely fabrics. Guests are welcome to relax in the large salon where there usually is a cozy fire. The dining room is Charlie's pride and joy as he is the chef and delights in creating delicious dinners for his guests. Much work is still needed to bring the entire chateau back to the standard of luxury it once enjoyed, and Charlie has an endless list of enthusiastic plans. *Directions:* Take D311 from Alençon toward Mamers and Chartres. Look for the sign to the chateau just at the end of Alençon.

CHÂTEAU DE SAINT PATERNE (Gîte de France)
Host: Charles Henry de Valbray
72610 Saint Paterne, France
tel: 16.33.27.54.71 fax: 16.33.29.16.71
2 room/3 suites, with private bathrooms
Double: 630-780F
Table d'Hôte: 230F per person
Closed January & February
Good English spoken
Region: Normandy, Michelin Map 231

Words are inadequate to describe the perfection of La Ferme des Poiriers Roses: it is an absolute dream. To begin with, the home is a "picture-postcard" perfect Normandy farmhouse: a fantasy facade of crooked wood beams and cream colored plaster, with a steep roof, enhanced by gabled windows beneath which pink geraniums spill over from blue window boxes. The home is even more incredible inside—a virtual fantasy of flowers. Every niche and cranny is filled with enormous, exquisitely arranged bouquets of fresh, fragrant flowers. In addition, an unbelievable assortment of dried flowers, cleverly tied with pretty ribbons, hang from the rough hewn beamed ceilings, creating a whimsical canopy of color. All the flowers come from the garden and are dried and arranged by Elizabeth and her three daughters. Each of the cozy bedrooms has its own personality and shows the loving hand and artistic flair of Elizabeth. There are antique accents in each of the bedrooms, and, of course, flowers, flowers, flowers. And, best of all are the owners whose happy nature permeates their little inn. The entire family opens their hearts to you in an unsurpassed welcome. I should not close without mentioning the breakfast...no, I will leave that as a surprise. *Directions:* From Lisieux go north on D579 for about 5 km to Ouilly-le-Vicomte where you turn right on D98 signposted to St Philbert. Go about 4 km, turn to the right on D284. The farm is first road on your left.

LA FERME DES POIRIERS ROSES
Hosts: Elizabeth & Jacques Lecorneur
14130 St-Philbert-des-Champs, France
tel: 31.64.72.14   fax: 31.64.19.55
7 rooms with private bathrooms
Double 400-450F, Suite 600F
No Table d'Hôte
Open all year
Some English spoken
Region: Normandy, Michelin Map 231

Old mills are almost always extremely appealing, and Le Petit Moulin du Rouvre, dating back to 17th Century, is no exception. The quaint stone building is backed by a forest. One enters directly into the dining room that is cozy as can be with a cradle in front of a large fireplace. Stone walls, tiled floors, country-French table and chairs in the middle of the room, a wonderful antique armoire, and colorful plates on the walls make the room very warm and appealing. An adjacent parlor, somewhat more formal in decor, has windows opening onto the pond. There are four bedrooms that are quite small and basic in decor, but immaculately clean. The choice bedroom is "les Amis," decorated in blues and with an opening where you can look below and see the old water wheel. An added bonus if you plan to stay at Le Petit Moulin du Rouvre—Madame Michel is renowned for her ability in the kitchen and has even been featured in several magazines. She uses only fresh produce from the garden and specializes in the cuisine of Normandy and Brittany. *Directions:* From Rennes take N 137 for 40 km north toward St-Malo. Take the St-Pierre de Plesguen exit, then take the D10 toward Lanhelin. Before you reach Lanhelin, you will see the road leading to Le Petit Moulin du Rouvre well sign-posted on the right side of the road. (Along the way you will see another B&B sign, but it has another name.)

LE PETIT MOULIN DU ROUVRE (Gîte de France)
Hostess: Annie Michel
35720 St-Pierre de Plesguen, France
tel: 99.73.85.84
4 rooms, with private bathrooms
Double 270-280F
Table d'Hôte: 95F per person, without wine
Open all year
No English spoken
Region: Brittany, Michelin Map 230

The Chateau de Roussillon is an old fortified castle, partially in ruins, that is perched on a rock outcrop high above a deep valley. The existing castle and towers date from the 13th and 15th Centuries, but were built on the remains of a far more ancient fortress. Madame Hourriez offers extremely romantic accommodation in the ancient tower chapel. The large guest room has a private bath and an independent entrance off the upper stone courtyard. A high stone vaulted ceiling and exposed stone walls lend a very medieval feeling to this spacious room furnished entirely in dark wood antiques, Oriental rugs and tapestry wall hangings. A comfortable double bed is found near a window, set deep into the thick rock wall, offering a spectacular view over the valley below. A cozy fireplace corner beckons in the evenings or on cool autumn afternoons. Madame brings breakfast every morning to the room or to the outdoor table and chairs in the courtyard garden. For longer stays, Madame Hourriez has an equally picturesque, fully-equipped apartment for up to six people. *Directions:* St-Pierre la Feuille is located about 8 kilometers north of Cahors. Take N20 towards Paris and, once in the village of St-Pierre, look for a sign pointing to the right for Chateau de Roussillon.

CHATEAU DE ROUSSILLON (Gîte de France)
Hostess: Madame Marcelle Hourriez
St-Pierre la Feuille
46090 Cahors, France
tel: 65.36.87.05
1 room with private bathroom
Single: 330F, Double: 350F, Triple: 470F
No Table d'Hôte
Open all year
Very little English spoken
Region: Lot, Michelin Map 235

The du Réau family has resided in this dramatic building since it was built in 1808. The current host is the very cultured, yet down-to-earth Jean du Réau who has taken great pleasure in renovating his family home so that he could offer Bed and Breakfast accommodation in this tranquil, authentic French country home setting. Monsieur du Réau offers breakfast in an intimate style in his country kitchen, seated at a long wooden table facing an old stone fireplace and copper pots filled with graceful yellow wildflowers. The epitome of the French country gentleman, Monsieur sports a handlebar mustache and is most often found smoking his aromatic pipe. He was actually born in one of the beds upstairs, in the same room where one can admire a lovely portrait of his mother, painted when she was five years old. All of the bedrooms have been freshly renovated with tasteful wallpapers and furnished with impressive family antiques, mostly from the Empire period. This is a very special Bed and Breakfast where guests may experience a deeply ingrained, authentic sense of the past, complete with gracious host and comfortable surroundings. *Directions:* St-Rémy la Varenne is located about 23 kilometers east of Angers on the Loire's south bank. Take D952 to the village of St-Rémy la Varenne where Chambres d'Hôtes signs lead the way to Monsieur du Réau's driveway.

CHATEAU DES GRANGES (Gîte de France)
Host: Monsieur Jean du Réau
Bourg, 49250 St-Rémy la Varenne, France
tel: 41.57.02.13
3 rooms, all with shower/basin, share one WC
Double: 380F
No Table d'Hôte
Open all year; in winter by reservation only
Some English spoken
Region: Loire Valley, Michelin Map 232

Each summer Martin and Beth Silvester left the rain and chill of their native England to holiday in France. On each visit they looked for a place to retire and finally found the perfect spot, a handsome stone manor house—bright and cheerful inside with tall windows (framed in light green shutters) letting in the sun. After extensive renovations, they have turned one wing of their home into a Bed and Breakfast. A fabulous old wooden spiral staircase (dating back to the 1700's) winds up to three bedrooms that, although not decorator perfect are homey and comfortable. Ask for the blue bedroom at the top of the stairs: it is the most attractive with a lovely antique wooden sleigh bed, antique dresser, rich planked wooden floors, a modern bathroom with skylight and French casement windows overlooking the terrace. In the front of the manor is a large swimming pool, a welcome respite for a hot day after sightseeing. Even if you speak French, it might be a welcome relief to slip back into English again for a few days and not have to tax your vocabulary skills. *Directions:* St-Romain is located 95 km northeast of Bordeaux. Take the D2 east from Chalais. Just before Aubeterre, when the road forks, turn left on D10 (signposted Montmoreau). Manoir de la Sauzade is about 1 km on the left side of the road.

LA SAUZADE (Gîte de France)
Hosts: Beth & Martin Silvester
16210 St-Romain, France
tel: 45.98.63.93 fax pending
3 rooms, with private bathrooms
Double: 350F
Table d'Hôte, 100 per person, includes wine
Credit cards: None
Open Easter to October
Fluent English spoken
Region: Atlantic Coast, Michelin Map 233

The Arredondo family's old stone farmhouse lies in a hilly, forested region 20 kilometers north of the medieval town of Carcassonne. Monsieur and Madame and their two grown sons raise veal, sheep, fowl, cows and horses, as well as plenty of friendly tabby cats. The Arredondos offer a true country Bed and Breakfast experience, complete with guided horseback tours of the region and Table d'Hôte dinners. Their own farm products are featured at meals, that might include homemade patés and sausage followed by a chicken dish, garden vegetables and salad, local cheese, and dessert. The dining room is rustic and intimate, with a stairway at the far end leading up to the guest bedrooms. Located in a renovated attic, the rooms are small but very fresh and clean. Madame Arredondo has decorated each room individually with charming flower print and lace curtains, beds and night tables. *Directions:* Saissac is located southeast of Toulouse and 20 kilometers north of Carcassonne. Leave Carcassonne on N113 in the direction of Castelnaudary. After about 7 kilometers, turn right onto D629 and continue through the village of Montolieu, following signs for Saissac and Revel. Just before entering the village of Saissac, look for a Chambres d'Hôtes sign and the right-hand turn up a hill. Leave town and travel about 3 kilometers on a country road looking for a Chambres d'Hôtes sign directing to their driveway on the left.

DOMAINE DE L'ALBEJOT (*Gîte de France*)
Hosts: Monsieur & Madame Arredondo
11310 Saissac, France
tel: 68.24.44.03
5 rooms, 2 w/pvt WC/bath, others share
Double: 200-260F
Table d'Hôte: 70F per person
Open all year
Very little English, fluent Spanish
Region: Midi Pyrénées, Michelin Map 235

The flower-filled medieval village of Salers is perched on a high point in the mountainous region of central France. Officially classified as one of the prettiest villages in France, it is a picturesque jumble of quaint, cottage-style houses and shops, all built from regional gray stone and with slate roofs. Young hosts Claudine and Philippe Prudent offer travellers comfortable and practical accommodation in a separate wing of their historic house. Bedrooms are all similar in decor, featuring country-style beds, tables and chairs and small alcoves with shower, wash-basin and WC. Exposed ceiling beams and dormer windows add character to the functional rooms. Guest quarters are accessed through a peaceful green garden that has a magnificent view over the surrounding hills and valleys. Breakfast in served here in this tranquil, natural setting or, if preferred, in guest bedrooms. *Directions:* Salers is located approximately 35 kilometers north of Aurillac. Take D922 north towards Mauriac on a winding, hilly road, turning right onto D680 towards Salers. Travel through the village on narrow cobblestone streets all the way to the central square. Turn left down the rue des Nobles and look for a Chambres d'Hôtes sign marking the Prudent's house.

CHEZ PRUDENT (Gîte de France)
Hosts: Claudine & Philippe Prudent
Rue des Nobles
15410 Salers, France
tel: 71.40.75.36
6 rooms, with private bathrooms
Double: 202F, Triple: 253F
No Table d'Hôte
Open all year
Some English spoken
Region: Auvergne, Michelin Map 239

A large, ivy-covered house on a hill overlooking peaceful pasture lands is the setting for the Domaine des Hautes Cimes Bed and Breakfast. The Prunet family live in a house next door, thus offering completely private guest accommodation. Breakfast is usually served in the light, airy dining room of the guest house, furnished in country antiques with inviting details such as an old stone fireplace and beamed ceiling. The guest house also has an inviting salon with a television and comfortable seating. One bedroom is filled with family antiques, but most have simple, country-style pine furniture and provide basic comforts. *Directions:* La Salesse is located approximately 35 kilometers southeast of Aurillac. Scenic winding roads are the only way to reach this lovely, yet isolated spot. Leave Aurillac in the direction of Rodez, turning off after 4 kilometers, just after Arpajon sur Cère towards Vezac and Carlat. At the town of Raulhac, turn left onto D990 and after about 3 kilometers turn right onto small country road towards Brommes. At the next intersection turn left on D79 towards La Capelle Barrez. Continue for 3 kilometers, then turn right up a TINY lane that winds up to La Salesse. As you enter the hamlet, the Prunet's gate is straight ahead, while the road veers to the left and into the village.

DOMAINE DES HAUTES CIMES (Gîte de France)
Hosts: Monsieur & Madame Prunet
La Salesse, 12600 Mur de Barrez, France
tel: 65.66.14.27
6 rooms, all w/bath or shower, 1 w/private WC
Single: 115F, Double: 140-155F, Triple 135
No Table d'Hôte
Open all year
No English spoken
Region: Auvergne, Michelin Map 239

Although only about 20 years old, Aguzan, a pretty tiled roof home almost entirely laced with ivy, exudes an aura of agelessness. The living room with large fireplace, beamed ceiling and family antiques, reflects a sophisticated yet very comfortable, home-like ambiance. There are three bedrooms for guests. Our favorites were the two upstairs: One is a very prettily decorated single room overlooking the garden, the other, a double, attractively decorated with red and white wall paper and coordinating fabric on the bed. The rooms have a wash basin in a small adequate room that is separate from the bedroom and share a separate WC and bath. One of the best features of the house is the park-like rear garden. The owners, Monsieur and Madame Langer, do not speak English, but are gracious hosts and their home has an ambiance of spaciousness and refinement. *Directions:* Located 9 km northeast of La Rachel. Once in La Rochelle, take the D9 toward Puilboreau-Luçon (street Maaius-la Croix). After the village St-Xandre, take the road on the right toward La Sauzaie. In La Sauzaie go in the direction of Usseau, then the first road on the right (street du Chateau). The second lane to your left leads to Aguzan.

AGUZAN (Gîte de France)
Hostess: Annick Langer
Rue du Chateau, La Sauzaie
17138 Saint Xandre, France
tel: 46.37.22.65
3 rooms share 1 WC & bath
Single: 190F, Double: 240F
No Table d'Hôte
Credit cards: None
Open all year
No English spoken
Region: Atlantic Coast, Michelin Map 233

Le Prieuré Ste Anne is a favorite on our list of Bed and Breakfasts, offering a warm welcome in a tranquil, appealing setting. This 15th-century cottage recalls the days of Joan of Arc with its low beamed ceilings, walk-in fireplaces and old stone walls. Madame Caré is a motherly hostess who obviously takes great pleasure in welcoming guests to her charming, ivy-covered home. Her well tended garden provides fresh flower bouquets throughout her rooms that are furnished in highly polished family antiques. Bedrooms are comfortable and extremely romantic with exposed stone walls, old fireplaces and charming stone window seats. Small paned, lead-glass windows look out over the peaceful courtyard and secret garden. A hidden path leads up to this green haven where one is tempted to spend a lazy afternoon with book in hand or simply listening to the occasional bird. It is the fortunate traveller indeed who has the chance to stay at this enchanting Bed and Breakfast. *Directions:* Savonnières is located about 11 kilometers west of Tours on the south bank of the Loire via D7 in the direction of Villandry. Once in the village of Savonnières look for Chambres d'Hôtes signs that lead to Madame Caré's driveway.

LE PRIEURÉ SAINTE-ANNE (Gîte de France)
Hostess: Madame Lucette Caré
10, rue Chaude
Joué les Tours
37510 Savonnières, France
tel: 47.50.03.26
1-2-bedroom suite with one bathroom
Double 275F
No Table d'Hôte
Open all year
No English spoken
Region: Loire Valley, Michelin Map 232

The Lethuilliers built their Norman dream house seven years ago near the picturesque port town of Fécamp and the spectacular cliffs of Étretat. The entire house is furnished in lovely antiques, complemented by pretty flowered wallpapers, Oriental rugs and fresh flower arrangements. Madame Lethuillier proudly displays her collections of brass and copper artifacts on the living room mantel, as well as a fine collection of old plates that once belonged to her grandmother. Madame Lethuillier is a talented seamstress, and her artistic flair is evident in every room, creating a pleasing feeling of home-like elegance. Breakfast can be enjoyed either in the inviting salon (complete with tabby cat curled up on a chair cushion) or, weather permitting, on the terrace overlooking the front garden and goldfish pond. The Lethuillers do not speak English, but their British daughter-in-law lives nearby and is happy to stop by to help with any communication difficulties. *Directions:* Senneville is located approximately 45 kilometers northeast of Le Havre via D940 changing to D925 after Fécamp: on D925 the route is well-marked by signs for Chambres d'Hôtes. Follow a country lane bordered by wildflowers, turning right at a small sign for Val de la Mer.

CHEZ LETHUILLIER (*Gîte de France*)
Hostess: Mireille Lethuillier
Val de la Mer, Senneville sur Fécamp
76400 Fécamp, France
tel: 35.28.41.93
3 rooms, 2 with private WC/shower
Double: 250F, Triple: 320F
No Table d'Hôte
Open all year
No English spoken
Region: Normandy, Michelin Map 231

Located in the heart of the Burgundy wine region, Maryse and Philippe Viardot's charming home is an ideal base from which to explore the surrounding countryside and sample the renowned local wines. Although their 200-year-old house is found in a small village, it remains a quiet haven; set back from the street and bordered by a peaceful garden. Madame is an energetic hostess with a real flair for decoration who has managed to capture just the right blend of contemporary design and old-fashioned ambiance in her home and guest rooms. Bedrooms are highly tasteful combinations of soft color schemes, pretty country antiques and carefully-chosen artwork. Fresh flowers and plants personalize the attractive rooms, making guests feel right at home. Warm, sunny mornings mean breakfast in the garden, while in cooler weather it is served in the shelter of a pleasant, glass-enclosed verandah. *Directions:* Senozan is located approximately 15 kilometers north of Macon. Take N6 towards Tournus, turning off after 10 kilometers following signs for Senozan. Just after entering the village, look for a small stone church on the right. Across the street you will see a stone entryway, set back between two houses, and marked with a Chambres d'Hôtes sign. Turn left and drive through this portal to the end of the driveway, passing the houses closest to the road.

CHEZ VIARDOT (*Gîte de France*)
Hosts: Maryse & Philippe Viardot
Rue du Chateau
Le Bourg Senozan 71260, France
tel: 85.36.00.96
6 rooms, 4 w/private bath, 3 share 1 bath/WC
Double: 255F, Triple: 310F
No Table d'Hôte
Open all year
Very little English spoken
Region: Burgundy, Michelin Map 243

The Jezequel family offers old-fashioned hospitality and delicious farm-fresh meals at the quaint Ferme Auberge de Sepvret. Their 300-year-old home is covered with ivy and surrounded by a pretty, flower-filled garden. Farm inn meals are served in the intimate and home-like dining room furnished with round wooden tables adorned with bouquets of fresh flowers and a cheerful selection of tablecloths. Traditional home-cooked fare features regional specialties such as farci poitevin, a type of soufflé made from garden greens (spinach, cabbage, parsley and sorrel), eggs, sour cream and spices. Simple country charm is felt throughout the house and in the guest bedrooms that are furnished with brass beds, old armoires and flowered wallpapers. Large windows open out to the back garden, letting in plenty of light and fresh air. Days usually begin with a romantic and peaceful breakfast enjoyed outdoors at a table set under the trees. *Directions:* Sepvret is located about 45 kilometers southwest of Poitiers. Take N10 towards Angoulême for 2 kilometers, then turn off onto N11 (that later becomes D150) and travel in the direction of Niort, la Rochelle and Saintes. Turn right after about 40 kilometers onto D108 to Sepvret. Once in the village, follow signs for Chambres d'Hôtes and Ferme Auberge that lead to the Jezequel's home.

FERME AUBERGE DE SEPVRET (Gîte de France)
Hosts: Françoise & Claude Jezequel
Sepvret, 79120 Lezay, France
tel: 49.07.33.73
5 rooms, 3 with private bathrooms
Double: 150-190F
Table d'Hôte, 65F per person, without wine
Open May to September
Very little English spoken
Region: Atlantic Coast, Michelin Map 233

Emile and Gilberte Moynier are wonderfully warm and solicitous hosts. Their 17th-century manor house is set back from the main road behind trees framing a magical view of the green valley and distant mountain peaks. Gilberte has decorated each of the guest bedrooms differently, combining classic country charm with her own personal artistic style. Les Hirondelles (The Nightingales) has dainty, mauve-flowered curtains and matching bedspreads on lovely old wooden beds complemented by a matching armoire, while Les Tilleuls (The Lime Trees) is bright and fresh with hand painted furniture and tall windows looking out over the front garden. A separate dining room/kitchen/lounge area is available for guests' use. Formerly a sheep stall, it now has a cozy ambiance created by low, vaulted ceilings and walls of exposed stone sheltering rustic country antiques and a cheerful fire blazing in the hearth. *Directions:* Serres is located approximately 34 km southwest of Gap. Take D994 past Veynes to the town of Aspres sur Bruech. Leave town on N75 going south towards Nice. About 6 km later, before the village of Serres, look for signs for L'Alpillonne and a sign advertising Chambres d'Hôtes; English spoken. The Moynier's driveway is on the left and is easy to miss.

L'ALPILLONNE (Gîte de France)
Hosts: Gilberte & Emile Moynier
La Plaine de Sigottier
Serres 05700 Sigottier, France
tel: 92.67.08.98
3 rooms, 1 w/private shower/WC*
*2 share 1 bath/WC
Single: 200F, Double: 250F, Triple: 300F
No Table d'Hôte
Open June 15 to September 30
Good English spoken
Swimming pool in garden
Region: Maritime Alps, Michelin Map 245

Le Chaufourg is a dream—absolute perfection. The home has been in the Dambier family "since the beginning" and today Georges Dambier has created from what was originally a rustic farmhouse dating back to the 1700's, an exquisite work of art. Although when Monsieur Dambier began remodeling the task was formidable, all the ingredients were there. The house, built of beautiful soft-yellow stone, already had charm, and its location on a bend of the Isle river, was idyllic. Although strategically located in the heart of the Dordogne and conveniently near access roads to all the major sites of interest, once within the gates leading to the romantic front courtyard, one feels insulated from the real world. The exterior of the house is like a fairytale cottage with its white shuttered doors and windows, laced with ivy and surrounded by masses of colorful flower gardens. Inside, the magic continues. Each guest room is entirely different, yet each has the same mood of quiet, country elegance with natural stucco walls of warm honey-beige, stunning antiques, and tones of soft whites and creams. Nothing is stiff nor intimidating—just the elegant harmony of country comfort created by an artist. And, Georges Dambier adds the final ingredient—the warmth of genuine hospitality. *Directions:* From Périgueux take N89 southwest in the direction of Bordeaux for about 32 km. to Sourzac (about 3 km before Mussidan). On the right side of the road, you will see the entrance to Le Chaufourg.

LE CHAUFOURG EN PERIGORD
Host: Georges Dambier
24400 Sourzac, France
tel: 53.81.01.56 fax: 53.82.94.87
9 rooms with private bathrooms
Double from 830-1,180F, suites from 1,430F
Open all year; 2 day minimum
Table d'Hôte, occasionally available
Credit cards: all major
Very good English spoken
Region: Dordogne, Michelin Map 233

Located in the heart of the Brittany countryside, the Lollier's farm is in a peaceful, scenic setting of wooded hills, pastures and streams. There is an inviting garden and front terrace leading up to this typically Breton, gray and white stone farmhouse. Inside, the attic guest rooms are simple yet charming, with sloping roofs and skylight windows. Two flights of a stairway that becomes narrow and steep at the top must be negotiated to arrive at the small sitting area on the top-floor landing that leads to the bedrooms. Furnishings are contemporary and tasteful, and the shared bathroom has fresh pine paneling. In the mornings, a bountiful breakfast is served downstairs in the cozy dining room: Madame Lollier's hot crepes, coffee cakes, homemade preserves, fruit juice, and coffee, tea or hot chocolate provide a delicious way to start the day. An old wooden chest is filled with a plate collection, while pretty wood floors, a country armoire, grandfather clock and dried flower arrangements combine to create a very inviting and welcoming ambiance. *Directions:* Spézet is located approximately 41 kilometers northeast of Quimper. Take D15 towards Gourin, turning left onto D82 towards Spézet after about 32 kilometers. Just after entering Spézet, turn right just before a restaurant, La Cremaillerie. Continue following Chambres d'Hôtes signs for about 1.5 kilometers to the Lollier's two-storey house on the right.

PENDREIGNE (Gîte de France)
Hosts: Monsieur & Madame Lollier
29540 Spézet, France
tel: 98.93.80.32
2 rooms, share bath & WC
Single: 140F, Double: 180F*
*Full English breakfast included
No Table d'Hôte
Open all year
No English spoken
Region: Brittany, Michelin Map 230

If you are looking for a Bed and Breakfast convenient to Paris and close to Fontainebleau, Vivescence, located in the pretty village of Thomery, makes a good choice. The home, ideally located on the main square opposite the church, looks like most of its neighbors from the front. However, a surprise awaits: the back of the house opens up onto an expansive park. The well-tended lawn sweeps to a rim of flowers and beautiful trees although it cannot compete with Fontainebleau, for a private home, the garden is truly outstanding. Vivescence is also a health center, and hosts various groups and fitness seminars. There are some guest rooms available in the annex where the conferences are held, but these do not have much personality. Ask for one of the large bedrooms in the main house overlooking the garden. An added bonus is a heated indoor swimming pool that opens onto its own pretty walled garden. In addition, there is a sauna that guests may use. *Directions:* Thomery is located 7 km east of Fontainebleau. From Fontainebleau Chateau, take the N6 east for approximately 4 km and then turn left on the D301 (signposted Champagne, Thomery) and follow the signs to Thomery centre. Vivescence is located on the main square across the street from the church.

VIVESCENCE (Gîte de France)
Hostess: Brigitte Stacke
9, Place Greffulhe
77810 Thomery, France
tel: 1.60.96.43.96 fax: 1.60.96.41.13
10 rooms, with private bathrooms
Double: 370F
Table d'Hôte: 120F per person, includes wine
Credit cards: VS MC
Open all year except Christmas
Fluent English spoken
Region: Ile de France, Michelin Map 237

The Juchereaus offer home-like accommodation in their rustic farmhouse, located on the edge of the scenic Marais de Poitevin. The Marais is a lush and verdant marshland full of canals and waterways where picturesque flat boats reminiscent of Venetian gondolas are used for transportation. The Juchereau's charming guest bedrooms are decorated with matching curtains and bedspreads and furnished with a harmonious mix of antiques and reproductions. These young hosts are friendly and solicitous of their guests, and offer Table d'Hôte dinners featuring fresh home cooking. Their informal, familial dining room has exposed stone walls and is furnished in a rustic style with ladder-backed chairs and a country chest filled with faience plates. On warm mornings, the sunny, peaceful back garden is a pleasant place to breakfast or simply give in to the beckoning lawn chairs. *Directions:* Le Thou is located approximately 18 kilometers east of La Rochelle. Take D939 towards Surgeres for about 15 kilometers, then turn right onto D5 in the direction of Rochefort. Two kilometers later turn left towards Le Thou. Follow signs to the small settlement of Maisonneuve and then look for a Chambres d'Hôtes sign marking the Juchereau's shuttered farmhouse.

CHEZ JUCHEREAU (Gîte de France)
Hosts: Monsieur & Madame Juchereau
11, rue Maisonette du Bois
Maisonneuve, Le Thou, France
17290 Aigrefeuille, France
tel: 46.35.72.91
4 rooms, all w/pvt shower/share 2 hall WCs
Double: 170F, Triple: 220F
Table d'Hôte: 60F per person
Open all year
Very little English spoken
Region: Atlantic Coast, Michelin Map 233

Located near the historical ruins of a fortified castle, Le Queffiou is an attractive, turn-of-the-century house with a large garden. Refined hostess Madame Sadoc offers a very warm welcome, along with highly comfortable accommodation including spotless, luxurious bathrooms supplied with big fluffy towels and sweet-smelling soap. The bedrooms are feminine and traditionally French in their decor and furnishings except for one that is a complete departure in style: high-tech modern. A solicitous hostess, Madame Sadoc pays great attention to detail and is a gourmet cook. Breakfasts are copious: the usual French bread and strong coffee, tea or chocolate accompanied by hot, buttery croissants, coffee cake and fresh fruit. Table d'Hôte dinners at Le Queffiou are enjoyable and delicious, served with style in the intimate dining room. *Directions:* Tonquédec is located approximately 25 kilometers northwest of Guingamp. Travelling on D767 from Guingamp, turn onto C2 just after Cavan towards Tonquédec. Go through the village, following signs for the Chateau de Tonquêdec. Five hundred meters before the chateau, there is a Chambres d'Hôtes sign directing you to turn left into the Sadoc's driveway.

LE QUEFFIOU (Gîte de France)
Hostess: Odette Sadoc
Route du Chateau
22140 Tonquédec, France
tel: 96.35.84.50
5 rooms, with private bathrooms
Double: 330-350F
Table d'Hôte: 150F per person
Open all year
Very little English spoken
Region: Brittany, Michelin Map 230

Manoir de l'Hormette is a beautiful farmhouse in Aignerville. The garden setting is very restful, protected and enclosed by the stone walls. The grounds are meticulous, beautifully groomed and planted. Inside, the warmth of the family and their welcome is evident in the decor and their thoughtful touches. There is a nice choice of accommodations: an apartment on the first floor in the main house with a double room, a twin room and a small single room with sleigh bed and TV. In addition, there are two separate cottages: "Le Petite Maison" and "La Bretonniere." The kitchen is a masterpiece and Monsieur's collection of homemade vinegars sits above the window ledge. The dining room is very handsome, and outside tables await a sunny morning for a wonderful breakfast repast. *Directions:* Located 15 kilometers northwest of Bayeux off the N13. Travelling the N13 from Bayeux to Isigny, take the Aignerville exit to the left. Six hundred meters from the highway, at the first cross-road, turn left. The Manoir is 150 meters on the right at the second white fence.

MANOIR DE L'HORMETTE (Gîte de France)
Hosts: Monsieur & Madame Yves Corpet
Aignerville
14710 Trévières, France
tel: 31.22.51.79 fax: 31.22.75.99
3 rooms, 2 cottages/duplex with kitchen, 1 Studio
Double: 490-940F (940F rate for 5 people)
Table d'Hôte: 250F per person
Credit cards: VS, MC
Open end of March to end of December
Some English spoken
Region: Normandy, Michelin Map 231

The Rocagel's contemporary chalet is found on a hillside overlooking a lovely Alpine panorama. Their pretty home was recently built, and has charming rustic touches such as flower-filled window boxes and a light-toned wood balcony and shutters. Inside, home-like knick-knacks and contemporary decor create an unsophisticated, informal atmosphere. Guest bedrooms have independent entries, modern furnishings and bright color schemes. Madame Rocagel is a very fastidious hostess who keeps her home spotlessly clean and takes a personal interest in her guests, offering a wealth of information on local sights and activities. She is rightfully proud of her culinary skills and enjoys offering Table d'Hôte dinners featuring regional specialties. We dined on a savory meal of sausage and potatoes with cheese and onions, accompanied by green salad, local cheeses and a strawberry tart. *Directions:* Trevignin is located approximately 10 kilometers east of Aix les Bains. Leave Aix crossing the overpass above the freeway to the village of Mouxy on the Route du Revard. At Mouxy, turn left onto D913, still following Route du Revard. Continue past Trévignin and turn left towards St-Victor at an intersection marked by a large stone cross. The Rocagel's two-storey home is the first house on the left.

LA REVARDIRE (Gîte de France)
Hosts: Monsieur & Madame Rocagel
Hameau de St-Victor
Trévignin 73100 Aix-les-Bains, France
tel: 79.61.59.12
3 rooms, 1 with private bathroom
Double: 265-350F
Table d'Hôte: 85F *
* Gourmet meal 190F per person
Open all year
No English spoken
Region: French Alps, Michelin Map 244

The Le Rouzic's attractive, contemporary house is situated on the picturesque Trinité inlet overlooking peaceful sailboats moored between gray rock cliffs and dark green pines. Monsieur and Madame are a young couple who have recently converted part of their home into comfortable Bed and Breakfast accommodation with scenic views over the water and surrounding countryside. The bedrooms are sparkling clean and furnished in a tasteful, modern style with fresh pine wood or wallpapered walls. The Le Rouzics invite guests to make themselves at home and enjoy the television and stereo in the casual salon. An adjoining glassed in verandah with a glorious southern exposure is a relaxing spot to enjoy breakfast above the pretty inlet. Early-morning guests are even treated to the sight of playful wild rabbits who inhabit the surrounding fields and hedgerows. *Directions:* La Trinité sur Mer and the village of Le Latz are located approximately 26 kilometers west of Vannes. Take N165 to Auray, then D28 towards Locmariaquer and La Trinité sur Mer. After crossing the Pont (bridge) de Kerisper, take the first right and continue straight ahead, following signs for Le Chateau du Lac. Take the dirt road that circles the chateau to the left, following it around to the right, and look for arrows directing you to Chambres d'Hôtes. The Le Rouzic's driveway and white Breton-style house will be on the right.

LA MAISON DU LATZ (*Gîte de France*)
Hostess: Nicole Le Rouzic
Le Latz, 56470 La Trinité sur Mer, France
tel: 97.55.80.91 fax: 97.55.86.03
4 rooms, with private bathrooms
Double: 250-300F, Triple: 400F
Table d'Hôte: 110F per person, without wine
Open all year
Very little English spoken
Region: Brittany, Michelin Map 230

In the heart of the Chateaux country is the well-priced Manoir de Chaix, where you can enjoy both real country ambiance and excellent accommodations. The handsome two storey farm house, dating back to the 16th Century, is owned by the hospitable Suzanne Fillon. She speaks no English, but you can communicate with her son and daughter, both who live on the farm and speak English. On the property are a swimming pool and clay tennis court. Madame Fillon can loan you rackets, and if you wish, her son can give you lessons. Dinner is served family-style in the large dining room. A private entrance leads to the spiral stone staircase that leads up the tower to the bedrooms that are decorated outstandingly. All have some antiques and headboards prettily upholstered in fabric that matches the drapes. My least favorite room is the most expensive one. So do not splurge, just take one of the "standard" rooms. Best of all I liked "La Varidaine," a lovely room with a stunning antique armoire, beamed ceiling, and gabled room overlooking the countryside. If you are on a tight budget, "La Touraine" is a tiny, but very pretty room that rents for 270F. In the morning Madame Fillon serves a delicious breakfast of fresh juice, home made jam and honey from the estate. *Directions:* From Tours, take N143 south to Truyes. Then turn east on D45 (toward Bléré) for 2 km and turn right at the Chambres d'Hôtes sign.

LE MANOIR DE CHAIX (Gîte de France)
Hostess: Suzanne Fillon
37320 Truyes, France
tel: 47.43.42.73
4 rooms, with private bathrooms
double 270-400F
Table d'Hôte 80F, includes wine
Open all year
Some English spoken by son & daughter
Region: Loire Valley, Michelin Maps 232, 238

The ancient Roman town of Vaison la Romaine is found in a hilly, wooded setting in northern Provence. Just outside of town on a high point affording panoramic views of the surrounding mountains and plains, the Delesse's 150-year-old stone house offers a refined haven for travellers. The guest bedroom is a bit removed from the main part of the house, well soundproofed by thick old stone walls and accessible from an independent entrance. French doors lead out to an intimate terrace overlooking a restful view of fields and distant hills. The room is tastefully decorated and very comfortable, with a writing table and bookcase stocked for guest enjoyment. Monsieur and Madame are both teachers, and specialize in French and English respectively, so communication with their English-speaking guests is no problem, and convivial breakfasts are enjoyed together in their cozy beamed breakfast room or outside in the tranquil front courtyard. A pool has been added since our visit. *Directions:* Vaison la Romaine is located about 18 kilometers north of Carpentras via D938. If coming from Avignon, follow signs to Orange, and then for Vaison la Romaine. Upon entering the town, turn left at the first traffic light, then take the first left at the high school, then right, then left again. The Delesse's driveway is on the right and is marked with a Chambres d'Hôtes sign.

CHEZ DELESSE (*Gîte de France*)
Francoise & Claude Delesse
Chemin de l'Ioou
Le Brusquet, 84110 Vaison la Romaine, France
tel: 90.36.38.38
1 room with private bath
Double: 250F, Triple: 320F (child)
No Table d'Hôte
Open all year
Very good English spoken
Region: Provence, Michelin Maps 245, 246

The Haute Ville of Vaison-la-Romaine, an unspoiled fortified village rising steeply from the banks of the L'Ouveze River, has a superb Bed and Breakfast, owned by the Verdier family. Jean, an architect, and Aude, his pretty wife, moved from Paris to the ancient walled city of Vaison-La-Romaine in 1975. They worked together to transform the ruins of what was once a part of the bishop's palace, into a gracious home for themselves and their three sons. Three of the bedrooms are kept for Bed and Breakfast guests who also have a private entrance onto the street and an exclusive lounge. Of the guest rooms, my favorites were the twin bedded rooms that have more of an antique ambiance than the double bedded room that has a bit of an art deco feel. Aude serves breakfast on an enticing terrace snuggled amongst the rooftops, or when the weather is chilly, in the family dining room. Although Aude and Jean speak only a smattering of high school English, their absolutely genuine warmth will guarantee a very special stay. *Directions:* Vaison la Romaine is located 45 km northeast of Avignon. When you reach the town of Vaison la Romaine, cross the river and climb the narrow road to the Ville Médievalé. The L'Évêché is on the right side of the main street, rue de L'Évêché.

L'ÉVÊCHÉ (Gîte de France)
Hosts: Aude & Jean Loup Verdier
Rue de l'Évêché, Ville Médievalé
84110 Vaison la Romaine, France
tel: 90.36.13.46 fax: 90.36.32.43
4 rooms, with private bathrooms
Double: 330-370F
No Table d'Hôte
Credit cards: None
Open January to December
Very little English spoken
Region: Provence, Michelin Maps 245, 246

In French, La Maison aux Volets Bleus means The House of the Blue Shutters—indeed, the bright cobalt shutters of the Maret's charming home can be seen from far below the hilltop town of Venasque. Follow a winding road up from the plains to this ancient town that is now a haven for painters and art lovers. An old stone archway leads to the Maret's doll-like walled garden and their picturesque home filled with colorful dried flower bouquets hanging from every available rafter. Each bedroom is unique and decorated with Martine Maret's artistic flair for harmonious colors, Provençal prints, and simple, attractive furnishings. Martine and her husband Jerome are an energetic young couple with many talents who enjoy welcoming guests into their home and to their table. Reserve well in advance in order to enjoy a stay with the Marets at the Maison aux Volets Bleus. *Directions:* Venasque is located approximately 8 kilometers southeast of Carpentras via D4 towards Apt. Look for the turnoff marked Venasque to the right up a hill. Continue to the fountain square (Place de la Fontaine) and look for a Chambres d'Hôtes sign to the left indicating the arched entry to the Maret's home.

LA MAISON AUX VOLETS BLEUS (Gîte de France)
Hosts: Martine & Jerome Maret
Place des Bouviers
Le Village, 84210 Venasque, France
tel: 90.66.03.04
6 rooms, with private bathrooms
Double: 280-350F
Table d'Hôte: 110F per person, without wine
Open March 15 through November 11
Good English spoken
Region: Provence, Michelin Maps 245, 246

The imposing, red-brick Chateau de Jallanges is skillfully looked after by Stéphane and Danièle Ferry-Balin. A fortified castle stood on this site in the 1200's, and the current castle built in 1480 reflects the beginning of the Renaissance period in French history. It is easy to take a mental journey back in time while enjoying a house specialty aperitif on the back terrace that overlooks a green lawn shaded by three stately old cedar trees. The Balins strive to maintain a relaxing, aristocratic ambiance and to offer their guests a chance to experience an authentic taste of life in a French Renaissance castle. Breakfasts are gourmet delights that include two kinds of fresh, homemade pastries and natural fruit juices in addition to the usual breakfast fare. The guest suites each have two small, intimate bedrooms furnished with a delicate feminine touch. One room features a romantic brass bed covered with a pretty lace bedspread. Also at guests' disposal are an elegant wood-paneled salon and a billiard room. Another wing of the castle is open to the public for tours and tastings of local wines. In addition "Promenades" with the chateaux own horses and coach are available as are balloon trips and helicopter rides. *Directions:* Vernou sur Brenne is located approximately 12 kilometers east of Tours on the north bank of the Loire. Take N152 to Vouvray, then D46 to Vernou sur Brenne. Follow signs for the Chateau de Jallanges.

CHATEAU DE JALLANGES (Gîte de France)
Hosts: Danièle & Stéphane Ferry-Balin
Vernou sur Brenne, 37210 Vouvray, France
tel: 47.52.01.71
3 rooms, 2 Suites, all with pvt bath/WC
Double: 650-850f, Suites 1300F
Table d'Hôte: 250F per person, includes wine
Open all year
Good English spoken
Region: Loire Valley, Michelin Maps 232, 238

The attractive and friendly Porret family offer travellers comfortable accommodation in a newly renovated part of their chalet-style house. Monique and Joseph paid close attention to detail when remodeling their guest quarters, adding welcome conveniences such as a pine-paneled kitchen and completely independent entry. The four guest bedrooms are all very similar, each with a private shower and WC and French doors leading to a private balcony. A fresh, clean feeling pervades the rooms that are tastefully decorated with warm, textured wall coverings and contemporary furniture. La Cascade is an ideal stopping place for travellers seeking reasonably priced, independent accommodation with modern comfort, located in the heart of the scenic French Alps. *Directions:* Vesonne is located approximately 30 kilometers south of Annecy via N508 in the direction of Albertville. About 3 kilometers before the town of Faverges, look for a sign for Col de la Forclaz (Forclaz Pass) to the left that leads through the village of Vesonne. Go through the village, following signs for Col de la Forclaz. Just after crossing a bridge, look for the Porret's driveway on the left that is marked with a Chambres d'Hôtes sign.

LA CASCADE (Gîte de France)
Hosts: Monique & Joseph Porret
83 Chemin de la Forge
Vesonne, 74210 Faverges, France
tel: 50.44.65.48
4 rooms, with private bathrooms
Double: 180F, Triple: 230F
No Table d'Hôte, but kitchen available
Open all year
Very little English spoken
Region: French Alps, Michelin Map 244

The location of the 17th-century Domaine des Jeanne is really prime. It has a superb setting, perched above the Aisen river with a lawn rolling right down to the water's edge. Another plus is that, although it is insulated by its own private park, the mansard-roofed manor is only steps from the quaint village of Vic-sur-Aisne. The entrance is not impressive: a hallway with a soccer pin ball machine (that undoubtedly some of the guests enjoy). Beyond is a parlor whose main attribute is its view of the river. By far the most attractive room in the house is the dining room with a massive, beautifully carved fireplace rising almost to the ceiling. On the far wall, windows open onto a stunning view of lawn, flowers, trees and the gentle river flowing by below. Madame Martner enjoys cooking and in the evening the tables are prettily set with fresh flowers, good linens, and the sparkle of wine glasses. The bedrooms are simple in decor, but each has a private bathroom, and best of all, a magnificent view over the park-like grounds to the lovely river. On the terrace behind the manor, also with a view out of the river, is a very nice swimming pool that offers a refreshing respite after a day of sightseeing. *Directions:* Take the tiny lane, sign-posted rue Dubarle, that is just off the main square in town. The Domaine des Jeanne is located just down the little lane on the right.

DOMAINE DES JEANNE (Gîte de France)
Hosts: Anne & Jean Claude Martner
Rue Dubarle
02290 Vic-sur-Aisne, France
tel: 23.55.57.33
5 rooms with private bathrooms
Double 320F, Triple 390F
Table d'Hôte 85F per person
Open May 15 to October
Very little English spoken
Region: Champagne, Michelin Map 237

Ginette and Yvon live on a sheep farm in an idyllic mountain setting of which most city dwellers can only dream. Their friendly white furry dog and several tabby cats cluster at the threshold of their charming old chalet of regional stone and weathered wood. A very casual, home-like atmosphere reigns inside the 158-year-old house where Monsieur and Madame have raised five children and now offer guest accommodation in two attic bedrooms on the third floor. Rooms are furnished with wooden beds, tables and chairs and each has a private shower and washing area. Old exposed beams, rafters and natural wood walls add a rustic, mountain feeling, that is enhanced by the lovely view from the balconies over green meadows dotted with trees and wildflowers. The soothing sound of a rushing stream provides a restful nighttime lullaby. Chez Avrillon is a good base for hikers and travellers seeking simple comforts in an unspoiled Alpine setting. *Directions:* Les Villards sur Thones is located approximately 25 kilometers east of Annecy. Take D909 in the direction of La Clusaz that passes right by the town of Les Villards sur Thones. Just after town, turn to the right off the main road following a sign for Chambres d'Hôtes with a green arrow. Turn left at the next intersection and look for a driveway leading to the Avrillon's chalet on the right.

CHEZ AVRILLON (Gîte de France)
Hosts: Ginette & Yvon Avrillon
Les Villaz
74230 Les Villards sur Thones, France
tel: 50.02.04.30
2 rooms with private showers, share 1 WC
Double: 160F
Table d'Hôte: 65F per person
Open all year
No English spoken
Region: French Alps, Michelin Map 244

Villars les Dombes is a small town located in the heart of a forested region that is dotted with thousands of small lakes. The George family lives in a quiet suburb on the edge of town where they offer Bed and Breakfast accommodation to travellers. Their house has thick stone walls and old beamed ceilings that attest to its 300-year history. The former attic has been renovated into a fresh, cheerful guest apartment offering a kitchenette, bedroom with private bath and a fold-out sofa in the sitting area. The bedroom is prettily decorated with blue flowered wallpaper and the bathroom is very modern, well-equipped and spotlessly clean. Exposed beams and a bouquet of daisies add charm to the kitchen and sitting area that is furnished in light pine furniture and pale green wallpaper. A stay with the Georges means a high level of comfort and privacy in a quiet setting. *Directions:* Villars les Dombes is located approximately 30 kilometers northeast of Lyon. Leaving Lyon, take N83, following signs for Strasbourg and Bourg en Bresse. Once in the town of Villars les Dombes, look for Chambres d'Hôtes sign in front of the pharmacy. Turn right and head out of town for about a half mile, until another Chambres d'Hôtes sign directs into the George's driveway on the right.

CHEZ GEORGE (*Gîte de France*)
Hosts: Therese & Maurice George
Les Petits Communaux
01330 Villars les Dombes, France
tel: 74.98.05.44
2 rooms with private baths
Double: 200F, Triple: 260F
No Table d'Hôte *
*kitchenette available to guests
Open all year
No English spoken
Region: Burgundy, Michelin Map 244

When Christine and Xavier Ferry bought Ferme du Chateau, it looked absolutely hopeless: no water, no electricity, cows and pigs living in the house. But, with the help of family and friends, they have transformed the derelict house back into a proper home. That they have also added three children, is quite evident. A sand box filled with buckets and little shovels is incorporated into the front lawn, a swing set is in the back garden, toys nestle under the window in the entry lounge. Christine and Xavier have boundless energy. He runs the farm, and when cows became unprofitable, he turned the grazing ground into a golf course. Christine is a busy mother, yet manages to offer four of her nicely decorated bedrooms to the public. She also is an exceptionally good chef and prepares an evening meal except on weekends (a time she sets aside to be with her children). From the back garden, that runs down to a little stream, the turreted house has maintained it castle-like ambiance. From the front, the building looks like a farmhouse flanked by stone barns, but from the rear garden with its own little stream, the house looks quite different: more like a small, turreted castle. *Directions:* From the A4, take the Dormans exit. Turn right toward Dormans, then right again back over the expressway, then right at the first road that leads to the Chateau.

FERME DU CHATEAU (Gîte de France)
Hosts: Christine & Xavier Ferry
02130 Villers-Agron, France
tel: 23.71.60.71
5 rooms, 2 with private bathrooms
Double 295F
Table d'Hôte: 78F, per person
Open all year
Fluent English spoken
Region: Champagne, Michelin Map 237

The Chateau de Villiers-le-Mahieu, whose origins date back to the 13th Century, will fulfill any childhood fantasy to live in a fairy-tale castle. The beautifully maintained castle is positioned in park-like grounds, manicured to perfection. Like a gem within this park, the chateau sits on its own little island surrounded by a moat. The main access is over a narrow bridge leading into the inner courtyard-garden, framed on three sides by the ivy-covered stone walls of the chateau. The Chateau de Villiers-le-Mahieu is not a homey little castle where one becomes chummy with the owners, but rather a commercial operation with 18 guest rooms in the chateau and 11 in the garden annex. Splurge and request room one, a grand room in the original castle, wallpapered in a handsome blue print fabric that repeats in the drapes the three tall French windows looking out to the gardens. In the park surrounding the castle there is a beautiful swimming pool and tennis courts. *Directions:* Located 40 km southwest of Paris. Take the A13 west from Paris. Exit south on A12 toward Dreux-Bois d/Arcy. Continue following the signs to Dreux until you come to Pontchartrain then take D11 signposted to Thoiry. As the road leaves Thoiry, turn left on D 45 toward Villiers le Mahieu and continue through the town and you will see signs to the chateau on the left side of the road.

CHATEAU DE VILLIERS-LE-MAHIEU
Host: M. Jean-Luc Chaufour
78770 Villiers-le-Mahieu, France
tel: 34.87.44.25 fax: 1.34.87.44.40
29 rooms, with private bathrooms
Double: 654-804F
Table d'Hôte: On request, 6 person minimum*
*per person from Price 320,000 F
Credit cards: AX, VS
Closed one week at Christmas
Good English spoken
Region: Ile-de-France, Michelin Map 237

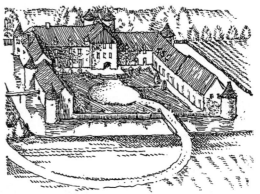

Monsieur and Madame Portal's contemporary home is found on a scenic plateau high above Aix les Bains, with spectacular views over the surrounding granite peaks. In this tranquil setting guests are two steps away from lovely walks on the wooded plateau, yet at the same time have the convenience of close-by civilization. Madame Portal is a very warm, cheerful hostess who makes sure her guests feel comfortable and at home. Bedrooms are attractively furnished in a contemporary style and all open onto a balcony above the Portal's restful garden. The house is built on a hillside, and there is a lower level where the Portals have installed a fully-equipped kitchen so that guests may prepare their own evening meals. A flagstone terrace with a table and chairs opens out to the garden for a pleasant dinner setting. *Directions:* You can go to Viviers du Lac by either N491 or N201. When you arrive in the village where there is a fountain, town hall and church, take the way Route des Essarts. Go straight for 700 meters, follow the curving road up a hill, weaving right when the road forks. At the top of the hill, look for the Portals brown gate on the left (1193 route des Essarts).

CHEZ PORTAL (Gîte de France)
Hosts: Monsieur & Madame Portal
1193 Rte des Essarts
73420 Le Viviers du Lac, France
tel: 79.61.44.61
3 rooms, 1 with private bath,
Other rooms share 1 bath/WC
Single: 192F, Double: 290F, Triple: 390F
* Discount for stays over 3 nights
No Table d'Hôte, kitchen available for guests
Open all year
A little English spoken
Region: French Alps, Michelin Map 244

James and Marie-Jose Hamel are a very friendly young couple who take great pleasure in welcoming guests to their manor home. Originally a fortress dating from the 12th Century, Le Chateau was rebuilt in 1450 and again in 1750 and has a colorful history. The Hamels are fond of recounting the story of their most famous visitor, Andy Rooney of 60 Minutes fame. He worked here as a journalist during World War II when the chateau was inhabited by the American Press Corps and recently revisited in 1984. Breakfast is served in the former press room complete with brass nameplate, in English, still intact on the door. A lofty ceiling, dark, pine-paneled walls and a lovely old tile floor provide intimate surroundings to begin the day or enjoy an evening aperitif. Guest bedrooms are tastefully furnished and decorated with handsome antiques and harmonious color schemes. The rooms are found in a separate wing of the chateau, thus affording guests a convenient, private entry. *Directions:* Vouilly is located approximately 25 kilometers west of Bayeux. Take D5 west to Le Molay Littry, then turn right, continuing on D5 in the direction of Isigny sur Mer until you reach Vouilly. Just after entering Vouilly, look for a Chambres d'Hôtes sign directing you to turn right onto a winding road, follow it to the Hamel's driveway.

LE CHATEAU (Gîte de France)
Hosts: Marie-Jose & James Hamel
Vouilly, 14230 Isigny sur Mer, France
tel: 31.22.08.59
3 rooms, all w/ pvt bath, 1 w/ pvt WC
Single: 210F, Double: 250F, Triple: 370F
No Table d'Hôte, Ferme Auberge nearby
Open all year
Very little English spoken
Region: Normandy, Michelin Map 231

Key Map

Pas-de-Calais

Picardie

2

Normandy

PARIS
Ile-de-France

3

Lorraine

Champagne

4

Alsace

Brittany

1

6

Loire Valley

Centre

Berry

Limousin

Burgundy

5 Jura

Atlantic Coast

Périgord

7

8

French Alps

Rhône Alps

Dordogne

Auvergne

Rhône Valley

Lot

9 Maritime Alps

Aquitane

Tarn

Provence

Côte d'Azur

Midi-Pyrénées

Languedoc-Rouissillon

Map 1

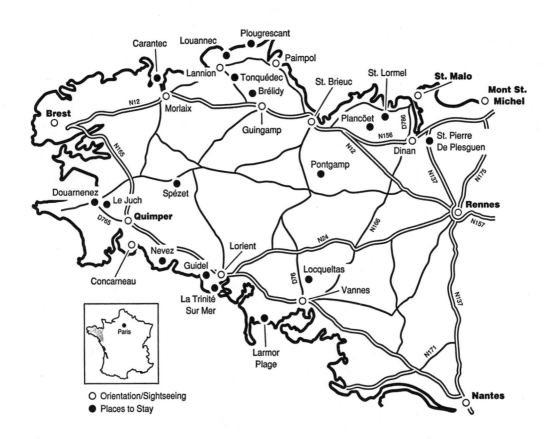

Carantec
Louannec
Plougrescant
Paimpol
Lannion
Tonquédec
St. Lormel
St. Malo
Brélidy
St. Brieuc
Mont St.
Michel
N12
Morlaix
Plancöet
St. Pierre
De Plesguen
Brest
Guingamp
N156
N12
Dinan
Pontgamp
N137
N175
Douarnenez
Le Juch
Spézet
N165
N166
Rennes
Quimper
D765
N24
N157
Nevez
Lorient
Locqueltas
Guidel
D76
Vannes
Concarneau
La Trinité
Sur Mer
N137
Larmor
Plage
N171
Nantes

Paris

○ Orientation/Sightseeing
● Places to Stay

220

Map 2

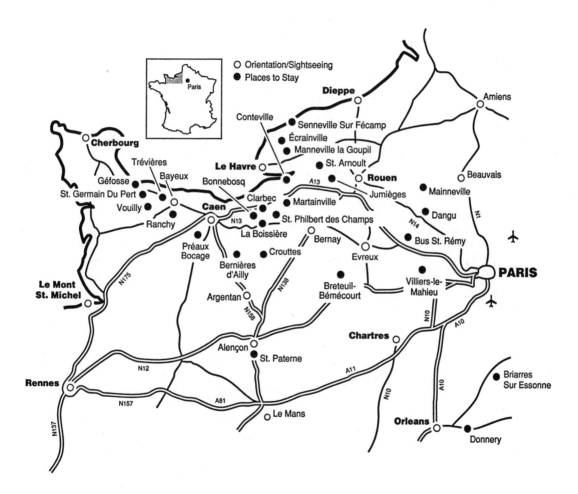

○ Orientation/Sightseeing
● Places to Stay

Dieppe
Amiens
Conteville
Senneville Sur Fécamp
Écrainville
Manneville la Goupil
Cherbourg
St. Arnoult
Trévières
Le Havre
Bayeux
Rouen
Beauvais
Géfosse
Bonnebosq
A13
Mainneville
St. Germain Du Pert
Clarbec
Jumièges
Vouilly
Caen
Martainville
Dangu
Ranchy
N13
St. Philbert des Champs
La Boissière
Bus St. Rémy
N14
Préaux
Bocage
Bernay
Crouttes
Evreux
Bernières
d'Ailly
PARIS
Le Mont
St. Michel
N175
Villiers-le-
Mahieu
Breteuil-
Bémécourt
Argentan
N138
N158
N10
A10
Chartres
Alençon
N12
St. Paterne
A11
Briarres
Sur Essonne
Rennes
N10
N157
A81
A10
N137
Le Mans
Orleans
Donnery

221

Map 3

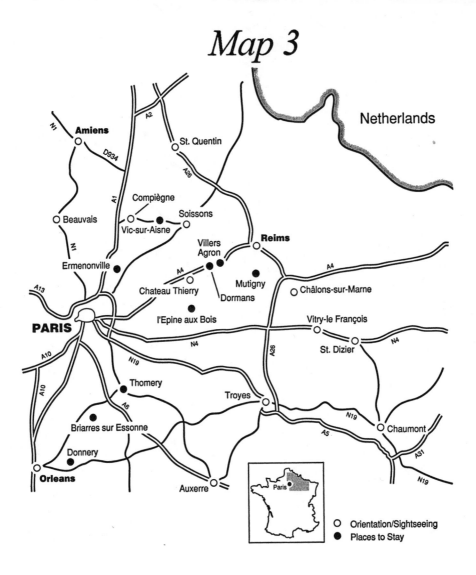

Netherlands

Amiens

St. Quentin

Compiègne

Beauvais

Soissons

Vic-sur-Aisne

Villers
Agron

Reims

Ermenonville

Mutigny

Châlons-sur-Marne

Chateau Thierry

Dormans

PARIS

l'Epine aux Bois

Vitry-le François

St. Dizier

Thomery

Troyes

Briarres sur Essonne

Chaumont

Donnery

Orleans

Auxerre

Paris

○ Orientation/Sightseeing

● Places to Stay

Map 4

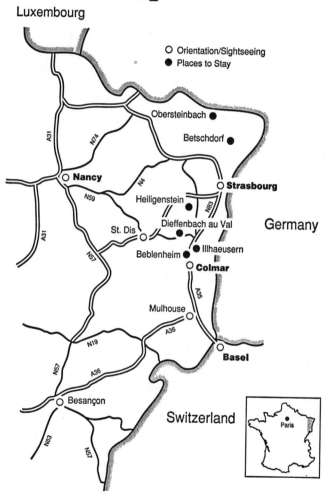

Luxembourg

○ Orientation/Sightseeing
● Places to Stay

Obersteinbach ●

Betschdorf ●

A31

N74

○ **Nancy**

N4

Heiligenstein ●

○ **Strasbourg**

N83

Germany

N59

St. Dis ○

Dieffenbach au Val ●

A31

N57

Beblenheim ● ● Illhaeusern

○ **Colmar**

A35

Mulhouse ○

A36

N19

N57

A36

○ Besançon

Switzerland

○ **Basel**

N83

N57

Paris ●

Map 5

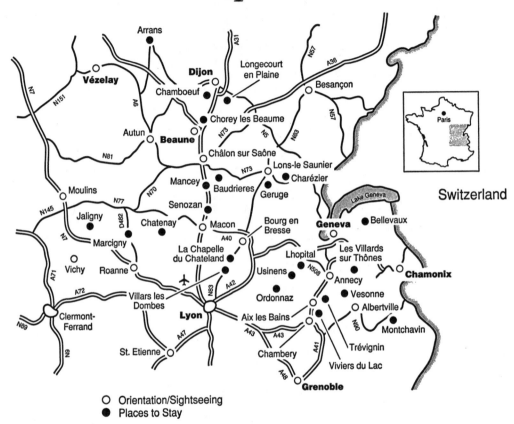

Arrans

A31

Vézelay

N7

N151

Dijon

Longecourt
en Plaine

Chamboeuf

N57

A36

Besançon

A6

Chorey les Beaume

Autun

N73

N5

N57

N83

Beaune

Châlon sur Saône

N81

Mancey

N73

Lons-le Saunier

Charézier

Baudrieres

Geruge

Lake Geneva

Switzerland

Moulins

N70

Senozan

N77

Jaligny

D482

Chatenay

Macon

Bourg en
Bresse

Geneva

Bellevaux

N145

N7

Marcigny

A40

La Chapelle
du Chateland

Lhopital

Les Villards
sur Thônes

Vichy

Roanne

Usinens

N508

Annecy

Chamonix

A71

Villars les
Dombes

N83

A42

Ordonnaz

Vesonne

A72

Clermont-
Ferrand

Lyon

Aix les Bains

Albertville

N89

N9

A47

St. Etienne

A43

A43

Chambery

A41

N90

Montchavin

Trévignin

Viviers du Lac

A48

Grenoble

Paris

O Orientation/Sightseeing
● Places to Stay

224

Map 6A

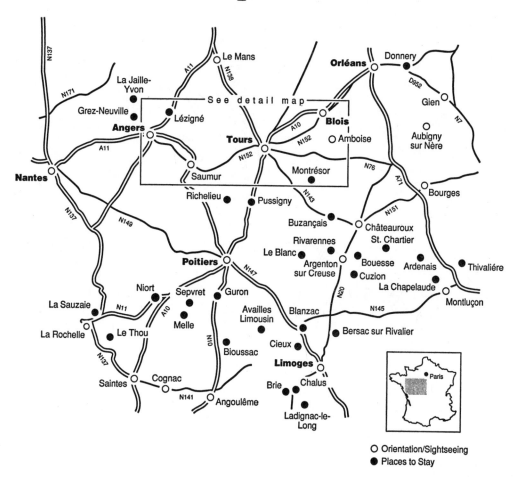

Map 6B

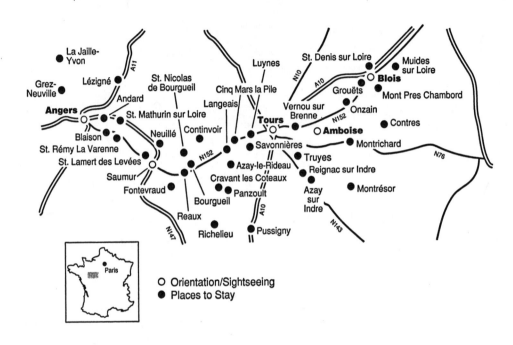

La Jaille-Yvon

Grez-Neuville

Lézigné

St. Nicolas de Bourgueil

Luynes

St. Denis sur Loire

Muides sur Loire

Blois

Andard

Cinq Mars la Pile

Grouëts

Mont Pres Chambord

Angers

St. Mathurin sur Loire

Langeais

Vernou sur Brenne

Onzain

Blaison

Neuillé

Continvoir

Tours

Amboise

Contres

St. Rémy La Varenne

Savonnières

Montrichard

St. Lamert des Levées

Truyes

Saumur

Azay-le-Rideau

Reignac sur Indre

Fontevraud

Cravant les Coteaux

Panzoult

Azay sur Indre

Montrésor

Bourgueil

Reaux

Pussigny

Richelieu

Paris

O Orientation/Sightseeing
● Places to Stay

226

Map 7

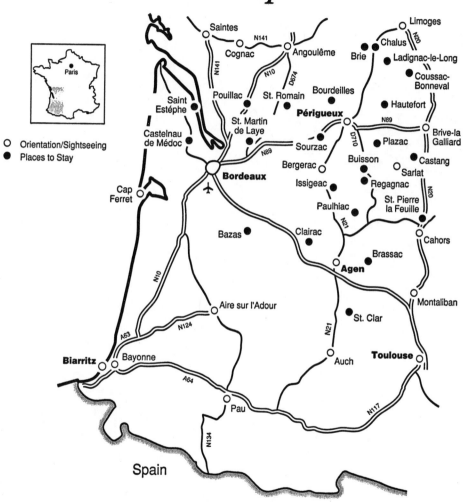

○ Orientation/Sightseeing
● Places to Stay

Saintes
Cognac
N141
Angoulême
Limoges
Chalus
N20
Brie
Ladignac-le-Long
Coussac-Bonneval
N141
N10
N10
D674
Pouillac
St. Romain
Bourdeilles
Hautefort
Saint Estéphe
St. Martin de Laye
Périgueux
N89
Brive-la-Galliard
Castelnau de Médoc
Sourzac
D710
Plazac
Bordeaux
N89
Bergerac
Buisson
Castang
Cap Ferret
Issigeac
Regagnac
Sarlat
Paulhiac
St. Pierre la Feuille
N20
Bazas
Clairac
N21
Cahors
Agen
Brassac
N10
Montaliban
Aire sur l'Adour
St. Clar
A63
N124
N21
Biarritz
Bayonne
Auch
Toulouse
A64
N117
Pau
N134
Spain

Paris

227

Map 8

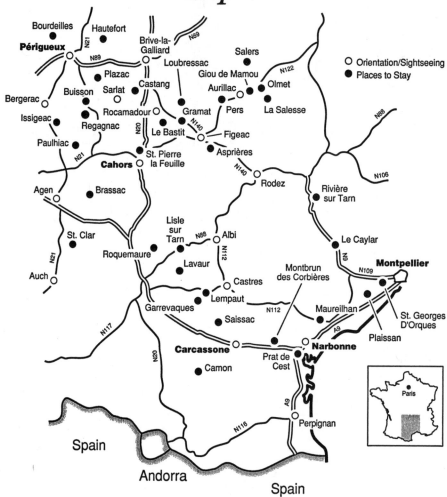

Bourdeilles
Hautefort
Périgueux
Brive-la-Galliard
Salers
N21
N89
N89
N89
Loubressac
Giou de Mamou
N122
Plazac
Aurillac
Olmet
Buisson
Sarlat
Castang
Bergerac
Rocamadour
Gramat
Pers
La Salesse
Issigeac
Regagnac
N20
Le Bastit
N140
Paulhiac
Figeac
N88
St. Pierre
la Feuille
Asprières
N21
Cahors
N140
Rodez
Rivière
sur Tarn
N106
Agen
Brassac
Lisle
sur
Tarn
N88
Albi
Le Caylar
St. Clar
N112
N9
Roquemaure
Lavaur
Montbrun
des Corbières
Montpellier
N109
N21
Castres
Maureilhan
St. Georges
D'Orques
Auch
Lempaut
N112
A9
Garrevaques
Saissac
Plaissan
N117
Prat de
Cest
Narbonne
N20
Carcassone
Camon
A9
Spain
Perpignan
N116
Paris
Andorra
Spain

○ Orientation/Sightseeing
● Places to Stay

228

Map 9A

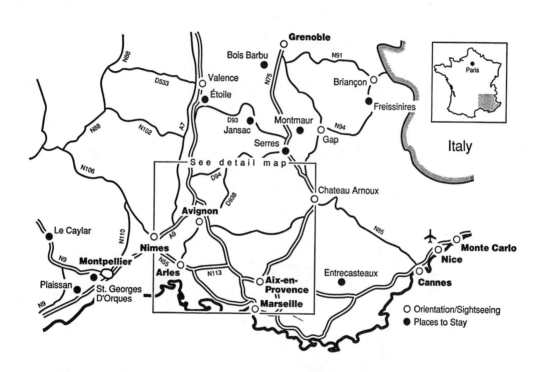

Map 9B

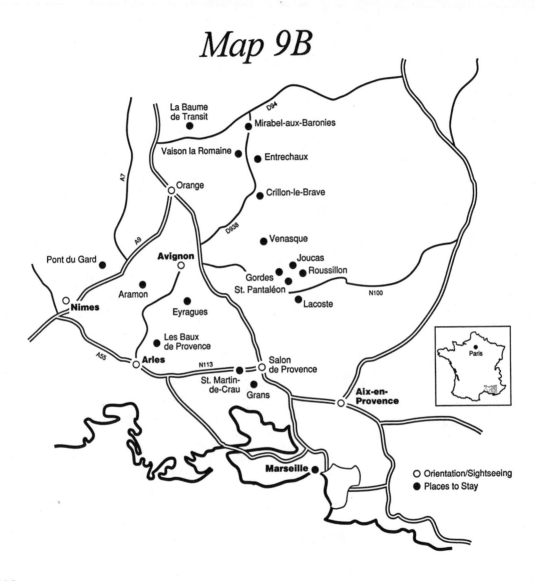

La Baume
de Transit

Mirabel-aux-Baronies

D94

Vaison la Romaine

Entrechaux

A7

Orange

Crillon-le-Brave

D938

Venasque

Pont du Gard

A9

Avignon

Joucas

Gordes Roussillon

St. Pantaléon

N100

Aramon

Nîmes

Eyragues

Lacoste

Les Baux
de Provence

A55

Arles

N113

Salon
de Provence

St. Martin-
de-Crau

Grans

Aix-en-
Provence

Paris

Marseille

○ Orientation/Sightseeing
● Places to Stay

Discoveries from Our Readers

Many of the new Bed and Breakfasts featured in this edition of "French Country Bed & Breakfasts" are those that travellers have recommended to us. We inspected them and agreed wholeheartedly with our readers' appraisals. However, on our research trip to France we did not have time to visit every place suggested to us. Since many of these "tips" sound too good to pass up, we're passing them on to you in this "Discoveries from Our Readers" section. Thank you for sharing your discoveries. Please keep them coming.

ADRETS DEL'ESTEREL "EGLISE"   HOTEL LE CHRYSTALIN

REGION: COTE D'AZUR, Chris and Alain, Hotel Le Chrystalin, Quartier Les Gieris, Chemin des Philippons, 83600 Les Adrets de L'Esterel "Eglise," France; tel: 94.40.97.56 fax: 94.40.94.66.

The following write-up recommendation sounds more like a hotel than a Bed and Breakfast, however since it is too simple to be included in our hotel guide and we need places to stay in the Cote d'Azur, we decided to share it with you. "People from Quebec who we met in Beaune had found this place and highly recommended it. There were two other couples there. All the rooms have full baths. The pool is wonderful and the views amazing. We swam and went down into Cannes and headed right back up...too hot and busy. We paid for a demi-pension which was 640F. The dinner, which included wine, consisted of four courses. Put this one in your book Karen—it is great. Our favorite of the trip." Recommended by Wendi Van Exan, Ontario, Canada.

ARTANNES   CHATEAU DE LA MOTHE

REGION: LOIRE VALLEY; Béatrice and Christian Lamy, Chateau de La Mothe, 9, rue de la Fontaine Sainte, 37260 Artannes, France; tel: 47.26.80.18, fax: 47.26.80.57; double 350F-450F; open April-September.

"The Chateau de la Mothe is a small chateau near Azay-le-Rideau, ideally located for touring the Loire area. Welcoming hosts Beatrice and Christian Lamy speak good English and are always happy to assist guests in planning their sightseeing. They offer one double room and two suites for four people, all with private bathrooms and WC. Our suite was very spacious, as was the bathroom, with lovely views over the countryside. The guest sitting room has an old tile floor, bookcases and a large stone fireplace. Most of the rooms are accessed from the central tower's circular stone staircase and have lots of historic ambiance." Recommended by Ambrose Wilson.

BOSC-ROGER-SUR-BUCHY   LE CHATEAU

REGION: NORMANDY; Katia & Jacques Preterre-Rieux, Le Chateau, Place de l'Eglise, 76750 Bosc-Roger sur Buchy, France; tel: 35.34.29.70; 4 rooms; double 320F; open March to January; English spoken; no restaurant.

"We so enjoyed our stay at Le Chateau that we'd like others to as well. Le Chateau is a large attractive house set on large grounds in a small, friendly village. Katia and her husband are cosmopolitan, warm hosts, friendly yet not intrusive, and speak good English. Our room was large and comfortable, with thoughtful extra touches such as magazines and little candies provided." Recommended by Chuck and Kaye Cook-Kollars, Beverly, Massachusetts.

BURES SUR DIVES   MANOIR DES TOURPES

REGION: NORMANDY; Michael Cassady, Manoir des Tourpes, Chemin de l'Église 14670 Bures sur Dives, France; tel: 31.23.63.47; 3 rooms with private bathrooms.

Michael Cassady, an American, and his French-born wife, recently moved from Paris to the Manoir des Tourpes, a manor house constructed in the 17th and 18th Centuries. The village of Bures is 15 km from Caen, situated on the river Dives which passes along one side of the property. Beyond the river, the house looks out onto the open marsh lands where cattle graze and fisherman dream along the banks of the many canals. At the time of the D-Day landings in June 1944, the river was the designated eastern perimeter of the invasion plan, however, in spite of very intense fighting in the area, the house was fortunately spared except for minor damage to the roof. Guests have a separate sitting room with a fireplace at their disposal. The decor and way of life is entirely French, although the Cassadys seem to understand what sort of comforts American travellers prefer.

CHATEAUNEUF-LA-FORET   LA CROIS-DU-REH

REGION: LIMOUSIN; Elisabeth and Patrick. McLaughlin, La Croix-du-Reh, 87130 Chateauneuf-La-Foret, France; tel: 55.69.75.37, fax: 55.69.75.38; 6 rooms, most with a private bathroom. Double from 300F. Table d'Hôtel 120F per person with wine.

The McLaughlin's home, set on 3 acres of a beautiful park, is located 34 kilometers from Limoges, in the tranquil wooded region of Limousin. In the low season, Elisabeth and Patrick operate a language course. In the high season, they open their home to guests on a Bed and Breakfast basis. This cozy ivy covered manor with steep pitched roof and dormer windows, looks more English than what one thinks of as typically "French."

CONTES - NICE   DOMAINE DU CASTELLAR

REGION: CÔTE D'AZUR; Francine Vélut, Domaine du Castellar, Route de Berre les Alpes, 06390 Contes, France; tel: 93.91.83.51; 2 rooms, approximate cost, double 330F

We are *VERY* eager to visit Domaine du Castellar, just a 20-minute drive from Nice. Until then, we will share some notes from our readers. "The last 4 nights of our holiday were spent at the home of Madame Vélut, at the Domaine du Castellar. We can testify that Madame Velut's home is delightful: set in a scented garden, comfortable, spotlessly clean. The breakfasts are the largest and most varied of anywhere that we stayed, and Madame Vélut herself is charming, helpful and most welcoming." Anonymous, Canada. "Madame Vélut offers two guest rooms in a pastel-pink stucco villa with the traditional light green shuttered windows and doors. The house opens onto a very pretty English garden." Another guest wrote: "We had a marvelous experience and only wish we could have stayed longer to enjoy the wonderful hospitality, the charming countryside, and the best breakfast in all of France." Recommended by Angie and Marilyn.

ENTRECHAUX   L'ESCLERIADE

REGION: PROVENCE; Marie-Jean and Vincent Gallo, L'Escleriade, Route de Saint-Marcellin, 84340 Entrechaux, France; tel: 90.46.01.32; 6 rooms, 4 with private bathrooms; double 250F; open all year.

"We wish to highly recommend L'Escleriade, run by Marie-Jean and Vincent Gallo. They have only been open a short while, but they are most charming hosts and their Bed & Breakfast is an absolute delight. It is a new building (built in the traditional style) in a most attractive setting. The bedrooms are prettily decorated. There are lovely views across the valley. We only intended to stay one night, but in fact stayed four nights. We found it difficult to leave the atmosphere and friendliness of our hosts, as did other guests who stayed even longer than we did." Recommended by Marie and John Shannon, England.

Discoveries from Our Readers

HAUTEFORT   L'ENCLOS

REGION: PÉRIGORD; Diana and Robert Ornsteen, L'Enclos, Pragelier, 24390 Hautefort, France; tel: 53.51.11.40, fax: 53.51.11.40.

We are happy to add the Niedner's suggestion for a Bed and Breakfast and in the idyllic Périgord, one of our favorite regions of France. "I would like to recommend L'Enclos, owned by Americans, Diana and Robert Ornsteen—great people, who speak French fluently and relate to people easily. Rooms and suites are very up to date and show great taste. One immediately gets the feeling of the French countryside. There is a pool and luxury, but the improvements are subtle. My wife and I loved the flowers, the farm land, and quaint buildings. One can walk into Tourtoirac easily. On a scale of 10, give it a 10. Great experience." Recommended by Charles & Priscilla Reilly Niedner, CT, USA.

JOSSELIN   CHEZ GUYOT

REGION: BRITTANY, Monsieur and Madame Guyot, Chez Guyot, Butte Saint-Laurent, 56120 Josselin; France, tel: 97.22.22.09; 3 rooms, Double 240F.

"This note is a follow up on our recent conversation singing the praises of a Brittany B&B we found on a recent trip to France. The Guyots are located in a new hilltop house with three bedrooms available in Josselin, a small town ideally suited for an overnight stop while travelling from St. Malo in Northern Brittany to Vannes in Southern Brittany (it is closer to Vannes). The Guyots do not speak English, but have a son (computer type) living in San Jose, CA. They are natural hosts. Breakfast consists of rolls, baguettes, croissants, home made jam and local honey, and Mme Goyot's crepes." Recommended by Paul E. Boudakian, D.D.S., Berkeley, California

LAPALUD   LA BERGERIE

REGION: PROVENCE; Simone and Gabriel Buet, La Bergerie, Les Iles, 84840 Lapalud, France; tel: 90.40.30.82, fax: 90.40.24.29; 2 rooms; 300F.

"I would like to recommend La Bergerie in Provence. We first stayed with Simone and Garbriel Buet 14 years ago and have gone back three times since. Their home is an ideal location for touring since it is close to so many sights. Both bedrooms, one with twin beds and one with a double, overlook the garden and are quite cozy and comfortable. We had dinner there in the evenings with fresh fruits and vegetables from the garden. Simone and Garbriel are both very warm, hospitable people who enjoy sharing their considerable knowledge about Provence. They are fluent in English and direct one to sights that the casual tourist would miss, such as the best local markets, chateaux, artists' studios, restaurants, picturesque villages, etc." Recommended by Fontaine Laing, Birmingham, Michigan, USA.

LOURMARIN   VILLA SAINT-LOUIS

REGION: PROVENCE; Monsieur and Madame Lasalette, Villa Saint-Louis, 25 rue Henri de Savournin, 84160 Lourmarin, France; tel: 90.68.39.18, 5 rooms, double 260-315F.

A reader wrote us while on the road in France: "I thought you might like to know about a very special country inn that I ran across in a beautiful French village called Lourmarin. I saw a sign saying "Chambre d'Hotes" and was really pleasantly surprised. I received an incredibly warm welcome from Madame Lasalette, who really mothered me during my three-day visit. She even gave me a mountain bike and showed me around the Luberon mountains. Her husband, Michel, is a well-known interior decorator, who has given La Villa Saint Louis its own distinctive character. Well worth a detour! Hope you like it." Recommended by Jeff Probst of Wisconsin.

MONTEILLE FERME DES VERGÉES

REGION: NORMANDY; Madame Claudine Guillaumin, Ferme des Vergées, Monteille 14270 Mézidon, France; tel: 31.63.01.13; 2 rooms, each with wash basin and toilet - share a bathroom; double 200F; open all year.

"Madame Claudine Guillaume speaks no English, but her daughter Christine, speaks English well. The house is a fascinating 300-year old Normandy farmhouse with barn in back, sheep in the meadow, apple orchard, corn, and cows. The surroundings are simply gorgeous. It is a short drive to the coast and all its towns and sights, and a joy to return to. Madame Guillaume prepares a special breakfast in a wonderful old room where the fireplace is as large as most kitchens. Truly a slice of heaven." Recommended by B.B., USA

MOULICENT LA GRANDE NOË

REGION: NORMANDY; La Grande Noë, Monsieur and Madame Jacques de Longcamp, 61290 Moulicent, France; tel: 33.73.63.30, fax: 33.83.62.92; three rooms with private bathrooms, double 420-630F.

American guests on their honeymoon recommended the following: "La Grand Noë, which has been in the same family since its construction in the 15th Century, has three guest rooms, all with antique furniture and decor. The owners personally welcome guests and enjoy having dinner with them. Their goal is not to have a professional hotel, but to restore their chateau and welcome guests from around the world into their home. The place is very quiet and peaceful—only the farm outside, and the nearby village, which is one kilometer away." From the picture we received, the chateau looks most inviting—stately and elegant. We look forward to more feedback. Anonymous, USA.

MONTHOU-SUR-CHER   "LES LILAS"

REGION: LOIRE VALLEY; Sheila and Dave Sands, "Les Lilas," Les Quatre Pierres, Monthon-sur-Cher, 41400 Montrichard, France; tel: 54.71.57.21; 4 rooms, Double 250F.

Just a few days before going to press, we received a recommendation for the Loire Valley that looks lovely and is very reasonable. "Sheila and Dave Sands from Eastbourne, Great Britain, are a lively, warm couple who have re-done a 1930's house and garden with loving care and expertise. It's comfortable and homey and open and bright. The Sands are totally accommodating. Real Talent! "Les Lilas" is located on the Vierzon Train line from Tours. Recommended by Gretchen Rachlin, South Orange, New Jersey, USA.

OLHABIDEA   BED AND BREAKFAST OLHABIDEA

REGION: BASQUE; Anne-Marie Fagoaga, Bed and Breakfast Olhabidea, 66310 Sare, France; tel: 59.54.21.85; Four rooms with private bathrooms, Double from 300F. Open March to November; Children over five years old accepted.

"In May 1992 we stayed at a new B&B in Sare, France, which is a short drive from St Jean de Luz and Biarritz. We urge you to do whatever fact-finding necessary to confirm our belief that it should be included in your next Bed and Breakfast publication. Olhabidea is operated by Madame Anne-Marie Fagoaga, an effervescent and "chaleuresuse" lady. She lives in a magnificent Spanish Basque-style home, exquisitely decorated. Each very large bedroom has its own large bathroom/bath and shower. The guests share a separate entrance, living room, dining room and kitchen decorated "a la Basque." The locale is on acres of land looking towards the mountains." Note: we have seen several photographs of Olhabidea and indeed the house seems very special—decorated with sophistication and charm: many French country-style antiques enhanced by colorful arrangements of fresh flowers, hanging baskets and plates hanging on the walls and pretty fabrics. Recommended by Bernice Shaposnick, Montreal, Canada.

PARCY   LE MOULIN GIRARD

REGION: NORMANDY; Jasmine and Roger, Le Moulin Girard, Le Chefresne, 50410 Percy, France; tel: 33.61.62.06; 2 rooms, from 200F; open all year.

"Le Moulin Girard is an old watermill that has been charmingly restored. It has two rooms available plus 'The Miller's Cottage' which is available for parties of six. The price includes French-style breakfast, but an English breakfast can also be arranged and excellent evening meals are available on request. Roger and Jasmine are English and know the area extremely well, which can be very useful when it comes to choosing places to visit (or avoid). You will get a very warm welcome here and most likely fall in love with this beautiful part of Normandy. The mill is situated some 3 kilometers due east of Percy." Recommended by Julian Day, London.

ST-SENIER-SOUS-AVRANCHES   CHATEAU DU CHAMP DU GENÊT

REGION: NORMANDY; Annette and Jean-Pierre Jouvin, Chateau du Champ du Genêt, Route de Mortain, 50300 St-Senier-sous-Avranches, France; tel: 33.60.52.67; 4 rooms, double from 195F.

"The Chateau du Genêt, situated just outside Dirmanches, is owned and run by the Jouvin family and is a gem. There are four charmingly decorated rooms, all with ensuite bathrooms. Breakfast is served in the banquet hall surrounded by superb antique furniture. The chateau, standing on its own grounds, is an island of peace and quiet. Jean Pierre and Annette (who speak a little English) make you very welcome." Recommended by Julian Day, London.

TOURETTES-SUR-LOUP   CHEZ MEIER-GAILLARD

REGION: CÔTE D'AZUR; Jean and Ani Meier-Gaillard, Chez Meier-Gaillard, 533 Route des Vallettes du Sud, 06140 Tourettes-sur-Loup, France; tel: 93.59.25.31; 1 double room.

"Jean and Ani Meier-Gaillard have a lovely home nestled in the hills above the Riviera, not far from St Paul de Vence. They have one bedroom with accommodation for two people and a lovely adjoining bathroom. Their having only one bedroom for guests allows for personal attention which Ani and Jean bestow graciously and generously. Breakfast can be served on the terrace. A swimming pool is in the process of being built. Ani paints and Jean plays the violin. They have a friendly German shepherd and a cat. They know the area well and can make suggestions for sightseeing. They are located 5 kilometers from a charming medieval village (Tourettes-sur-Loup), whch has about 25 ateliers and several restaurants. We noticed in your book that the Riviera is a lean area for B&Bs and hope you can use this recommendation in your next edition " Note: We rarely include places to stay with only 1 bedroom, but, as Gay Marshall correctly stated, we do need more B&Bs in the popular Côte d'Azur region. Recommended by Gay Marshall, Pennsylvania, U.S.A.

URRUGNE   CHATEAU D'URTUBIE

REGION: PYRÉNÉES-ATLANTIQUES (BASQUE); Comte and Comtesse de Coral, Chateau d'Urtubie, 64122 Urrugne (Pyrénées-Atlantiques), France; tel: 59.54.62.49; or (winter) 1.39.54.30.894; 9 rooms, from 600F; open July to mid-September.

The Count and Countess de Coral have a home in Versailles, but spend the summer in the Basque country at their Chateau d'Urtubie where they welcome guests. The chateau is set in a beautiful 14-acre park which shelters a tennis court. In addition, for the sports enthusiasts, there are golf courses nearby and beaches three kilometers away. The stately, turreted castle dates back to the 14th Century. (We welcome more feedback on this castle.)

VENASQUE AUBERGE LA FONTAINE
===

REGION: PROVENCE: Ingrid and Christian Soehlke, Auberge la Fontaine, Place de la Fontaine, 84210 Venasque, France; tel: 90.66.02.96, fax: 90.66.13.14; 5 suites: approximate cost double 800F.

We received an enthusiastic letter about what sounds like a superb "restaurant with rooms" in one of our favorite villages. "The Auberge la Fontaine, owned by Christian and Ingrid Soehlke, is located in Venasque, a small, very picturesque, partially-walled old village. Christian Soehlke is the chef. He makes guests welcome and converses easily in at least four languages. The food is marvelous. Mr. Soehlke is very talented and has a passion for excellence. During the dinner hours he is calm and easily accessible to the diners, but this belies the fact that he puts in long days, beginning early in markets of nearby and not-so-nearby towns, searching for the best ingredients on which to build his menu. The auberge exhibits of the works of artists and photographers from throughout Europe, many of whom have been friends of the Soehlke. Periodically concerts are presented in the dining room. These concerts are intimate, very civilized affairs. Always featuring artists of stature, which is surprising for such a necessarily small audience. The exterior of the auberge is very understated with a simple, small sign. Although it is a large building, you could overlook it. Most of the suites have terraces, but they are so cleverly arranged that you would not guess from the street that they existed. We have been "Karen Brown" followers since the guides were first published and know the kind of places that merit your recommendation. We think the Auberge would be an excellent addition and think your other readers will gratefully agree. Anonymous, Wisconsin, USA.

REGION: Ile de France, Pierre Lansard and son, Manuel, La Residence du Berry, 14 rue d'Anjou, 78000 Versailles, France; tel: 1.39.49.07.07, fax: 1.30.50.59.40; 38 rooms; approximate cost double 380F to 440F.

"The Lansard Family who run the Hotel du Berry were the friendliest of all the owners we met on our last trip to France. The father let me check out many of the rooms until I found *the perfect one*, a large room on the upper floor with a beamed ceiling. Everyone was extremely helpful recommending places that were cooperative for car service, laundry, banking and dining. They made our stay in Versailles memorable. We made a great side trip to Fontainebleau and Vaux Le Vicomte (the latter gardens should not be missed). We also did Paris from there by train, which avoided the brutal Paris traffic on weekdays." Recommended by Dr. and Mrs. Weeks, Oakland, California.

Index

Index

DISCOVERIES FROM OUR READERS

If you have a favorite hideaway that you would be willing to share with other readers, we would love to hear from you. The type of accommodations we feature are those with old world ambiance, special charm, historical interest, attractive setting, and, above all, warmth of welcome. Please send the following information:

1. Your name, address and telephone number.

2. Name, address and telephone number of your discovery.

3. Rate for a double room including tax, service and breakfast.

4. Brochure or picture (we cannot return material).

5. Permission to use an edited version of your description.

6. Would you want your name, city, and state included in the book?

Please send information to:

KAREN BROWN'S GUIDES
Post Office Box 70, San Mateo, CA 94401, U.S.A
Telephone (415) 342-5591   Fax (415) 342-9153

Karen Brown's Guides

For Europe And California

The Most Reliable & Informative Series On Charming Places To Stay

U.S.A. Order Form

Please ask in your local bookstore for KAREN BROWN'S GUIDES. If the books you want are unavailable, you may order directly from the publisher.

California Country Inns & Itineraries $14.95

English Country Bed & Breakfasts $13.95

English, Welsh & Scottish Country Hotels & Itineraries $14.95

French Country Bed & Breakfasts $13.95

French Country Inns & Itineraries $14.95

German Country Inns & Itineraries $14.95

Irish Country Inns & Itineraries $14.95

Italian Country Bed & Breakfasts $13.95

Italian Country Inns & Itineraries $14.95

Portuguese Country Inns & Pousadas (1990 edition) $6.00

Spanish Country Inns & Paradors (1989 edition) $6.00

Swiss Country Inns & Itineraries $14.95

Name _____ Street _____

City _____ State ___ Zip_____ tel. _____

Credit Card (MasterCard or Visa) _____ Exp: _____

Add $3.50 for the first book and .50 cents for each additional book for postage & packing. California residents add 8.25% sales tax.   Order form only for shipments within the U.S.A.

Indicate number of copies of each title; send form with check or credit card information to:

KAREN BROWN'S GUIDES
Post Office Box 70, San Mateo, California, 94401, U.S.A.
Tel: (415) 342-9117   Fax: (415) 342-9153

KIRSTEN PRICE, author of French Country Bed & Breakfasts, was born and raised in the San Francisco Bay area where she has been a friend of Karen's since grade-school days. Kirsten, who has a gift for foreign languages, has divided her time for the past 12 years between Colorado, New Zealand and Europe—teaching skiing, leading bike tours to France, working in the resort/travel industry and researching for the Karen Brown guides. Kirsten now lives in San Francisco. California.

CLARE BROWN, CTC, has many years of experience in the field of travel and has earned the designation of Certified Travel Consultant. Since 1969 she has specialized in planning itineraries to Europe using charming small hotels in the countryside for her clients. The focus of her job remains unchanged, but now her expertise is available to a larger audience - the readers of her daughter's Country Inn guides. Clare lives in the San Francisco Bay area with her husband, Bill.

BARBARA TAPP, the talented artist responsible for all of the hotel sketches and delightful illustrations in this guide, was raised in Australia where she studied in Sydney at the School of Interior Design. Although Barbara continues with freelance projects, she devotes much of her time to illustrating Karen's Country Inn guides. Barbara live s in the San Francisco Bay area with her husband, Richard, their two sons, Jonothan and Alexander, and young daughter, Georgia.

JANN POLLARD, the artist responsible for the beautiful painting on the cover of this guide, has studied art since childhood, and is well-known for her outstanding impressionistic-style water colors which she has exhibited in numerous juried shows, winning many awards. Jann travels frequently to Europe (using Karen Brown's guides) where she loves to paint old world architecture. Jann lives in the San Francisco Bay area with her husband, Gene, and two daughters.

Karen Brown's
French Country Inns & Itineraries

The Choice of the Discriminating Traveller to France

Featuring Charming Small Hotels and Inns
And Detailed Itineraries for Exploring the Countryside

French Country Inns & Itineraries is the perfect companion guide to Karen Brown's *French Country Bed & Breakfasts.* Whereas the Bed & Breakfast guide has "hand-picked" the choice places to stay in private homes, the *French Country Inns & Itineraries* book features accommodations with great charm in small hotels and inns. All the pertinent information is given: description of the accommodation, sketch, price, driving directions, maps, if there is a restaurant, owner's name, telephone and fax number, dates open, etc.

French Country Inns & Itineraries does not replace *French Country Bed & Breakfasts -* together they make the perfect pair for the traveller who wants to explore the countryside of France. Both feature places to stay with charm, warmth of welcome and old world ambiance: *French Country Bed & Breakfasts* features places to stay in private homes; *French Country Inns & Itineraries* features small hotels and inns PLUS the added bonus of 11 itineraries, handy for use with the bed & breakfast guide. Each book uses the same maps so it is easy to choose a combination of places to stay from each, adding great variety for where to spend the night.

SEAL COVE INN - LOCATED IN THE SAN FRANCISCO AREA

Karen Brown Herbert (best known as author of the Karen Brown's Guides) and her husband, Rick, have put sixteen years of experience into reality and opened their own superb hideaway, Seal Cove Inn. Spectacularly set amongst wild flowers and bordered by towering cypress trees, Seal Cove Inn looks out to the ocean over acres of county park: an oasis where you can enjoy secluded beaches, explore tide-pools, watch frolicking seals, and follow the tree-lined path that traces the windswept ocean bluffs. Country antiques, original-watercolors, flower-laden cradles, rich fabrics, and the gentle ticking of grandfather clocks create the perfect ambiance for a foggy day in front of the crackling log fire. Each bedroom is its own haven with a cozy sitting area before a wood-burning fireplace and doors opening onto a private balcony or patio with views to the distant ocean. Moss Beach is a 35-minute drive south of San Francisco, 6 miles north of the picturesque town of Half Moon Bay, and a few minutes from Princeton harbor with its colorful fishing boats and restaurants. Seal Cove Inn makes a perfect base for whale-watching expeditions, salmon-fishing excursions, day trips to San Francisco, exploring the coast, or, best of all, just a romantic interlude by the sea, time to relax and be pampered. Karen and Rick look forward to the pleasure of welcoming you to their hide-away by the sea

Seal Cove Inn, 221 Cypress Avenue, Moss Beach, California, 94038, U.S.A.
telephone: (415) 728-7325   fax: (415) 728-4116